AA

100
Great Wonders of the World

AA Publishing

Writers: Dr John Baxter, Rosemary Burton, Richard Cavendish, Dr Peter Clarkson, Dr Elizabeth Cruwys, Dr Beau Riffenburgh and Nia Williams

Produced by AA Publishing
First published 2004, reprinted 2005 (three times)
Reprinted 2006

Relief maps created from an original supplied by Getty Images/
The Studio Dog

Published by AA Publishing (a trading name of Automobile Association Developments Limited, whose registered office is Fanum House, Basing View, Basingstoke, Hampshire RG21 4EA; registered number 1878835).

ISBN 10: 0-7495-4228-4
ISBN 13: 978-0-7495-4228-3

A03047

The AA's website address is www.theAA.com/bookshop

A CIP catalogue record for this book is available from the British Library.

Design layouts for AA Publishing by Nautilus Design
From an original concept by Andrew Milne Design
Origination by Keene Group, Andover
Printed and bound in Dubai by Oriental Press

AA

100 Great Wonders of the World

Contents

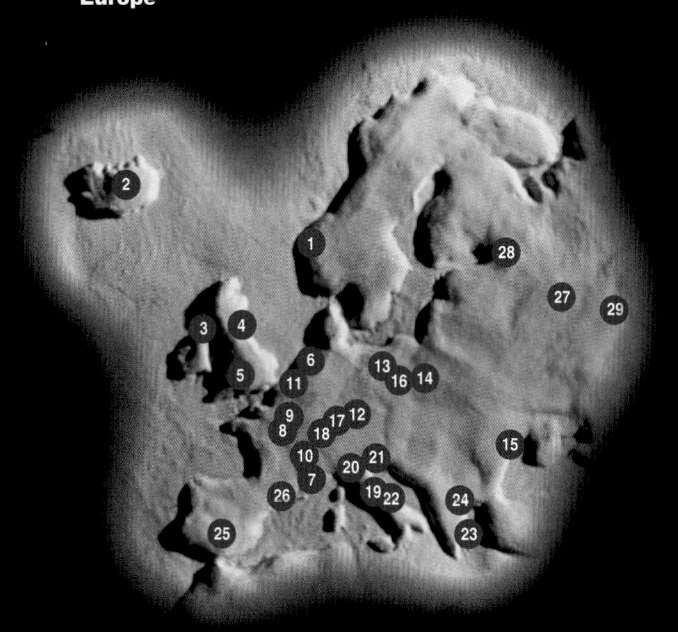

Europe
1
2
3
4
5
6
7
8
9
10
11
12
13
14
15
16
17
18
19
20
21
22
23
24
25
26
27
28
29

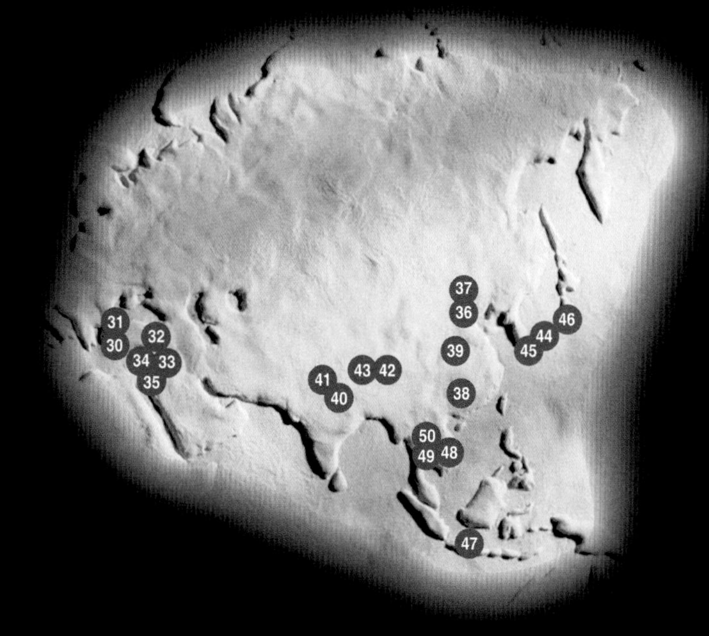

Asia
30
31
32
33
34
35
36
37
38
39
40
41
42
43
44
45
46
47
48
49
50

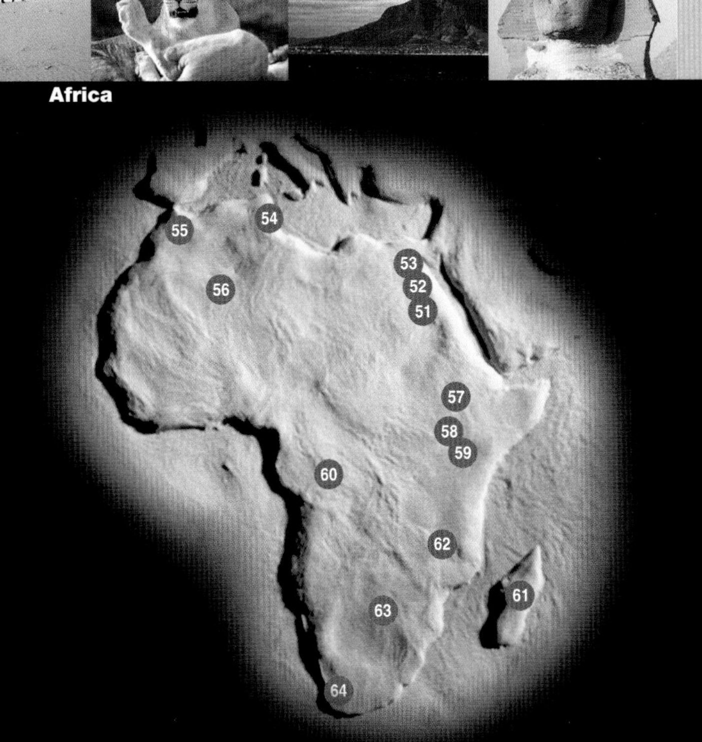

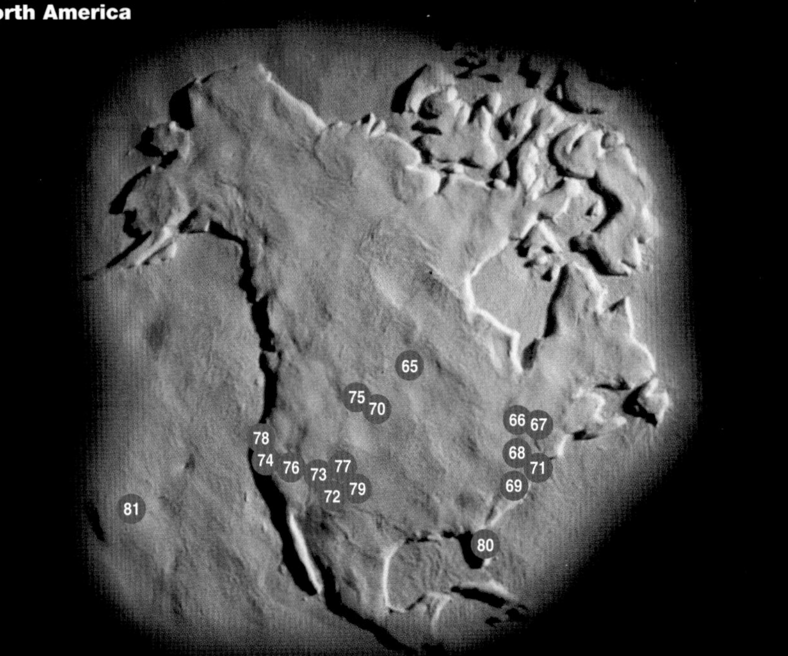

AFRICA

NORTH AMERICA

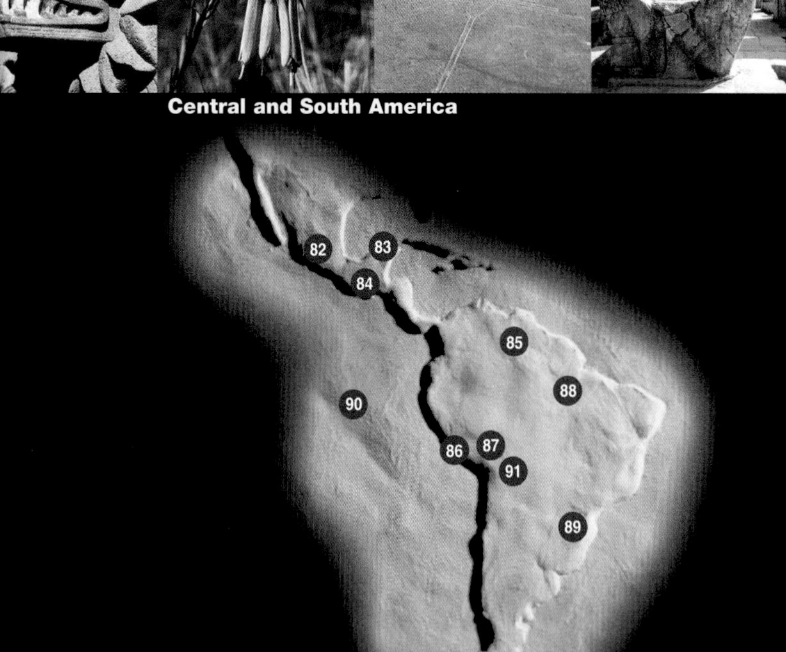

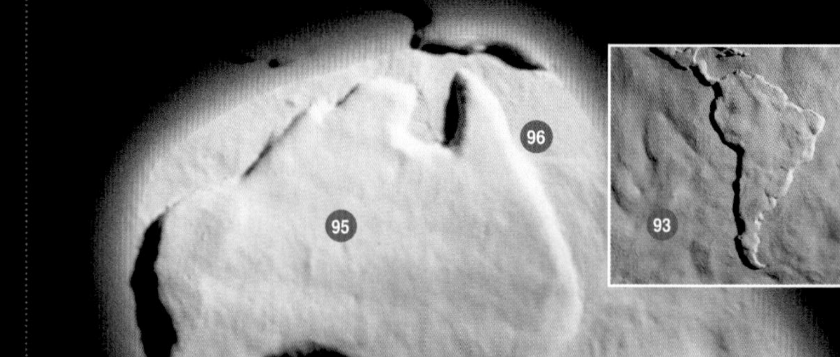

CENTRAL AND SOUTH AMERICA

AUSTRALIA AND OCEANIA

ANTARCTICA

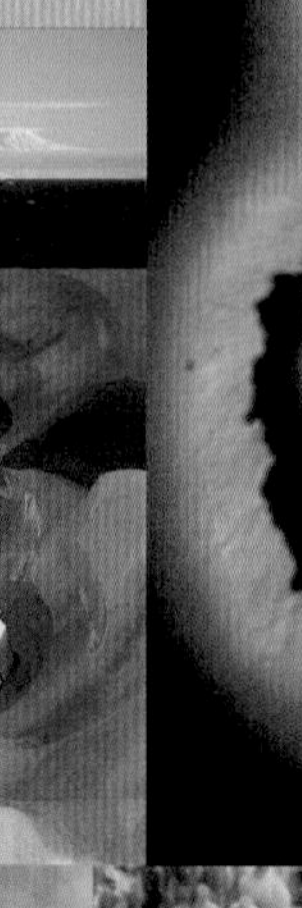

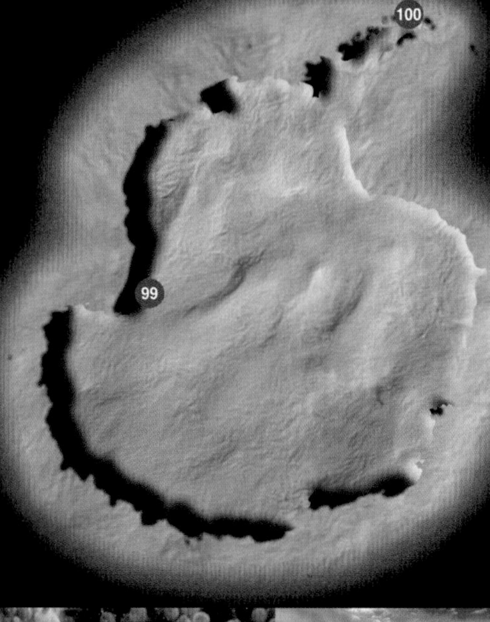

Introduction

Every feature and structure in this book is a cause of wonder. Even in a time of mass and instantaneous communication, when images of the globe's farthest and most remote reaches can be transmitted into every sitting room, the feats of human ingenuity and skill, and the extremes of the natural world can still astonish. The manmade achievements celebrated here span thousands of years of human history, while the Earth's natural splendours illustrate millions of years of upheaval, movement and erosion.

THE DESIRE TO BUILD

Everywhere in the world there has always been a delight in the spectacular and an urge to burden our groaning planet with the tallest, heaviest, largest constructions that imagination and technology would allow, from Stonehenge to the Three Gorges Dam. The CN Tower in Toronto, swaying slightly in the wind, rises more than 553m (1,815ft) into the sky. It dwarfs the Empire State Building in New York City, which, for more than 40 years, enjoyed the prestige of being the world's highest building. Like the elegant Eiffel Tower and the soaring spires of medieval cathedrals, it shows what human beings can do when they aim for the skies.

Some wonders are marvels of engineering, which conquer distance and tame nature. The Trans-Siberian and the Canadian Pacific Railway represent the pioneering impulse to cover vast distances and establish links across apparently impenetrable terrain. Some wonders, such as Stonehenge and the Great Wall of China, are astonishing structures completed without the benefit of modern machinery. Others illustrate the power of faith to overcome the challenges presented by seemingly inaccessible places—like the Metéora monasteries in Greece and the mysterious religious settlement at Machu Picchu, built by the Incas. Power and status have prompted the raising of monuments too—from the colossal, scattered statues of Nemrut Dag to the stone faces of American presidents hewn into Mount Rushmore. The more enigmatic the structure, the more awe-inspiring. Was Stonehenge an observatory or a funereal temple? Were the patterns in the desert at Nazca drawn for alien spaceships? Who lived in the Mayan temple-cities, in the jungles of the Yucatán? And who are the stone figures gazing mutely from Easter Island? A dozen theories can be found for every question, but these ancient manmade wonders keep their secrets safe.

PARADISE ON EARTH

Many vast constructions in stone and marble display the glory of kings, from Versailles to the Kremlin. Some become gilded prisons—like the Forbidden City of the Chinese emperors in Beijing, or the Potala Palace of the Dalai Lamas at Lhasa—in which the ruler becomes a puppet, cut off from real life. Such buildings may also be attempts to create an earthly paradise. 'If there is a paradise on earth,' said Shah Jehan, builder of the Red Fort in Delhi, 'it is this, it is this, it is this.' The Alhambra in Spain was designed with the same intention, and at Versailles, Louis XIV's architects and landscape designers set out to build a palace of ideal proportions, which would demonstrate not only the Sun King's majesty, but also the order of the world.

The same is true of great religious buildings—cathedrals, mosques and temples—created as symbols of the divine order. The colossal temple-mountains of the East, like Borobudur in Java and Angkor Wat in Cambodia, are stone lessons on the true nature of the universe. They demonstrate the indefatigable human ambition to match earthly wonders with wonders of the human spirit.

Hence the importance of orientation: of aligning a building with the order of the world. The Great Pyramid in Egypt was built so that its four sides accurately faced north, east, south and west. On the other side of the world, 3,000 years later, the city of Teotihuacán in Mexico was laid out in similar fashion. Sometimes orientation was used to spectacular symbolic effect. At Chichén Itzá, also in Mexico, the steps and terraces of the pyramid-temple represent the days and months of the year, so that at the spring and autumn equinoxes the shadows and patterns of sunlight made it look as if its serpent-god was coiling and writhing its way out of the temple.

GLORIES OF NATURE

Many of the sites explored in this book represent the attempts of humankind to travel across land and sea, or to make a mark on previously uninhabited territory. Yet it is not long since whole continents on Earth remained more or less unexplored by humanity. Antarctica is the world's last real wilderness on land, and much of the ocean floor is still a mystery. Our small planet, one of millions of stars in the galaxy, which is itself one of millions of galaxies in the universe, is an astoundingly beautiful place. Think of the Grand Canyon (the almost unbelievably vast gorge in the Arizona Desert, worn more than 1.6km/1 mile deep by the Colorado River), the bewildering array of life among the corals of the Great Barrier Reef, the delicate beauty of snow-topped Mount Fuji and the fiery rage of the young Hawaiian volcanoes.

Extremes of nature have always been a source of fascination. The formidable peaks of the Himalayas, the world's highest mountains, have provided daunting goals for mountaineers—not only the highest peak of all, Mount Everest, but the sheer ascents of Annapurna I and Nanga Parbat—the highest and longest wall climbs, respectively, in existence. The Dead Sea marks the lowest point on the earth's land surface and attracts crowds of visitors to marvel at its strange clusters of mineral salts and to wallow in the mudbaths and hot springs at its southern reaches. The world's biggest desert, the Great Sahara, is astonishing for the range of landscapes and life contained within its nine million sq km (3.5 million square miles), though best known for the ethereal beauty of its sweeping, golden sand dunes. And in the same continent the world's longest river, the Nile, flows more than 6,436km (4,000 miles) across Africa to its delta, one of the most fertile places on Earth, where fields and crops are irrigated by its waters today as they have been for thousands of years.

THE CHANGING WORLD

Nature is always changing, as is evident from the growing Hawaiian Islands and Iceland's steaming vents. The drift of continents, the ravages of weather and the natural extinction and evolution of species continues inexorably from millennium to millennium. Other changes, not always

positive, have been brought about by human activity. This activity hastens the pace of change and damages many of the planet's wonderful places. The Amazonian rainforest—only one example of many endangered forests around the globe—is being felled and cleared at an alarming rate, and before many native species have even been identified. The ozone layer is being depleted—at least in part by industrial emissions—and the increased ultra-violet radiation affects plants, animals and even the polar ice caps. Some animal species are on the verge of extinction as their habitats disappear. Increased travel, itself an element in these changes, has also opened the eyes of millions to the wonders of their planet. With proper care millions more will be able to appreciate this world's magnificent sites.

As for manmade monuments, cities and temples, they will crumble in time and be replaced by new wonders. Their remains may linger to perplex future generations, just as the ruined legacies of past ages, half-smothered by jungle growth, eroded by weather or pilfered for new structures, continue to intrigue us today. Sometimes the ravages of war threaten to destroy our wonders before their time—as at Angkor Wat, where scarring and bullet holes tell of recent hostilities. Sometimes the actions of individuals, governments or states are blamed for the defacement of great buildings. An example is Athens, where controversy still rages over the removal of the Elgin Marbles from the city's landmark Parthenon.

EARTH AND BEYOND

Looking ever outwards and upwards, mankind continues its search for the astounding and the extreme, for new challenges to meet and for new technologies. The great adventure into space has only just begun and already we have images of previously unimaginable wonders such as giant, spiralling columns of stardust, planets of fire, planets of ice, the birth of stars and stars on the point of death. But however many marvels we discover beyond our planet, and no matter how many planets there may be, there is no denying the beauty of our own small planet. There is also no denying its fragility. It is worth celebrating the wonders of our world for they must surely be at least as amazing as those of any other world.

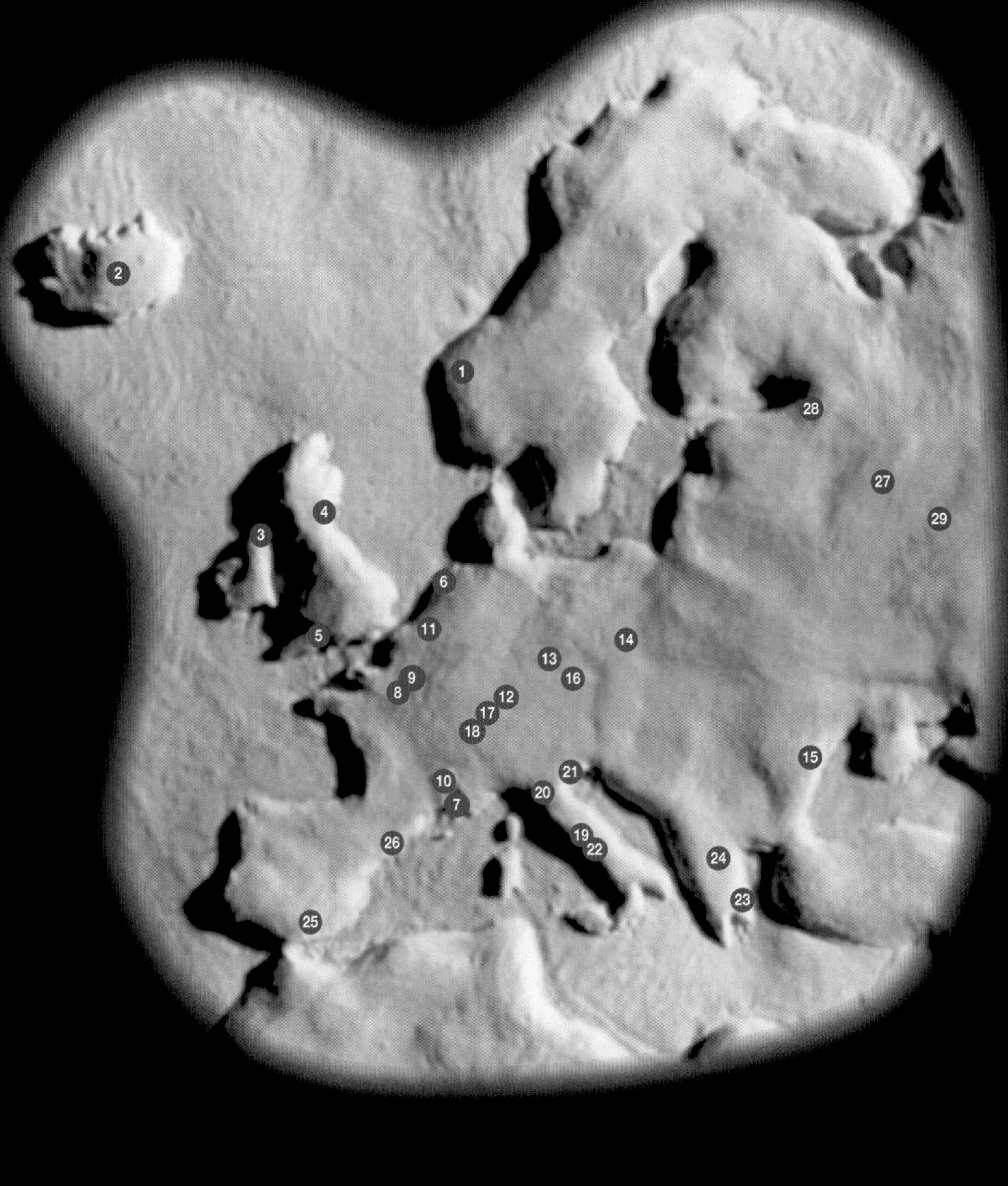

1 **The Great Fjords**
2 **Volcanic Iceland**
3 **The Giant's Causeway**
4 **Edinburgh Castle**
5 **Stonehenge**
6 **The Waddenzee**
7 **The Camargue**
8 **Versailles**
9 **The Eiffel Tower**
10 **The Pont du Gard**
11 **Grand' Place**
12 **Neuschwanstein**
13 **Golden Lane**
14 **The Wieliczka Salt Mines**
15 **The Danube Delta**
16 **The Hofburg**
17 **Kapellbrücke**
18 **The Matterhorn**
19 **The Colosseum**
20 **The Leaning Tower of Pisa**
21 **The Grand Canal**
22 **St Peter's Basilica**
23 **The Parthenon**
24 **Meteóra Monasteries**
25 **The Alhambra**
26 **The Sagrada Família**
27 **The Kremlin**
28 **The Great Palace**
29 **The Trans-Siberian Railway**

Europe

Since the great temple of Stonehenge was raised 5,000 years ago there have been many great feats of design and engineering in Europe—some built to induce awe, fear or respect, some to glorify deities and some to glorify monarchs and emperors. From the 5th century BC until the 4th century AD the Greek and Roman civilizations exerted a profound influence on Western culture. In Athens the Parthenon, temple of its protecting goddess, symbolized the Hellenistic ascendancy, and when Roman power extended across Europe and North Africa, the Colosseum provided an impressive monument to imperial grandeur and savagery.

After the fall of Rome in AD476 a new Western European civilization emerged, bringing with it soaring cathedrals and palaces, while in Granada the Muslim conquerors of Spain built a paradise on earth among the shaded courts of the Alhambra.

The genius of Greece and Rome took hold of Europe afresh during the Renaissance. In Rome, at the heart of Western Christendom, the vast Basilica of St Peter heralded the grandiose baroque style. The merchant princes of Venice, who controlled European trade with the East, constructed waterside palaces along the Grand Canal, while their northern equivalents in the Low Countries created the sumptuous Grand' Place in Brussels. Renaissance influence spread as far as Moscow, where the cathedral of St Michael the Archangel was built in the citadel of the Kremlin.

The evolution of the modern nation-state required palaces appropriate to the rulers' status. In Vienna the Hapsburg dynasty ruled an empire from the Hofburg, and Versailles made a noble setting for the Sun King, Louis XIV, and his successors in France.

A new age dawned with the 18th-century Industrial Revolution, which transformed the rural economy of Western Europe into an economy of machines, factories, teeming towns and mass production of consumer goods. The Eiffel Tower in Paris and the rails of the Trans-Siberian Railway, stretching from Moscow to the far coast of Asia, are two potent symbols of this age of machinery.

1 The Great Fjords, Norway

the facts

- Norway's coastline is 21,347km (13,264 miles) long.
- *Fjord* is a Norwegian word meaning 'an arm of the sea', and is applied to any long, narrow land indentations flooded by the sea.
- Sognafjorden is around 1,212m (4,000ft) at its deepest point and 610m (2,000ft) at its highest.

The Great Fjords

BELOW: *Dramatic scenery reflected in the still waters of Sognafjorden.*

Sitting in a small boat between the grey and forbidding walls of the great Norwegian fjords, it is easy to see how the legends of Valhalla and the brooding Nordic gods arose. On a dull and misty day, it is also not difficult to imagine the Viking longships in these mysterious waters, oars dipping into the still waters as the Norsemen headed off to explore the coasts of more gentle lands.

Fjords Great and Small

Sognafjorden is the biggest fjord in Norway. This finger of the sea is 180km (112 miles) long, although it is seldom more than 5km (3 miles) wide. It has several branches, including Naeroyfjord, where the walls crowd so closely together that ships sailing down it seem to disappear into a tunnel.

The great fjord carves its way through barren, desolate scenery to the highest mountains in Norway. Most of the way, the flanking mountains loom over the water and it always seems to be in twilight.

One of the smallest but most spectacular fjords is Geirangerfjord, snaking along 16km (10 miles) to the sea with sheer waterfalls cascading down its slopes and a village at each end—Geiranger and Hellesylt.

RIGHT: *The spectacular views are best enjoyed from the water.*

ABOVE: *A waterfall tumbles in steep cascades into Sognafjorden.*

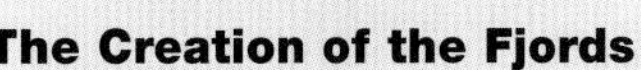

The Creation of the Fjords

Scandinavia's fjords were created many thousands of years ago during the ice ages, when glaciers ground their way across the land, carving deep U-shaped valleys. Sheer cliffs at the water's edge show tell-tale signs of scratching and scouring by the ice, and the fjords are shallower at the point where they enter the sea—here, the glaciers ran out of the power necessary to gouge through the bedrock. Not all geologists accept that the fjords were formed entirely by glacial action; the beds of some of the deepest fjords, such as Sognafjorden, in Norway, are considered too far below sea-level to have been wholly carved in this way.

Norway's Fjords

The Norwegian coast is deeply indented with fjords from Stavanger, in the south, to the border with Russia. Bergen, easily accessible by air and by ferry, makes a good base for exploration. Unlike the country's cold and mountainous interior, the coastal climate is temperate, modified by the North Atlantic current. Some 150,000 islands lie offshore, many supporting small settlements.

Fjords lead inland, to where great icecaps once lay. Little remains of the icecap that ruled supreme until 10,000 years ago, only isolated patches of ice, such as the Jostedalsbreen to the north of Sognafjorden. The pressure of the icecaps forced ice to flow seaward in individual valley glaciers. This process can be seen today at the vast Søndre Strømfjord on Greenland's west coast, where a glacier still flows over its head, producing green-blue icebergs.

In Norway the fjords make communication by land difficult, for villages that may lie just a few miles apart by boat are sometimes hundreds of miles apart by road. In the past many settlements had no land communications at all because the steep-sided fjords made permanent roads impossible. Some remote places still rely on sea-going vessels such as the *Hurtigruten* for contact.

The *Hurtigruten*

The *Hurtigruten* is a fjord ship that sails regularly from Bergen to Kirkenes, in the far north, following the rugged coastline and stopping at more than 30 settlements along the way. The voyage takes 12 days in all and brings communication and supplies to isolated communities, ranging from towns to hamlets, some of which are on tiny offshore islands.

For over 110 years the *Hurtigruten* has been an essential coastal service. In recent years, it has also doubled as a tourist attraction, as passengers take the opportunity to enjoy the cruise past dramatic fjord scenery from the fertile south to the Arctic Circle.

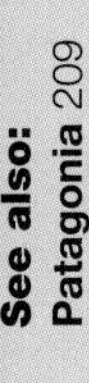

See also: **Patagonia** 209

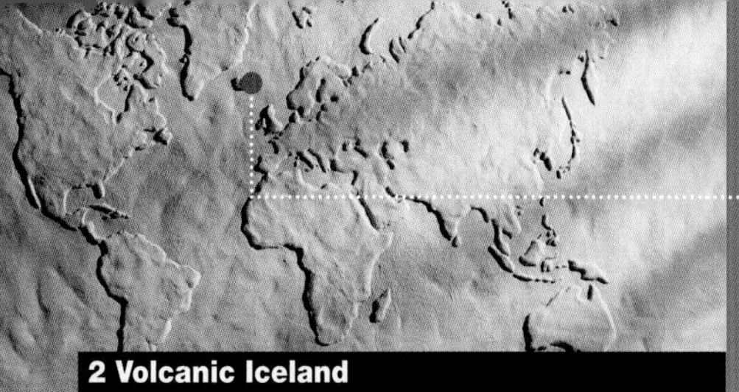

the facts

- Iceland's highest point is Hvannadals-hnúkur, 2,119m (6,952ft) up, on Öræfajökull in the south.
- Hraunhafnartangi, the northernmost point of Iceland, just touches the Arctic Circle.
- In 1963 a fissure eruption created Surtsey, a new island off the south coast.

Volcanic Iceland

Iceland is a land like no other. Only the southern coastal plains support much vegetation, and most of the farms are found here. The interior of the country is a barren, lunar-looking landscape, almost uninhabited, especially in winter. The vast majority of the country's population of just over 262,000 lives in the capital, Reykjavík. Iceland is a volcanic island with no native natural building materials such as wood. There are few stone buildings here, and the roofs are mainly corrugated iron. The land itself is still being built by nature—constantly pulled into two parts because of its position. It lies across the vast undersea split known as the mid-Atlantic ridge, which is stretched as Greenland and Scotland continue to move apart and cause sudden upheavals. Eruptions due to the mid-Atlantic ridge have included Eldgjá (896) and Laki (1783).

The Birth of Iceland

The opening of the Atlantic Ocean began some 180 million years ago, and Greenland began to separate from Scotland 60 million years ago, giving rise to the Tertiary volcanic provinces of northern Ireland, northwest Scotland and southeast Greenland. The oldest rocks in Iceland are less than 60 million years old and the island has continued to grow since that time, piling sheet upon sheet of lava from long fissure eruptions that provided the foundation for the active volcanoes of today. Despite the internal heat of Iceland, the island was covered by a sheet of ice during the

BELOW: *Icebergs floating on the glacial lagoon of Jökulsárlón.*

Explosive Landscape

Evidence of volcanism is everywhere, from the major active volcanic cones such as Hekla (major eruption in 1947, lesser eruptions in 1991 and 2000) to extinct craters, many with spectacular lakes and extensive hot spring areas. These springs range from sulphurous pools of boiling mud to crystal clear, turquoise-blue siliceous springs and geysers. Stóri Geysir (Great Geyser) at Geysir has given its name to all other spouting springs, and although it spouts less frequently today, it still performs spectacularly.

Hot water is Iceland's geological heritage and its value has long been recognized. Reykjavík is centrally heated by the island's subterranean hot water which is pumped to all public and domestic buildings.

last ice age and the remnants of that sheet form the icecaps and glaciers seen here today. Of the 102,797sq km (39,690 square miles) or so that Iceland covers, about 11.5 percent is made up of icecaps and glaciers.

Vatnajökull, on the southeast of Iceland, is the largest icecap in Europe, covering many geothermal sources. One of these gives rise to Grimsvötn, a unique lake within the icecap with a surface that is normally frozen solid. The source of the Jökulsá á Fjöllum River lies beneath the northern part of Vatnajökull, with hot springs under the ice keeping a chimney open to the lake above. In 1983 a canoeing expedition lowered its boats down the chimney and then paddled through the ice tunnel to the open river and down to the North Atlantic Ocean.

Settlement in Iceland

In the ninth and tenth centuries AD settlers from Scandinavia and from Norse communities in Britain arrived at Iceland, the last European country to be settled. The first to make a home here was Ingólfur Arnarson, a Norwegian chieftain, who brought his extended family in 874 and set up a farm on the present site of Reykjavík. In 930 Icelandic society was firmly established and the Althingi (parliament) was instituted, meeting once a year to adopt laws and deliver judgements.

Icelandic adventurers discovered Greenland in the late tenth century, and in about 1000 Leifur Eiríksson was the first European to set foot on the American continent.

See also:
Beppu 103
Deception Island 236-7
Hawaiian Islands 182-3

3 **The Giant's Causeway,** Northern Ireland

the facts

- There are about 40,000 basalt columns making up the Giant's Causeway.
- The tallest columns rise about 12.2m (40ft) from sea level.
- At some points in the cliffs they are 27.4m (90ft) thick.
- Molten basalt has been recorded flowing downhill at speeds of more than 48km (30 miles) per hour.

The Giant's Causeway

The strange columns of the Giant's Causeway in County Antrim, Northern Ireland, seem to have been fashioned as part of a vast, manmade architectural monument. Wedged tightly together, they descend in tiers, forming irregular stepping stones from the cliffside and out into the sea. Most of the columns are strictly hexagonal, though some have four, five, seven or eight straight sides. Their creation is, inevitably, the theme of legend, but in fact they were the result of the reshaping of an active landscape.

Formation of the North Atlantic

In the early days of the North Atlantic Ocean, the newly formed seaway flowing between the recently separated continents of North America and Europe was a still-developing feature: the body of the North Atlantic was in place, but its edges were still being formed and re-formed. The western coast of Greenland separated from Canada about 80 million years ago but the southeastern coast was still firmly attached to the opposing northwestern coast of the British Isles. Some 20 million years later these coasts began to separate and there were major volcanoes on what are now the islands of Skye, Rum, Mull and Arran, on the Scottish mainland at Ardnamurchan Point, and also to the south in Ireland at Slieve Gullion, Carlingford and Mourne. These ancient volcanoes must have been splendid sights in their prime, but the greatest record of this episode lies in the flood, or plateau, basalts. Basalt is a particularly hot, fluid lava, able to spread across large areas relatively easily, and constitutes the bulk of lava features found in this whole volcanic area.

BELOW RIGHT: *The Giant's Causeway steps down from the cliffs into the crashing waves of the Atlantic Ocean.*

RIGHT: *The basalt columns form a natural, and very convenient, seating area.*

Fingal's Cave

Columnar basalts are not confined to Northern Ireland, and another of the best known examples of this phenomenon is in the Inner Hebrides, off Scotland's west coast.

On Staffa, the columns are well developed over a large part of the island, and a huge cave where the sea has eroded the columns is known as Fingal's Cave, after a mythical giant.

Fingal's Cave has figured in many poems and novels over the centuries, and a rather rough boat trip to the island in 1829 by the composer Felix Mendelssohn inspired his famous orchestral overture, known as *The Hebrides.*

Any hot liquid contracts as it cools, and molten lava is no exception. However when lava eventually cools sufficiently to crystallize, it tends to crack in a regular pattern, usually a hexagonal design similar to the cracks formed in the bottom of a muddy pond that dries out in a hot summer. The significant difference with lava is that the cracks extend right down through the flow from top to bottom. The result is a distinctive network of basalt columns, all packed incredibly closely together with just the thinnest of gaps between. Geologists refer to these cracks as 'joints' and to the whole as 'columnar basalt'. The width of the columns is typically about 46cm (18in), but larger and smaller columns are known. The Giant's Causeway is a particularly fine example of this unique phenomenon—a grand causeway, fit for giants.

The Myth of the Giant's Causeway

Legend has it that the Giant's Causeway was built by the Irish giant Finn Mac Cool, who drove the columns into the sea bed one by one so that he could walk to Scotland to fight his rival Finn Gall. When his work was finished, Finn Mac Cool decided to take a rest. Meanwhile, Finn Gall walked across to Ireland to size up his opponent, and was amazed and frightened by the size of the sleeping giant, especially after Mac Cool's wife told him that this was, in fact, only the giant's baby.

Fearing for his life at the thought of how big the baby's father might be, Finn Gall beat a hasty retreat, destroying the causeway behind him. All that remains of it today is on the Antrim coast.

See also:
Devil's Tower 172-3
Uluru (Ayer's Rock) 218-19

the facts

- The One O'Clock Gun is fired every day except Sunday at 1pm and is used by locals as an infallible time-check.
- The Scottish crown dates from 1540 and is of Scottish gold set with 94 pearls, 10 diamonds and 33 gems.
- A small fountain in the Esplanade marks the spot where those convicted of witchcraft were killed.

Edinburgh Castle

The high basalt rock that looms over Edinburgh has probably been the site of a fort since the Iron Age. Edwin, King of Northumbria, rebuilt the original fortifications in the seventh century and some 400 years later Malcolm III and his queen, Margaret, took up residence there. Only one building, named in tribute to the pious Queen, remains from that period: St Margaret's Chapel, the oldest surviving structure in the city. The rest of the castle was demolished in 1314 to foil invading English armies.

The castle now seen by about a million visitors a year is a conglomeration of buildings added, embellished and rearranged over the course of around 700 years. An L-shaped keep, known as King David's Tower, was built at the southeast corner of Castle Rock and later partly incorporated into the 16th-century Half Moon Battery, which was raised on a platform for the defence of the castle's northeastern flank. The King's Lodging and great hall were added in the 15th and 16th centuries and altered in the 17th century. Making up the fourth side of the square of palace buildings within the castle complex is the Scottish National War Memorial, constructed shortly after World

BELOW: *Canons on guard at the 16th-century Half Moon Battery.*

RIGHT: *Edinburgh Castle, sitting atop its great volcanic crag, domintes the city.*

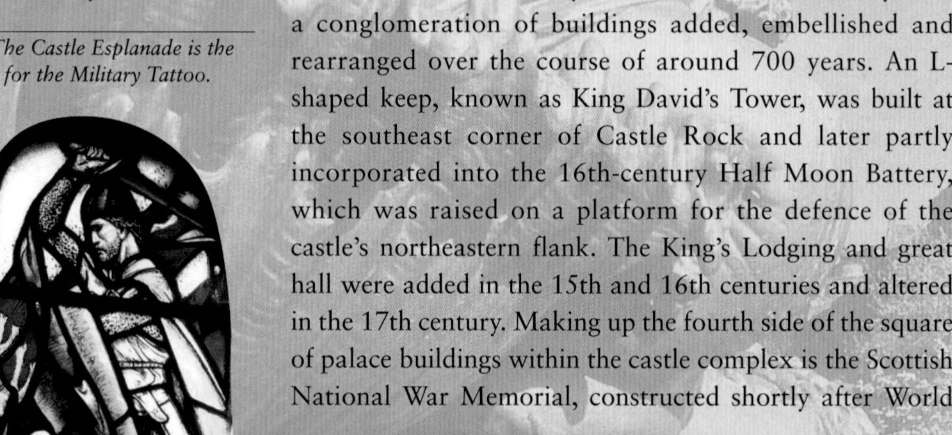

LEFT: *The Castle Esplanade is the venue for the Military Tattoo.*

LEFT: *William Wallace is depicted in a stained-glass window inside St Margaret's Chapel.*

Mons Meg

This mighty cannon was made for the Duke of Burgundy in Belgium in 1449. The Duke duly passed it on to his nephew, King James II of Scotland, who employed it in 1455 against his enemies the Douglas family at their stronghold, Threave Castle, bringing a two-month siege to an abrupt end. Mons Meg's last action came in the 17th century when the cannon exploded while firing a salute.

For over a century it was kept in the Tower of London, but writer Sir Walter Scott called for its return to Scotland in the 19th century and Meg found a retirement home at Edinburgh Castle in 1829.

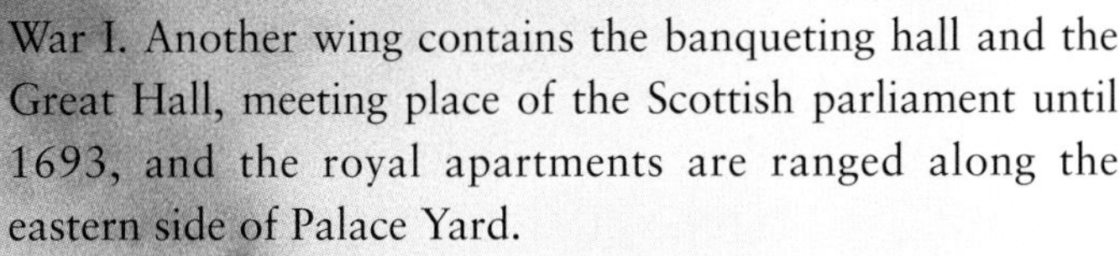

War I. Another wing contains the banqueting hall and the Great Hall, meeting place of the Scottish parliament until 1693, and the royal apartments are ranged along the eastern side of Palace Yard.

Among the royal apartments is the tiny room where Mary, Queen of Scots gave birth to the future King James VI of Scotland and James I of England in 1566. She had fled to the castle to have her child in safety, after the shocking murder of her secretary and suspected lover, David Rizzio (1533-66), by a band of conspirators who included the Queen's own husband, Henry Stuart, Lord Darnley. In 1603, on the death of the childless Elizabeth I, James succeeded to the throne of England and moved his court to London. From then on Edinburgh Castle, former royal residence, became an occasional stopover for monarchs and served largely as a military fortress and prison. During the wars with France in the 18th and 19th centuries, French prisoners of war were held in its vaults and the graffiti they etched into the walls can still be seen.

The Scottish regalia—crown, sceptre and sword of state—were walled up here after the union of Scottish and English parliaments in 1707, and are now on display in the stone-vaulted Crown Room.

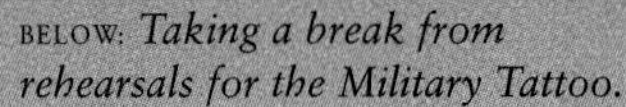

BELOW: *Taking a break from rehearsals for the Military Tattoo.*

The Esplanade

For three weeks in August the Castle Esplanade, the ceremonial parade ground outside the castle entrance, hosts the Edinburgh Military Tattoo, a world-famous military and musical display.

The Esplanade was built in 1753. In the early 19th century it was made wider and given walls and railings, signifying the castle's transition from military barracks to symbolic landmark. The castle is always guarded, nevertheless, and acts as the headquarters of the Scottish Division and several regiments and military museums.

The first Edinburgh Tattoo was presented on the Esplanade in 1950 and since then over 11 million people have joined the audience at the castle, not to mention the 100 million television viewers who tune in to watch it every year.

See also:
The Hofburg 37
Neuschwanstein 32-3

Some stones are 8m (25ft) high and weigh 40 tonnes.

The bluestones within the sandstone ring are thought to have been transported from the Preseli Mountains of South Wales, possibly on rafts along water routes.

The trilithons were deliberately shaped to be wider in the middle, giving them an even appearance from below.

Stonehenge

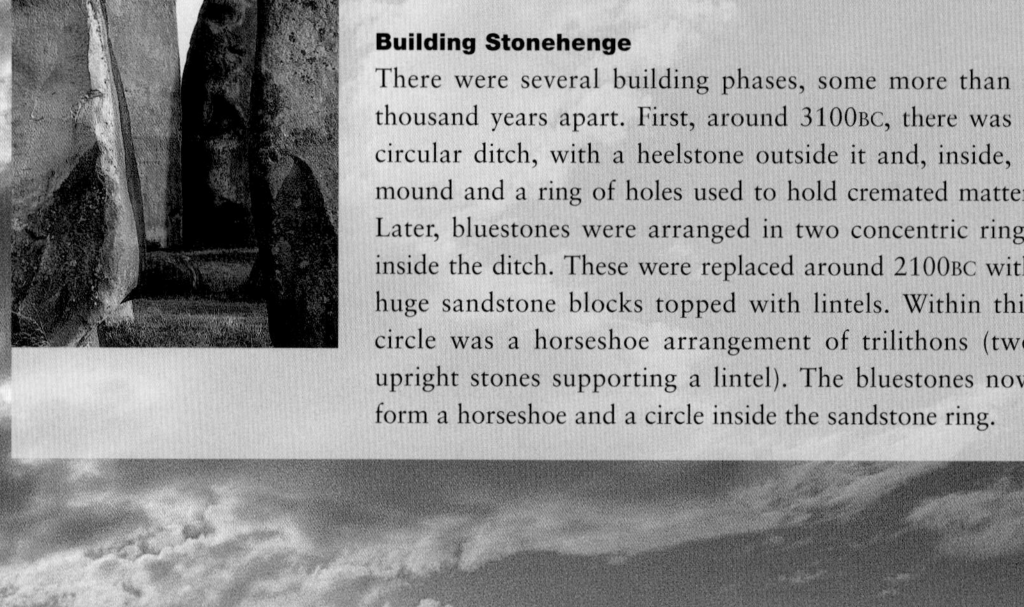

One of many theories about Stonehenge suggests that it was a prehistoric astronomical observatory. The axis of the inner horseshoe of stones and an ancient approach road to the site are aligned with the midsummer sun. Whatever their original purpose, these giant monoliths from another age still evoke a powerful atmosphere.

Building Stonehenge

There were several building phases, some more than a thousand years apart. First, around 3100BC, there was a circular ditch, with a heelstone outside it and, inside, a mound and a ring of holes used to hold cremated matter. Later, bluestones were arranged in two concentric rings inside the ditch. These were replaced around 2100BC with huge sandstone blocks topped with lintels. Within this circle was a horseshoe arrangement of trilithons (two upright stones supporting a lintel). The bluestones now form a horseshoe and a circle inside the sandstone ring.

Avebury

A few miles from Stonehenge, at Avebury in Wiltshire, is a stone circle thought to be the largest in the world. An estimated 247 standing stones form outer and inner rings; another 97 or so pairs formed an associated avenue. A huge ditch around the outer stone circle, 21m (70ft) wide, encloses an area of nearly 12ha (30 acres). The outer circle of about 100 stones surrounds two smaller circles, and each of the smaller circles had another stone or stones arranged within it.

Like Stonehenge, Avebury defies all attempts to solve its mysteries. Sun or moon worship, fertility rites—the list of theories is endless. The Avebury stones date from about 2600BC, but the area shows signs of earlier activity.

6 **The Waddenzee,** Netherlands/Denmark

the facts

- The Waddenzee extends over 488km (310 miles), from the Netherlands to Denmark.
- Its waters are 2m to 3m (6ft to 10ft) deep.
- The total area covered is around 10,101sq km (3,900 square miles).

The Waddenzee

ABOVE: *The Waddenzee is home to many species of duck including mallard.*

The Waddenzee is one of Europe's most important and productive wetland areas. The shallow waters and extensive intertidal areas of sand and mud flats, shallow sandbanks and salt marsh are protected from the forces of the North Sea by a string of offshore islands. More than ten million birds from as far afield as northeast Canada, Greenland, Iceland and Siberia congregate here to feed, and many birds breed here during the summer, especially on the many remote islands. Over 100 species of fish, and both common and grey seals, also rely on the Waddenzee for at least part of the year.

Environmental Concerns

Much of the coastline of the southern North Sea is under considerable developmental pressure. The construction of ports and embankments to protect against rising sea levels has resulted in the loss of much of the original salt marsh. Nonetheless, what remains still represents the most extensive wetland area in Europe.

Vulnerable Wildlife

The population of the common seal in the Waddenzee, as elsewhere in the North Sea, has been severely reduced in recent years. A ban on seal-hunting and a reduction of some pollutants had led to an increase in numbers to 10,000 by the early 1980s, but in 1988 large numbers of dead common seals were reported around the North Sea, including around 7,000 in the Waddenzee. The seals were victims of the distemper virus. Manmade compounds and pesticides don't degrade easily and accumulate in the tissues of animals like seals, reducing the effectiveness of their immune system and making them more susceptible to such infections.

Seal numbers are recovering slowly, but the incident is a reminder of the vulnerability of wild populations to such events.

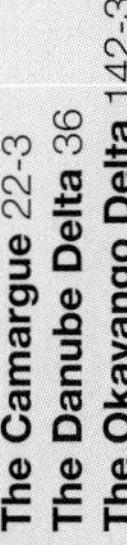

See also:
The Camargue 22-3
The Danube Delta 36
The Okavango Delta 142-3

- The Camargue lies at the mouth of the River Rhône, in the Golfe des Saintes-Maries in the South of France.
- It extends over 1,466sq km (566 square miles).
- More than 300 species of migrant birds have been recorded here. Nesting birds include the collared pratincole, which breeds nowhere else in France.

the **facts**

ABOVE: *A buzzard poised for flight in the Camargue.*

RIGHT: *Flamingos are a familiar and exotic sight on the lagoons.*

The **Camargue**

This huge coastal wetland area is one of the most important of its type in Europe. When the Roman and Greek empires were at the height of their powers, the Mediterranean coast supported a mosaic of wetlands, which remained largely intact until the 19th century. Large areas were then drained to create agricultural land and to destroy the breeding grounds of the mosquito. As a result, very little remains,

Brine Shrimps

Very few animals can adapt to highly saline waters. Those that have done so usually occur in very large numbers and the brine shrimp, *Artemia salina*, is no exception.

This shrimp, no more than 15mm (0.6in) long, can live in salt levels ranging from less than a third of that of sea water to over six times as much. This enables it to survive periods of inundation by fresh water as well as times of extreme drought. It achieves this feat by having a skin which is impermeable to both salt and water, and transfer of both is restricted to very confined, strictly controlled areas of its body.

BELOW: *The beach at Étang de Vaccarès.*

but the Camargue has survived more or less intact—although human intervention, such as the development of the salt pans, has brought changes to the landscape.

A Rich Habitat

The Camargue is an intricate mix of beaches, sand dunes, reed beds, brackish lakes, riverine forest and pasture lands, together with the extensive salt pans. This array of varied habitats, combined with the strategic geographic location of the Camargue, makes it a vital staging post in the migration routes of many bird species. Millions of ducks, geese and waders visit each year from as far afield as Siberia and northern Europe. Some of these birds are merely transient visitors on longer journeys; others come here to nest and breed, attracted by the combination of suitable roost sites and the adjacent feeding areas. Ducks spend a large part of the day in relative safety on the many brackish ponds in the region. In the early morning and late evening they can fly to the nearby marshes to feed. Many of these marshes are privately managed and wild fowling is permitted. As a result the numbers of birds over-wintering on the Camargue have dropped by 50 percent during the last ten years.

Perfect Conditions

The unusual conditions of very high salinity created by the salt pans make the area especially suitable for the brine shrimp, an important food for some species of bird, particularly the pink or greater flamingo. These strikingly beautiful birds are a symbol of the success of the management of the Camargue: since 1944 the number of breeding pairs of greater flamingos has risen steadily. Central to their success is the presence of secure nest sites in the salt pans and the proximity of rich feeding areas.

The Camargue is also famous for its local breed of black cattle and, more particularly, for the celebrated roaming herds of semi-wild white horses, thought to be direct descendants of primitive horses.

BELOW: *Distinctive white horses are bred in the Camargue.*

Salt Pans

One of the easiest ways of obtaining salt, historically an important trading commodity, is by allowing the sun to evaporate sea water, which leaves a residue of salt and other trace elements. In the salt pans of the Camargue, sea water is moved by pumps through a series of shallow ponds or pans, becoming more and more salty at each stage, until it reaches the final pan, where the last of the water evaporates to leave the crystalline salt.

The complete predictability of this artificial system guarantees suitable conditions for birds to roost, feed and breed. It is this manmade system that has given the Camargue its importance as a major site for the greater flamingo, as well as for other avian visitors.

See also:
The Danube Delta 36
The Okavango Delta 142-3
The Waddenzee 21

the facts

- The gardens of Versailles cover 101ha (250 acres).
- The garden frontage of the palace is 640m (2,100ft) long, and the Hall of Mirrors is 72m (235ft) long, 10.6m (35ft) wide and 12.8m (42ft) high.
- Construction of the palace started in 1661.

Versailles

Versailles, less than 24km (15 miles) from Paris, was chosen by King Louis XIII (1601–43) as the site for a modest chateau that would serve him as a base for his hunting expeditions. His son, Louis XIV (1638–1715), also enjoyed hunting but had more elaborate plans for the estate. Dissatisfied with other palaces available (including the Louvre and the Tuileries), he decided, in 1660, to turn Versailles into a vast royal enclave. Everything was to be the ultimate in magnificence, and he would build on such a scale that eventually the whole French court could be accommodated.

Work began in 1661, and in the course of two years Louis XIV, who came to be known as the Sun King, spent a vast amount of money, provoking anguished protests from the

BACKGROUND: *The focal point of the park is the ornamental pool with a magnificent bronze sculpture of the sun god Apollo driving his chariot.*

BELOW: *Le Nôtre designed the gardens along geometric lines.*

Outdoor Theatre

Parisian nobility flocked to the gardens during the early years of the Sun King's reign, and in 1664, 1668 and 1674 the grounds became the backdrop for elaborate artistic extravaganzas, featuring operas by Lully and plays by Molière and Racine. The whole place was like a stage set, with entire re-created landscapes, such as the 'Grand Canal', with its own 'Little Venice'.

This tradition of make-believe was continued by Louis XIV's successors, most notoriously by Marie Antoinette. She had her own theatre built within the grounds and even created a rustic hamlet, stocked with animals and staffed by shepherds and other country people, where she and her friends could play at being peasants.

treasury. In fact, building was to continue for decades, involving many thousands of workmen and ever-increasing expense. The original architect, Louis Le Vau, was succeeded by Jules Hardouin Mansart, who worked on Versailles for 30 years. André Le Nôtre was responsible for the landscaping, and his grand design for the gardens so surpassed the original chateau that it was decided to turn it into a far more sumptuous palace.

Very Royal Reflections

At the heart of the building is the Hall of Mirrors, a huge gallery with 17 windows overlooking the gardens, matched by enormous mirrors on the opposite wall. Paintings by Charles Le Brun present a flattering account of the reign of Louis XIV between 1661 and 1678; this artistic celebration of the king helped to enhance the aura of royalty that Louis was determined to cultivate. Versailles became his permanent residence in 1682, and the French court was soon established there. Complex rituals developed, and precise rules of etiquette were observed. Hopeful courtiers would come to Versailles and wait, sometimes in vain, for an opportunity to witness the king's *Levée* or *Coucher*—the rising or retiring to bed.

Louis XIV died in 1715. Louis XV (1710–74) engaged the architect Gabriel to carry out further work, including the building of an opera salon and the palace known as the Petit Trianon. Under Louis XVI (1754–93) a fine library was added and his queen Marie Antoinette (1755–93) took over the Petit Trianon. But in October 1789 revolutionaries reached Versailles and the palace was invaded.

The Gardens

Versailles' gardens were designed to house a wealth of sculpture. The Water Parterre, in front of the Hall of Mirrors, has two lakes, each with four statues representing rivers of France. The Loire and Loiret are by Regnaudin, the Saône and the Rhône are by Tuby, the rivers Marne and Seine are by Le Hongre, and the Garonne and the Dordogne rivers are by Coysevox.

A magnificent work in lead by Tuby depicts Apollo, god of the sun, driving his horses and chariot out of a lake. The Fountain of Enceladus by Gaspard Marsy, dating from 1676, portrays the tortured figure of the Titan Enceladus virtually buried beneath rocks.

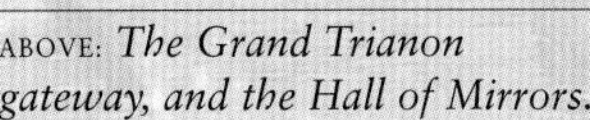

ABOVE: *The Grand Trianon gateway, and the Hall of Mirrors.*

RIGHT: *A copy of Giovanni Battista Foggini's statue* The Knife Grinder *in the gardens at Versailles.*

See also:
The Great Palace 64-5
The Hofburg 37
Neuschwanstein 32-3

The Eiffel Tower

For over a hundred years the Eiffel Tower has been synonymous with Paris, its silhouette instantly reconizable throughout the world. Visible far and wide throughout the city, it soars above the River Seine, opposite the Trocadero Palace by the Pont d'Iéna. Its slender grace and strength combine in a symbol of the achievements of the industrial age—a daring demonstration of the skills and ambitions of engineers and designers in the late 19th century.

Building techniques and materials accelerated the pace of change in the 19th century, and the challenge preoccupying many engineers—and politicians—of the day was to build a structure over 300m (1,000ft) high. French engineer Gustave Eiffel (1832–1923) and his company produced plans for such a tower at the end of 1884—largely the work of Eiffel's head of research, Maurice Koechlin. When a competition was announced two years later for schemes suitable for the 1889 Paris Exposition, over 100 schemes were submitted, but it was Eiffel who was chosen to create the world's tallest structure.

Eiffel had built a number of railroad bridges and had a reputation for solving the most technically challenging problems. He was unusual among his peers for his reliance on calculation and precision, and his understanding of environmental stresses such as windforce led to the ingenious use of filigree iron, reducing the surface area to a minimum.

Over 18,000 separate components were used in the construction of the tower, many of them prefabricated and produced with the aid of detailed technical drawings. The tallest tower in the world was built by a team of around 250 men at a speed that still seems

BELOW: *The various stages of the construction of the Eiffel Tower in 1888.*

the facts

- The entire structure weighs about 10,668 tonnes (11,760 tons) and contains 2.5 million rivets.
- The base of the tower encloses an area of 1.6ha (4 acres).
- About three million visitors go up the tower every year.
- There are 1,665 steps to the top of the tower. Visitors now take an elevator from the second floor.

the history

1884
Eiffel produces plans for a '300m Tower'.

1886
Competition announced for Paris Exposition designs.

1889
Tower opens on 31 March.

1926-36
Illuminated Citroën advert displayed on the tower.

1935
Tower becomes the city's TV transmission antenna.

1964
Eiffel Tower proclaimed an historic monument.

phenomenal: just 26 months. This rapid construction was possible only because of Eiffel's ability to plan ahead with the utmost precision. The 16 piers on which the tower stands (four to each leg of the base) incorporated hydraulic jacks to allow for exact alignment when the first platform came to be built. Only very minor adjustment was necessary, but without this facility it might never have been possible to complete the building.

For all the tower's social and curiosity appeal, it had a serious function from the start. Gustave Eiffel was a scientist, who recoiled from the idea that his tower was a mere ornament. He installed meteorological equipment at the top in order to investigate weather conditions at altitude and compare readings with those on the ground; and he also used the tower to conduct experiments in aerodynamics, constructing a wind tunnel at the base. The Eiffel Tower continued to facilitate pioneering scientific experiments, being used in radio transmission and housing the country's first radio and TV stations.

SUPPORTERS AND DETRACTORS

When the Eiffel Tower began to rise, a group of writers and artists signed a letter protesting about the effect that it would have on the Paris skyline and claiming that it was an insult to the city's great buildings. At one point building work was halted because of the fears of local residents that both their lives and their property were in danger: a mathematician had claimed that the whole structure would collapse before it reached 229m (750ft). Eiffel, who was already bearing the majority of the cost of the project, agreed to continue construction entirely at his own risk.

During the Paris Exposition two million visitors felt safe enough to take the elevator to the the first, second and third platforms. Later the first platform housed a restaurant, and author Guy de Maupassant is said to have frequented it because it was the only place on Paris from which he did not have a view of the tower. *Le Figaro* newspaper even opened an office on the second platform, 116m (380ft) up.

LEFT AND BELOW: *The Eiffel Tower was originally built by Gustave Eiffel as a temporary attraction for the 1889 Paris Exposition.*

See also:
The CN Tower 152-3
The Leaning Tower of Pisa 44-5

- The Pont du Gard is a UNESCO World Heritage Site.
- Only one of the lower six arches actually spans the river, and the arches in each tier are not identical.
- The aqueduct was built with a total drop of about 17m (55ft) between the water source and the city.

the **facts**

The **Pont du Gard**

The Pont du Gard was built by the Romans to carry fresh water across the Gardon River to Nîmes in southern France. Measuring 49m (160ft) high and 274m (900ft) long, it was part of a system of conduits and bridges that stretched 48km (30 miles) from Uzés. It was built by the Roman general and proconsul Agrippa (c.63-12BC), ally of the Emperor Augustus, and probably dates from 19BC.

The Pont du Gard has three tiers of arches, with 6 at the bottom, 11 in the middle, and 35 along the top directly below the water channel. Its stone blocks were laid without mortar, and rough knobs protruding from the sides were used to attach wooden scaffolding—essential for carrying out maintenance work when mineral deposits accumulated in the water channel. A modern visitor centre shows how the channel was built and maintained, and you can still cross the Pont via the adjacent bridge.

Roman Waterworks

In the first century AD a man called Frontinus was the superintendent of Rome's water supply. The technical handbook he wrote on the subject, *De Aquis*, goes into great mathematical detail about the dimensions of pipes and the construction of aqueducts, but also gives an insight into some of the sharp practices he encountered.

He tells of landowners who intercepted the public water supply running past their fields and diverted it to irrigate their crops. Confiscation of the land in question was a possible penalty for those caught in the act. Frontinus also reveals that a secret and elaborate network of pipes was detected beneath the streets of Rome, illicitly supplying water from public sources to private premises and shops.

the facts

- The original wooden guild houses on the site were replaced in flamboyant baroque style following a 36-hour French bombardment in 1695, when 16 churches and thousands of houses were destroyed.
- There's a flower market every day in the square, and a caged-bird market on Sunday mornings.

Grand' Place

Grand' Place, in Belgium's capital, Brussels, is a stage-set of pinnacles, curlicues, statues, gargoyles, medallions and heraldic beasts. Work started on the town hall, the Hôtel de Ville, which occupies most of one side, in 1402. The dazzling 91m (300ft) spire, designed by Jan van Ruysbroek, dates from the 1450s. On the façade are more than 100 statues which are 19th-century replacements of the originals. Inside are sumptuously decorated rooms hung with Brussels tapestries and paintings.

The Maison du Roi, opposite, was once the guild house of the bakers. It was used by the Spanish-appointed governors of the Low Countries and rebuilt between 1873 and 1895 in 16th-century style. Among the other gold-scrolled merchants' guild houses is La Louve (The She-Wolf), No. 5, which belonged to the Guild of Archers and displays a relief of Romulus and Remus being suckled by a wolf. The gable shows a phoenix, the emblem of Brussels.

ABOVE: *Workmen laying a carpet of flowers attract an audience in Grand' Place.*
RIGHT: *There are plenty of pavement cafés where you can relax and admire the setting.*

Manneken Pis

On the Rue de l'Etuve, not far from the Grand' Place, is the little bronze figure of a small boy passing water into the marble basin of a fountain. The 61cm (2ft) statue dates from the 19th century, but replaces much older figures. One legend about Manneken Pis has him naughtily bedewing the front steps of a wicked fairy, who retaliated by turning him to stone.

The statue is dressed up on special occasions. His first costume was presented to him in 1698 by the Elector of Bavaria, and in 1747 Louis XV of France sent him a suit of brocade embroidered in gold. Over 250 of his costumes are displayed in the Maison du Roi.

See also: Golden Lane 34

the facts

- Neuschwanstein took 17 years to build.
- Fifteen men worked for four and a half years just carving the king's bed.
- In 1886, only three months after moving in, King Ludwig II was declared unfit to rule, and soon afterwards was found dead in Lake Starnberg.

Neuschwanstein

Neuschwanstein is a fantasy made real—a fairy-tale castle festooned with balconies and turrets, rising high above the trees in the Bavarian Alps. Vast and substantial, it is the work of a leading set-painter called Christian Jank, and was commissioned by King Ludwig II of Bavaria (1845-86) as a backdrop against which he might act out the stuff of German romantic legend.

Ludwig had grown up in the nearby castle of Hohenschwangau, a medieval fortress restored by his father, Maximilian II, and decorated with wall paintings depicting, among other subjects, the legend of Lohengrin.

ABOVE: *Candelabras light up the grand Concert Hall.*

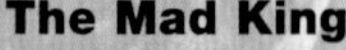

The Mad King

Ludwig appears to have identified with Lohengrin, the Knight of the Swan, and he developed an obsession with German mythology. A performance of Richard Wagner's opera *Lohengrin* in 1861 left him enchanted, and when he succeeded to the throne three years later, at the age of 18, one of his first acts was to summon Wagner for an audience. Now, with money at his disposal and all the power of a king, Ludwig became Wagner's patron, paid his debts, and promised to provide the composer with his longed-for theatre and festival, in the little town of Bayreuth. Wagner would create the German legend on stage on a grand scale and enact struggles between good and evil in front of an audience. Meanwhile, Ludwig would create a fantastic fairy-tale castle worthy in every way of the ancient German knights. This sort of thing was of limited appeal in Germany at the end of the 19th century. Ludwig was called the Mad King and seen as a man with no grasp of reality, although some were willing to credit him with clear-headed sense. His eccentric reputation was confirmed by his love of dressing up and his singular habits—he slept all day and reputedly entertained the ghost of Louis XIV at the dinner table.

The interior of the castle is a riot of different architectural styles, a Moorish-Gothic-baroque confection that incorporates stalactites, a throne room of outrageous Byzantine decadence, and a huge Singers' Hall, elaborately lit and intended for Wagnerian performances. Ludwig's taste for the medieval did not prevent him adding modern technology, however. The castle has an advanced heating system and a kitchen with hot and cold running water.

LEFT: *Pillars support the vaulted ceiling in the kitchens.*
RIGHT: *Built in the late 19th century, the castle is an amazing fantasy in stone.*

Linderhof

Ludwig had other extravagant palaces. Linderhof, near Oberammergau, stands in magnificent parkland where there are various structures including a temple of Venus and a Moorish kiosk that Ludwig bought while visiting the Paris Exhibition of 1867. Linderhof was built between 1869 and 1879, and here too the stage designer Jank was employed.

In the kiosk the King installed an outrageous peacock throne, and he is said to have dined on peacock from time to time and to have requested supplies of the bird from the Shah of Persia. Most astonishing of all is the Linderhof Venusberg Grotto, an artificial cave complete with lake and stalagmites and stalactites, and decorated with a huge painting of a scene from Wagner's opera *of 1845 Tannhauser.*

LEFT: *Intricate paintings decorate the Singers' Hall.*

Herrenchiemsee

Ludwig bought an island in Chiemsee Lake in 1873 with the idea of creating his own version of Versailles. He built a bigger and, to his mind, better Hall of Mirrors and a more sumptuous version of Louis XIV's Versailles bedroom, supposedly reserved for the use of that long-dead monarch.

The gardens were in the French style too, but after seven years' work the money ran out and the palace was never completed.

See also:
Edinburgh Castle 18-19
The Hofburg 37
Versailles 24-5

the **facts**

Franz Kafka (1883–1924) lived in Golden Lane between November 1916 and March 1917, and wrote many of the stories later included in *Ein Landarzt (A Country Doctor)*.

The Hradcany castle-palace complex, once the home of the rulers of Bohemia, has more recently served as the official residence of the Czech president.

Golden Lane

Golden Lane, formerly known as the Street of the Alchemists, huddles against the walls of Hradcany Castle in Prague. Its narrow, cobble-stoned street is lined with small, pastel-painted houses with diminutive doors and windows, low roofs and a crowd of chimneys. In the 1590s, in the time of the Hapsburg emperor Rudolf II who ruled from 1575 to 1612, these houses were occupied by guards from the castle. Later the street was taken over by goldsmiths.

At one end of the street is the Daliborka, a tower built in 1496. The story goes that it was named after its first prisoner, Dalibor of Kozojedy, who had joined a peasants' revolt. Imprisoned in chains, he taught himself to play the violin, which he did so sweetly that people would gather below the tower to listen. One day they waited in vain: Dalibor and his violin had been silenced. The 19th-century Czech composer Bedrich Smetana based his opera *Dalibor* on this moving story.

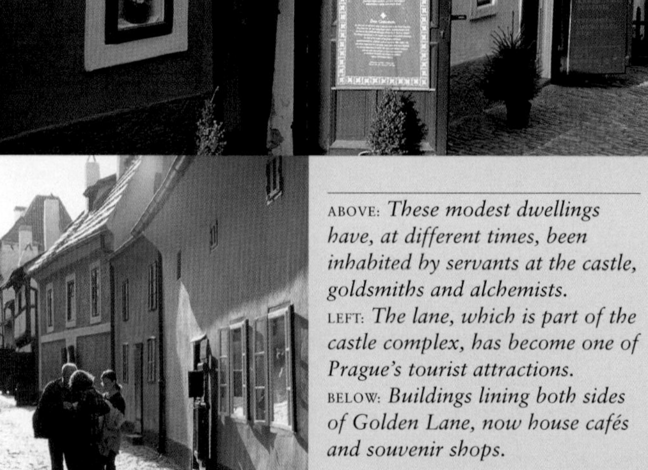

ABOVE: *These modest dwellings have, at different times, been inhabited by servants at the castle, goldsmiths and alchemists.*
LEFT: *The lane, which is part of the castle complex, has become one of Prague's tourist attractions.*
BELOW: *Buildings lining both sides of Golden Lane, now house cafés and souvenir shops.*

The Philosopher's Stone

Rudolf II was deeply preoccupied with alchemy, chemistry, astrology and astronomy. Born in Vienna in 1552, he was crowned King of Bohemia in 1575 and succeeded his father, Maximilian II, as Holy Roman Emperor the following year.

He suffered from severe bouts of depression, and shut himself away in Prague castle to concentrate on alchemical experiments. Meanwhile his court poet was ordered to write verse in praise of the fabled Philosopher's Stone, which reputedly turned base metals to gold and prolonged human life indefinitely. It was even said that the Emperor had discovered it himself.

In 1606 his family declared him incapable of ruling and tried to install his brother in his place. After several years of internecine strife, Rudolf died in Prague in 1612.

the facts

- There are over 200km (124ft) of underground passages on nine underground levels.
- More than 2,000 excavation chambers are linked together by the passages.
- The chambers reach depths of 327m (1,073ft) below the surface.

The Salt Mines of Wieliczka

Locals have been using the naturally occuring salt in Wieliczka, near Krakow in Poland, since prehistoric times, boiling off the briny spring water to leave the salt as a deposit. From the 13th century farmers began sinking small shafts during the winter, and by the time Wieliczka's modern mines closed in the 1990s they had developed into a vast network of passages and chambers, where the rock salt had been carved by generations of miners into sculptures and statues, churches, altars and bas-reliefs.

The largest of many chapels, the Chapel of the Blessed King is a spectacular space over 50m (164ft) long and 12m (39ft) high, scooped out of the rock 101m (331ft) below ground level. In the 19th century brine baths were provided to treat everything from catarrh to love-sickness, and from the late 1950s sufferers of respiratory problems could come here to benefit from the mines' microclimate. In 1996 the mines were opened for tourists to view the works of art.

BELOW AND INSET: *The tunnels and chambers are filled with sculptures carved out of the rock salt by the miners.*

Mines in Danger

Rock salt starts dissolving when the air around it reaches a relative humidity of about 75 percent.

Several of the Wieliczka salt sculptures are now beginning to dissolve, having absorbed an excess of water vapour from the air that ventilates the mine. As a result their surfaces are being eroded, and it is also possible that chemicals in the atmosphere may be changing the nature of the salt itself. Teams of scientists and engineers from Poland and the US have been examining ways of dehumidifying the mine, and there is constant monitoring of the underground chambers for levels of potentially threatening pollutants such as sulphur dioxide, nitrogen dioxide, nitric acid and hydrochloric acid.

See also:
The Camargue 22-3
The Dead Sea 75

15 The Danube Delta, Romania

the **facts**

- The Danube is the second longest river in Europe after the Volga.
- It flows for 2,761km (1,716 miles) from its source in the Black Forest in Germany to Romania.
- The delta where the waters enter the Black Sea covers 6,000sq km (2,317 square miles).

The **Danube Delta**

Delta in Danger

For centuries the Danube has been a vital trade route, and for much of this time man and nature have survived in relative harmony. However, in more recent years, the Danube Delta has suffered from the commercial forces and pollution of modern civilization.

The waters of the delta and the adjacent coastal seas support a large number of fish species, many of which have been exploited. Over half the fresh-water fish harvest of Romania is taken from the Danube Delta, including carp and caviar-yielding sturgeon. Increased drainage for agricultural land—which in turn has meant increased pollution— has resulted in the decline of many indigenous species. Steps are now being taken to reverse some of the damage and protect this vital ecological unit.

BELOW: *Pelicans in flight above the Rosca-Buhaiova Reserve on the Danube Delta.*

This vast area of wetland straddles the border between Romania and Ukraine. Above all else the Danube Delta is famous for its bird life, with over 300 species recorded here. About 180 species breed in the area, and the remainder—from as far apart as the Arctic, China, Siberia and the Mediterranean—use the delta as an over-wintering area or a stopover on longer migrations. Large proportions of the remaining world populations of four species in particular depend on the delta: the pygmy cormorant, of which there is a colony of around 12,000 pairs; the red-breasted goose, of which the entire world population can sometimes be found wintering in the area; 150 pairs (10 percent of the total world population) of the very rare, silvery-white Dalmatian pelican; and a substantial number of white pelicans. The floating islands and reed beds of the Danube Delta provide essential safe nesting and feeding for the two species of pelican found there.

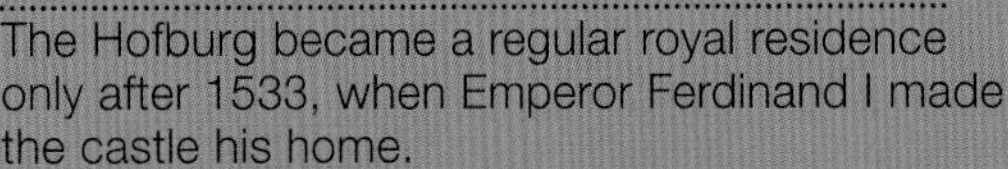

the facts

- The Hofburg became a regular royal residence only after 1533, when Emperor Ferdinand I made the castle his home.
- The oldest part of the Hofburg palace is the Schweizerhof, which is named after the Swiss guard that garrisoned it.

The Hofburg

This sprawl of buildings ranging from the 13th century to the 19th was the Viennese residence of the Hapsburgs, Holy Roman Emperors and subsequently rulers of the Austro-Hungarian Empire. Parts are still government offices, while others house the Hapsburg collections. Among rooms open to the public are the imperial audience chamber; the simple bedroom of Emperor Franz Josef, who died in 1916 after a reign of almost 80 years; the gymnasium where his wife, Empress Elizabeth, kept fit; and the Treasury, which houses the gem-studded tenth-century imperial crown and the Holy Lance, which reputedly pierced Christ's side on the cross. The famous Spanish Riding School, where stately white Lipizzaner horses perform, was completed in 1735.

The Albertina contains a superb collection of graphic art, and near by is the court's parish church, the Augustinerkirche, where the ill-fated Marie Antoinette was married to the future Louis XVI, and where the hearts of Hapsburgs are interred.

LEFT: *The Hofburg, residence of the Hapsburg emperors until 1918.*

LEFT: *Equestrian statues in Heroes' Square in front of the crescent shaped Neue Burg (New Palace).*

BELOW LEFT: *The main entrance to the former Court Library, which now houses the Austrian National Library.*

City of Music

The Hofburg's collection of musical instruments is a reminder that no other city is home to as many great composers as Vienna. Christoph Gluck (1714–87) wrote operas for the Hapsburg court; Mozart (1756–91) and Haydn (1732–1809) both lived and composed in Vienna. Beethoven (1770–1827) settled here in 1792; and Schubert (1797–1828) lived and died here.

The city's socialites swayed to the waltzes of the Strauss family in the 19th century and hummed to the operettas of Franz Lehar (1870–1948). Brahms (1833–97) and Bruckner (1824–96) both settled in Vienna in the 1860s. Gustav Mahler (1860–1911) was director of the court opera, and Arnold Schönberg (1874–1951) and Alban Berg (1885–1935) were also both sons of Vienna.

See also:
Edinburgh Castle 18-19
Neuschwanstein 32-3
Versailles 24-5

the facts

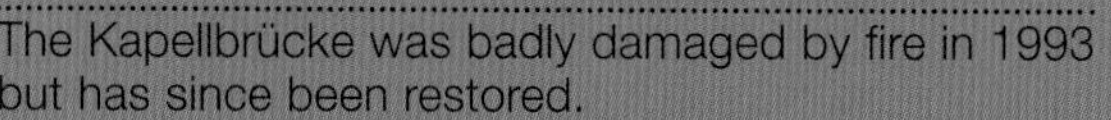

The Kapellbrücke was badly damaged by fire in 1993 but has since been restored.

The Wasserturm may once have served as the lighthouse (*lucerna*) that gives the town its name.

The Kapellbrücke

BACKGROUND: *Lucerne's 14th-century Kapellbrücke spans the River Reuss, with an octagonal water tower.*

Lucerne (Luzern), in the German-speaking part of Switzerland, sits below the mountains at the northwest corner of Lake Lucerne. The town's main defence is now its main attraction: Europe's oldest wooden bridge, the Kapellbrücke (Chapel Bridge), built in 1333 and extending diagonally a little over 198m (650ft) across the Reuss River. Towards its southern end is the octagonal, tile-roofed Wasserturm (water tower), which has served as a prison, a torture chamber, and the treasury.

The Road to Swiss Independence

High up in the rafters of the bridge are 112 paintings dating from the early 17th century and restored in the early 1900s. They depict Lucerne's history and the brave deeds of the people of this area, who played a crucial part in the struggle for Swiss independence, and illustrate the lives and legends of Lucerne's two patron saints, St Léger and St Maurice.

The Dying Lion

Lucerne's famous Löwendenkmal (Lion Monument) was designed by the great Danish sculptor Bertel Thorwaldsen and completed in 1821. It commemorates an event from the French Revolution.

Swiss mercenaries were employed as bodyguards for the French king, Louis XVI, and his family. In 1792 an angry mob stormed the Tuileries Palace in Paris, threatening the lives of the royal family. Over 700 Swiss soldiers were killed in the ensuing conflict—unaware that the King and his wife and children had escaped the building. The monument depicts a wounded lion, which lies dying in a niche carved out of a hillside.

Lucerne made its fortune in the 13th century, becoming a major commercial site with the opening of the Alpine route through the St Gotthard Pass between northern Italy and the Rhineland. Switzerland was the first democratic state in Europe, and the cradle of Swiss democracy was the area around Lake Lucerne. In the Middle Ages Switzerland was part of the Holy Roman Empire, but the settlements among the remote mountains and forests were largely self-governing, resisting the centralizing policies of the Hapsburg emperors.

In 1291 the representatives of three forest states, or cantons, close to the lake signed a treaty of mutual assistance. This was seen as the founding moment of the Swiss Confederation, which Lucerne joined in 1332 to protect its commercial interests. Other communities joined the confederacy, and the Swiss eventually won their independence. During this period Lucerne's main fortifications were built—the bridge and the wall with its watchtowers, which still stand, on the north bank of the Reuss.

Visible from the Kapellbrücke are the twin spires of the Church of St Léger and St Maurice, consecrated in 1644. Further west is the Spreuerbrücke (Mill Bridge) from 1407 which is adorned with 17th-century paintings.

BELOW LEFT: *Gable paintings run the length of the bridge.*

Wagnerian Idyll

Just outside Lucerne, on a promontory above the lake, is the house, Tribschen, where Richard Wagner (1813–83) lived from 1866 to 1872. He moved there from Weimar, having fled France after taking part in the 1848 uprising. It is now a museum devoted to the life and works of the composer, who wrote most of his opera *Die Meistersinger* there and part of his great *Ring* cycle. It was there that the *Seigfried Idyll* was first played, on Christmas morning 1870, to Wagner's wife, Cosima.

The philosopher Friedrich Nietszche (1844–1900) was a frequent visitor to the house, though his sister Elizabeth disliked the Wagners' taste, complaining of an excess of pink satin and cupids.

See also:
Golden Gate Bridge 170-1
Sydney Harbour Bridge 217

18 The Matterhorn, Switzerland/Italy

the facts

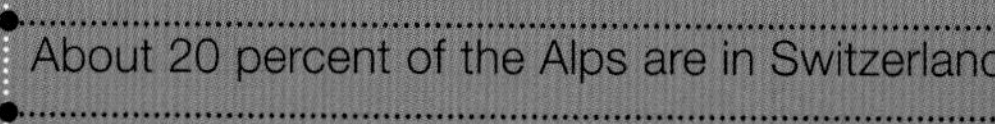

- About 20 percent of the Alps are in Switzerland.
- Around 100 peaks are nearly or more than 4,000m (13,125ft) high.
- The Matterhorn is known in France as Mont Cervin and in Italy as Monte Cervino.

The Matterhorn

The Matterhorn is not the highest mountain in the Alps, but it is surely the most dramatic, its classic pyramidal peak towering over the Italian-Swiss border. A road runs to the mountain on the Swiss side, following the River Rhône as it flows towards Lake Geneva (Lac Léman). The town of Zermatt sits under its northern face. On the Italian side there is access from Turin and Aosta.

Glacial activity formed the Matterhorn in the ice ages over the last 2 million years. Four tapering faces of rock converge at its peak, faces so difficult to climb that an ascent was not completed until 1865. The south face remained unconquered until 1931. Its distinctive shape is the result of cirques, ground out by glaciers,

Alpine Peaks

The Alpine mountains have fascinated generations of visitors for their beauty and for the challenge they present. The highest mountain is Mont Blanc in France, which is 4,807m (15,771ft) high. The Jungfrau is considered one of the most spectacular of the snow-capped mountains.

The Eiger has achieved its place of importance because of the difficulty of its climbs: the almost sheer north face, 1.6km (1 mile) high, was not mastered until 1938. In Austria the towering Zugspitze is the tallest of the Bavarian Alps and is popular with skiers and climbers. In the valley below, Garmisch-Partenkirchen, site of the 1936 Winter Olympics, has tramways to the crest of the mountain.

converging on an ever-narrower point to the sharp tip of the mountain, known as a pyramidal peak.

The Alps themselves were formed when the tectonic plate of Africa was forced north to collide with southern Europe. The process began about 180 million years ago, and reached a climax about 40 million years ago when the earth's crust buckled and rose to form the great spine of mountains that are the Alps. The mountains' core contains hard rocks such as granite, mica schist and gneiss, with softer rocks such as sandstones and shales at the edges. Europe's great rivers—the Rhine, the Rhône and the Danube—originate in these mountains, and famous lakes such as Maggiore and Lucerne lie in the hollows gouged by the glaciers of the last ice age.

ABOVE: *A mirror image of the Matterhorn at sunset.*

Reaching the Top

On 14 July 1865 the first successful team of climbers, led by Englishman Edward Whymper, reached the top by traversing a ridge on the Swiss side. Three days later an Italian team under the leadership of Giovanni Carrel arrived at the summit via a ridge on the Italian side. The Italians later claimed that Whymper's team had thrown rocks at them, an allegation the Englishman vigorously denied. Today cables and artificial footholds help amateurs to the top of the peak that was once the domain of the hardy few.

Another climber associated with the Matterhorn was Hermann Perren, a Zermatt guide whose ambition was to climb the Matterhorn 150 times. Tragically he fell to his death at the age of 68, a few climbs short of his goal.

LEFT: *The Gornergrat–Monte Rosa railway gives one of the best close-up views of the mountain peak.*

Scaling the Matterhorn

The Matterhorn is one of the world's most frequently climbed mountains. Every part of it has been tackled, and the most popular routes have fixed ropes, ladders and huts. However, this should not fool anyone into thinking of it as an easy climb: the Matterhorn also has one of the highest death rates—indeed, on the way down from the first successful ascent, three of Edward Whymper's party fell to their deaths.

Local guides now take most climbers along the easiest and first ascent, Hornli Ridge, and Lion Ridge, which have sections of fixed climbing aids. More experienced climbers go for the Zmutt and Furggen ridges, and the North Face presents the greatest challenge of all. Inexperienced climbers are advised to leave this mountain to the experts.

See also:
The Himalayas 100-1
Mount Everest 100-1
Mount Kilimanjaro 134-5

- The Colosseum is nearly 0.5km (0.3 mile) in circumference and over 55m (180ft) high.
- It was built of travertine stone, tufa and brick.
- Seating and access were efficiently arranged, as spectators' ticket numbers showed which part of the stadium to enter.

the facts

The Colosseum

BELOW: *Peaceful today, the Colosseum was once the venue for popular bloodthirsty spectator sports. A labyrinth of underground passages can be seen under the arena.*

Man v Beast, Man v Man

In the Villa Borghese in Rome are mosaics showing scenes of combat in the arena. Bulls, stags, lions and even ostriches were considered fair game for the *bestiarius*, a man not unlike the modern matador. (Some surviving Roman amphitheatres are used today for bullfighting.) The Roman fascination with unfamiliar animals seems to date from the time when Carthaginian elephants were displayed in the city, long before the Colosseum was built.

Contests between gladiators were also part of a long tradition thought to have developed from Etruscan funeral ceremonies. Gladiatorial fights were sometimes highly professional affairs between trained and evenly matched men, and sometimes pathetic displays involving unwilling captives.

The amphitheatre was a Roman design borrowed from the Greeks. Its elliptical area was surrounded by tiers of seats from which huge crowds could look safely down on spectacular displays of combat and carnage. Here gladiators fought and exotic animals from all corners of the world were paraded, stared at, and then slaughtered. Rome had amphitheatres before the Colosseum, but after the great fire of AD64 a new one was needed. Vespasian, who became emperor in AD69, ordered the construction of a massive, permanent building that would bear his family name of Flavius and be bigger and better than any other.

The Flavian Amphitheatre

Known as the Flavian Amphitheatre, the new arena was built on the bed of a lake that had belonged to his predecessor Nero's absurdly opulent Golden House. The choice of site was a wise one structurally, and it also demonstrated that an era of monstrous self-indulgence was at an end. Vespasian built on as grand a scale as Nero, but he did so as a public gesture. Ironically, Nero has his posthumous revenge. Ever since the 8th century the Flavian Ampitheatre has been known as the Colosseum, a title thought to recall the colossal statue of Nero that once stood nearby. (Rather than demolish this, Vespasian had ordered a head transplant and renamed the statue Apollo).

ABOVE: *Narrow arches form tiers at four levels.*

It was opened by Vespasian's successor, Titus, in AD80, with a ceremony that involved 5,000 wild beasts. Even then work was not complete, and it was only during the reign of the next emperor, Domitian, that the final tier was added.

Crowd Control

The building is remarkable, and its design reveals an ingenious response to the question of crowd control. Although some 50,000 people could be accommodated, the system of staircases and corridors ensured trouble-free progress to and from the banks of seating. Still more important was the careful control of the animals. A network of passages and elevators delivered wild creatures directly to the arena from their cages below stage. Much of this infrastructure can still be seen, as can sockets and brackets for the top tier, which once held the masts from which a huge awning could be stretched over the open top. This elaborate arrangement of canvas, pulleys, and ropes was operated by sailors recruited specially for the task.

LEFT: *The outer shell of the great amphitheatre is surrounded by the bustle of the city.*

Christians and Lions

In 1744 the Colosseum, which had become Church property in the 13th century, was consecrated in memory of the Christians said to have died for their faith in front of crowds of baying Romans. The Colosseum has long been associated with Christian martyrdom, but there is actually very little evidence to link the two. Nonetheless, a cross stands in the arena to this day, and indeed it was its reputation and significance to the Church that eventually saved the Colosseum from obliteration.

As it was, much of its stone was plundered by the authorities for use as building material in new palaces and churches, leaving the dull shell that remains today, without its originally dazzling stone coat.

See also:
Pont du Gard 30

the facts

- The tower is 55m (179ft) high.
- Circular in plan, it rises in eight tiers, including the bell chamber.
- The delicate arcading surrounding the tower's six central stages may have been influenced by Byzantine or Islamic architecture.

The Leaning Tower of Pisa

Pisa's famous Leaning Tower (Torre Pendente) is actually the campanile, or bell tower, of the city's cathedral, part of a magnificent ensemble of cathedral, bell tower, baptistery and cemetery. If it stood upright, its fame would probably be limited mainly to historians of art and architecture. But because it is structurally flawed, its image is known throughout the world.

An inscription records that the tower was begun in 1174, but as the Pisan calendar was a year in advance of conventional dating, the true date was 1173. The original architects, Bonnano Pisano and William of Innsbruck, did not live to see the work completed—the tower had no bell chamber until the second half of the 14th century.

The Tower Complex

The tower is part of a complex of buildings in the Piazza del Duomo, which includes the duomo (cathedral), the baptistery and the *campo santo*, or cemetery. The baptistery is a circular building of marble begun in the middle of the 12th century in Romanesque style, but with some later Gothic work. The pulpit dates from 1260 and has remarkable carvings depicting scenes from the life of Christ.

The cemetery was begun in the late 12th or early 13th century, using earth brought by ships from Calvary. Gothic arcades are decorated with frescoes and, despite troubling themes such as the Triumph of Death, Hell and the Last Judgment, this is a place with a peaceful atmosphere.

Some have suggested that the tower was always intended to lean, a daring demonstration of the skill of the architects. This idea is scarcely believable, and it is much more likely that the designers knew they would be building on less than solid ground and made some allowance for this in their plans, constructing foundations that would tolerate a certain amount of subsidence. Seeing the tower today, and experiencing the odd, disorienting sensation of being pulled to one side while climbing the 294 steps, one can only marvel at the fact that it still stands at all.

The Leaning Tower was built as the bell tower of Pisa's cathedral, which was begun a hundred years earlier, following a naval battle in 1063 in which the Pisans defeated the Saracens at Palermo. The style of architecture is known as Pisan Romanesque, and Islamic influence can once again be detected in the exterior bands of alternating red and white marble. There are arcades rising one above the other into the gable, and the dome over the crossing of the nave and the transepts was a later addition.

Gravitational Pull

In 1564 the scientist Galileo was born in Pisa, and he is said to have made use of the Leaning Tower for one of his experiments, dropping objects from the top in order to demonstrate that the speed of their acceleration would be the same, regardless of weight. There is no doubt that Galileo proved this point, but whether he did so from the Leaning Tower is less certain. On the other hand, it would have offered an ideal setting for experiments with gravity, as it apparently defies gravity itself.

Correcting the Lean

The tower started leaning very early in its history, and blocks of masonry were incorporated to try and pull it back. Between 1278 and 1360 its southward tilt is thought to have increased from just over half a degree to 1.6 degrees. This probably speeded up at an alarming rate with the addition of the seventh level and the bell chamber. At the beginning of the 20th century, the tower was 4.3m (14ft) out of perpendicular; by the end of the century it was 4.6m (15ft) out. An injection of grout in 1934 caused a 10mm (0.4in) lurch and draining groundwater in the 1970s increased the lean by 12mm (0.5in). Careful soil extraction in 1999 seems to have enjoyed more success, reducing the tilt by half a degree.

ABOVE: *The Tower leans away from the cathedral next to it.*

See also:
The CN Tower 152-3
The Eiffel Tower 26-9

- The Grand Canal snakes in a broad S-shape for about 4km (2.5 miles) from the train station in the northwest of Venice to the Punt della Salute in the southeast.
- Three bridges cross the canal, with the Ponte Rialto being the oldest and best-known.
- Gondolas act as taxis on the canals.

the facts

The Grand Canal

At the height of summer, with thousands of tourists swarming on and off the *vaporetti* (water buses), or on a damp, grey winter morning, with fog rolling in from the lagoon—under whatever conditions you see it, the Grand Canal in Venice is magical. It is difficult not to be totally overwhelmed by the city as everywhere you turn, there is a building of note, a magnificent juxtaposition of brick and marble, a fine example of delicate Gothic tracery or of outrageous baroque overstatement. And almost everywhere there is water, lapping the edges of the buildings, reflecting the glories of the architecture, and serving as a thoroughfare for floating traffic of every kind.

The Gondola

Unique to Venice and a symbol of the city's romantic reputation, the gondola is artfully designed to travel in shallow water, and to carry the maximum load with the minimum draught. Eight types of wood are traditionally used in its construction. Its asymmetrical design allows it to be steered easily with one oar by one person standing at the stern.

A letter written in 1094 by the Doge Vitale Falier contains the earliest known reference to the gondola, which was probably being used, then as now, to ferry passengers around. In the 18th century there were perhaps as many as 14,000 gondolas on the canals in Venice, making these some of the busiest waterways in the world. Now there are only about 500.

From its position among the lagoons at the head of the Adriatic, Venice built up one of the greatest commercial empires in history on the basis of its flourishing maritime trade. Water was its life, and every year on Ascension Day this was affirmed when the Doge 'married' the sea by casting a gold ring into it, in the spectacular ceremony of the Spozalizio del Mar.

Venice is built on thousands of islands, which originally were little more than mud flats. The city rose on millions of wooden piles, and a unique style of architecture evolved to suit these maritime conditions. The palaces lining the Grand Canal display Venetian grandeur of every era, from the 13th century to the 20th.

A Lifetime of Marvels

The visitor could journey along the canal every day for a year, even for a lifetime, and still find something new to marvel at. The 16th-century Ca' d'Oro is perhaps the most celebrated palace of all. Now an art gallery and open to the public again after years of restoration work, the building is a supreme example of Venetian Gothic architecture. It is said to owe its name to the fact that it was originally adorned with gilt. A slightly later and quite different building on the Grand Canal is the Palazzo Dario, with a façade studded with polychrome marble.

At the southeastern end of the Grand Canal stands the Church of Santa Maria della Salute, designed by Longhena and completed in 1687 to commemorate deliverance from a plague that afflicted the city. Each November, a bridge of boats is constructed across the canal, allowing people to walk over to the church to celebrate its annual festival.

The Fondaco dei Turchi (built at the beginning of the 13th century but heavily restored), the Ca' Giustinian (mid-15th century), the Ca' Rezzonico (17th and 18th century, now a museum), the Ca' da Mosto (13th century)… the list of buildings to be seen along the Grand Canal is as long as the canal itself.

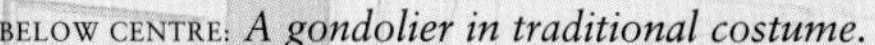

LEFT: *Gondolas at their distinctive moorings of striped poles along the length of Venice's Grand Canal.*
BELOW LEFT AND RIGHT: *The waters lap unremittingly at the stone façades of the grand palaces lining the canal.*
BELOW CENTRE: *A gondolier in traditional costume.*

Piazza San Marco

The most beautiful street in the world leads to what Napoleon called the finest drawing room in Europe. St Mark's Square (the one and only piazza in Venice) is bordered by buildings of different dates and styles, and yet the combined effect is perfectly harmonious. The 11th-century basilica of St Mark is an astonishingly rich building with a profusion of fine mosaics and inlaid marble floors. It was originally the private chapel of the Doges of Venice, whose palace is another of the major sights of the city.

The late 15th-century clock tower has a surprisingly modern-looking digital display of the time, and two bronze figures strike a bell to announce the hour to crowds and pigeons in the square below.

See also:
The River Nile 120–1

22 St Peter's Basilica, Italy

St Peter's Basilica

Almost all the celebrated architects of 16th-century Italy had a hand in the construction of this vast church. It took 170 years for the basilica to be completed, as its plans were passed from hand to hand and its design revised or replaced. The building that stands in the heart of Rome today is awe-inspiring in its dimensions. Even more remarkable, given the saga of its construction, is the fact that it was ever completed at all.

St Peter's has its origins in the martyrdom of the apostle Peter, crucified by Emperor Nero and buried in a public cemetery in about AD64. Peter's tomb became a place of pilgrimage, and Constantine (AD274-337), the first Christian emperor, built a basilica around it, which stood for a thousand years. When the structure began to crumble Pope Nicholas V planned a replacement, but he died in 1455 before work began. Work on the new St Peter's was to continue for nearly two centuries, interrupted at intervals as yet another pope or architect died and one scheme replaced another. The subsequent design of nave, façade and portico was ill-advised and ruined the view of the dome originally planned by Bramante and reintroduced 30 years later by Michelangelo.

Bernini's Contribution

The piazza in front of St Peter's was built later and much more swiftly, between 1656 and 1667. The work of Giovanni Bernini (1598-1680), it has 284 Tuscan columns arranged four deep with statues of saints above. Inside St Peter's, Bernini constructed a less universally admired bronze baldacchino, set canopy-like over the papal altar and supported on serpentine columns 29m (95ft) high.

It is possible to inspect St Peter's literally from top to bottom: to look down on Rome from a balcony attached to the lantern on top of the dome, and to descend beneath the

ABOVE *Members of the papal bodyguard, the elite Swiss Guard, wear a uniform designed by Michaelangelo.*

the facts

- St Peter's covers an area of 22,300sq m (240,000sq ft).
- The dome is 138m (453ft) high and 42m (138ft) in diameter.
- There are 284 columns in the colonnade.
- During construction the workforce numbered up to 2,000.

NOREM·PRINCIPIS·APOST·PAVLVS·V·BVRGHESIVS·ROMANVS·PONT·MAX·AN·MDCXII

the **history**

1506
Donato Bramante begins construction with Greek cross plan and dome.

1514-20
Raphael put in charge and abandons dome.

1539
Antonia da Sangallo draws up a new scheme which is not implemented.

1546
Michelangelo appointed to the project and reinstates dome.

1564
Giacomo della Porta succeeds Michelangelo and alters the design again.

1626
Church consecrated on 18 November by Pope Urban VIII.

high altar and view the excavations of the pagan necropolis that lay beneath the original basilica. One monument discovered here may mark the site of St Peter's grave, although there is not sufficient archaeological evidence to allow conclusive arguments for or against this.

Built on a massive scale and heavily ornate in much of its internal decoration, St Peter's is, for some visitors, overly elaborate and even oppressive. The initial impression on walking into the building, which stretches 189m (620ft) ahead, is sometimes one of bewilderment. There is so much to take in that you can't appreciate it all at once. Unqualified admiration may not be everyone's verdict, but as a whole it excites wonder and contains some exquisite works of art, such as Michelangelo's *Pietà*, a marble statue of the Virgin Mary with the dead body of her son in her arms.

LEFT: *An impression of St Peter's in the 18th century.*

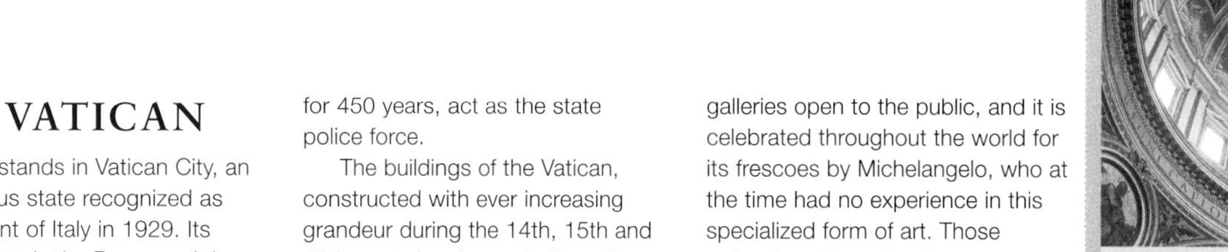

BELOW: *St Peter's and the arched bridge of Vatican City reflected in the calm waters of the River Tiber.*

THE VATICAN

St Peter's stands in Vatican City, an autonomous state recognized as independent of Italy in 1929. Its head of state is the Pope, and the Vatican has its own radio and TV stations, a train station, and an entitlement to diplomatic representation abroad. Swiss Guards, in distinctive uniforms which have remained unchanged for 450 years, act as the state police force.

The buildings of the Vatican, constructed with ever increasing grandeur during the 14th, 15th and 16th centuries, house half a million books and what is said to be the biggest collection of ancient art anywhere in the world.

The Sistine Chapel, built for Pope Sixtus IV around 1473, is part of the complex of rooms and galleries open to the public, and it is celebrated throughout the world for its frescoes by Michelangelo, who at the time had no experience in this specialized form of art. Those painted on the ceiling between 1508 and 1512, depict biblical scenes and characters before the Flood. Twenty years after their completion the artist went on to paint the Last Judgement on the chapel's east wall.

RIGHT: The Pietà *(1499), a marble group by Michelangelo.*
BELOW: *Bernini's ornate bronze canopy above the High Altar.*

See also:
Church of the Holy Sepulchre 78
Haghia Sophia 73
Sagrada Familia 60-1

In the 14th century a new generation of artists and architects began to look back to the Classical age, when Greece and Rome dictated styles and aesthetics across their imperial territories. For designers of monuments it was back to basics: to the beauty of geometry and symmetry, the pure simplicity of the circle and square.

the facts

- The Banqueting House on Whitehall in London was built by Inigo Jones (1573–1652) for James I as a demonstration of the principles of Palladianism.
- Michelangelo's funerary monuments in the Church of San Lorenzo, Florence, depict living figures instead of the reclining figures of medieval tradition.

Renaissance Europe

THEORY AND PRACTICE

Renaissance practitioners based their designs on the theories of Vitruvius, a first-century BC Roman engineer whose treatise *De Architectura* set out Greek architectural principles. These defined the three Orders—Doric, Ionic and Corinthian—and laid down the rule of proportions, relating all dimensions to each other arithmetically.

These rules dictated the grand Venetian church designs of Andrea Palladio (1508–80), whose work would, in turn, inspire 17th-century British architects including Sir Christopher Wren.

CLOCKWISE FROM TOP: *Frescoes by Benozzo Gozzoli in Palazzo Medici-Riccardi in Florence; a model of a flying machine by Leonardo da Vinci on display in his home village of Vinci;* The Holy Family *by Michelangelo in the Uffizi Gallery in Florence.*

THE ITALIAN JOBS

Filippo Brunelleschi (1377–1446) set the pace with the vast dome of the cathedral in Florence (*duomo*). Moving away from Gothic style, he based his work on sketches of Roman temples and basilicas. Florence became a Renaissance showpiece, attracting all of the talented artists and architects of the time.

Leon Battista Alberti (1404–72) spread the word across the rest of Italy, supervising the rebuilding of Rome under the patronage of Pope Nicholas V.

NEW WAYS

In 1505 Pope Julius II commissioned a new church over St Peter's tomb. The designer was Donato Bramante (1444–1514), a devoted adherent to Renaissance principles. His original plan for St Peter's basilica employed the Classical rules of simplicity and the Orders, but a sequence of changes after his death culminated in a compromise that moved away from the strict use of proportion toward the flamboyance of baroque.

CLOCKWISE FROM TOP: *Detail of bronze doors made by Lorenzo Ghiberti for the Florence Baptistery; intricate wrought-iron railings on a balcony in Sicily; Michelangelo's funerary monuments in the Medici Chapel of the Church of San Lorenzo in Florence; cameo of scientist Galileo Galilei; cameo of Leonardo da Vinci.*

See also:
Grand Canal 46-7
St Peter's Basilica 48-51

23 The Parthenon, Greece

the facts

- The Parthenon stands on the Acropolis, the ancient city on a hill above modern Athens.
- It was built on the foundations of an earlier temple to Athena.
- Athena was the goddess of wisdom and the patron of Athens.

The Parthenon

Descriptions of the Parthenon have always been littered with superlatives. This temple to Athena Parthenos, the patron deity of Athens, is regarded as the supreme example of classical architecture, an artistic and sculptural masterpiece. The building belongs to the middle of the fifth century BC. By then the Persians, who in 480BC succeeded in storming Athens, had been decisively defeated, and the city, under the influence of the statesman Pericles, was brimming with pride and self-

Who's Who?

The birth of the goddess Athena was celebrated annually at Athens, and every four years there was a special ceremony involving a procession and the presentation of a new robe for the statue of the goddess. The Parthenon frieze has long been thought to represent this procession, and many of the details support such an interpretation.

Yet there are some anomalies, and one theory is that the frieze shows the 192 Greek heroes who died fighting the Persians at the Battle of Marathon in 490BC. The presence of a whole assembly of gods, in addition to Athena, seems to show that this is a ceremony of unusual significance and that the heroes of Marathon are being presented to the gods of Olympus.

The Big Frieze

If the Parthenon was a temple, it was also something of an art gallery, a perfect setting for a collection of sculpture. The pediments and entablature were covered with figures visible from outside, but the celebrated 152m (500ft)-long Parthenon frieze, half of which was removed to London by Lord Elgin and bought by the British Museum in 1816, ran around the solid outer walls of the *cella* at a height of about 12m (40ft).

Around half the panels of the Parthenon frieze can be seen on display at the British Museum, although there are repeated calls for the restoration of the so-called Elgin Marbles to Greece.

confidence. This mood was reflected in a lavish building project, funded by tributes exacted from Athens' allies.

Classical Style

The Parthenon is a temple in the Doric style, 69.5m (228ft) long and 30.5m (100ft) wide. The peristyle, or outer colonnade, enclosed an inner building, the *cella*, containing the shrine that housed a giant statue of the goddess made of gold and ivory. The peristyle had 46 columns—8 visible across the front of the temple, 17 along the sides—each fluted, composed of a number of massive drums, and tapering toward the top. The columns were marble, as were the pediments and entablature they supported, but the roof of the temple was wooden. The building style had developed from that used for simple timber structures, and the Parthenon displays in stone all the elegance of those early solutions to engineering problems. But its simplicity of line and form is deceptive. The architect, an Ionian Greek called Iktinos, was a master of perspective, calculating exactly how a building must be shaped if it is to please the human eye gazing up at it from below.

The Parthenon Past and Present

The modern image of Greek temples as gleaming white buildings is a false one. The Parthenon was originally painted in bright, not to say gaudy, fashion. In recent years, however, the marble has suffered badly from the effects of Athens' smog and from the sheer number of tourists who crowd onto the Acropolis.

The building has had many different uses, serving as both Greek Orthodox and Roman Catholic churches and as a mosque. In 1687 the Turkish army was using it as a gunpowder store when besieging Venetian forces blew it up. Dubious 19th-century restoration schemes were resisted and today, despite all of these factors, the Parthenon is still a truly breathtaking sight.

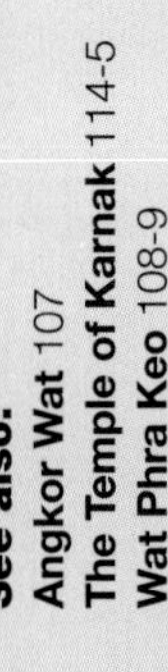
See also:
Angkor Wat 107
The Temple of Karnak 114-5
Wat Phra Keo 108-9

The Greek Orthodox monasteries were strictly for monks, but there were also nunneries, such as Agios Stephanos, reached by a bridge over a terrifying chasm.

St Athanasios, who founded the Great Metéoron, came from Mount Athos in northern Greece, an important site of the Orthodox Church.

the **facts**

Metéora Monasteries

ABOVE: *The perched monastery of Roussanou is accessed via a bridge.*

Metéora means 'in the air', and the monasteries are indeed up in the sky—perched on sheer pillars and pinnacles of rock up to 549 m (1,800ft) high on the edge of the Pindus Mountains, looking out over the valley of the Pinios River in Thessaly, in central Greece. Until the 1920s visitors either had to climb perilous and rickety ladders, 30.5m (100ft) or more long, fastened to the rock, or were hauled up by rope in a swaying net.

Supplies are still hauled up in nets, but the monasteries began attracting tourists after World War I, and especially after the 1960s, when a new road was built from the town of Kalabáka to make them easier to reach. Access now is by long flights of steps cut into the rock and across bridges over dizzying precipices. Many monks have moved away to regain privacy, and the sites today are more like museums than living communities.

The Wild Horsemen

From ancient times the broad plains of Thessaly in central Greece were well known as an important horse-breeding district. Inhabitants of the plains even entered Greek mythology. They were pictured literally as horse-men, or centaurs, each having a human head and torso growing out of the body of a horse, and were usually characterized as lusty and fond of strong drink—personifying the animal urges in human nature.

Among their numbers, however, was a rather different character—a wise old shaman named Chiron, said to have taught the heroes Achilles and Jason in their youth.

The Life of Prayer

From late in the third century AD, Christian ascetics retreated into the deserts of Egypt and Syria to lead lives of prayer and meditation. They were also well away from the growing authority of the Church. Their numbers increased in the fourth century when Christianity, now the official religion of the Roman empire, became more identified with the power of the state.

The most famous of these early hermits was St Anthony of Egypt, celebrated for the attacks made on him by armies of evil spirits in grotesque and horrible forms, a concept that furnished a lively theme for generations of painters of devotional art.

Another famous figure was St Simeon Stylites, who spent 40 years perched on top of an 18m (60ft) pillar in the Syrian Mountains.

Ascetics had been living on top of rock pillars in the region since the 12th century. According to legend, when St Athanasios, the founder of the principal monastery, the Great Metéoron, arrived in about 1350, he was lifted to the top of the pillar on which the monastery stands by an angel or an eagle. His pupil, Joasaph, a son of the king of Serbia, enlarged and enriched the foundation 30 or 40 years later.

Decline and Fall

Many more communities—over 30 in all—were founded in the 15th and 16th centuries after the Turks conquered Thessaly, but a long, slow decline set in during the 17th and 18th centuries and most of them have not survived. In the 19th century the monasteries attracted the attention of adventurous visitors, and word of them began to spread.

Built of stone, with red-tiled roofs and wooden galleries projecting vertiginously over deep abysses, the monasteries had a cramped cell for each monk, a church and a refectory for meals. Cisterns were cut in the rock to catch rainwater. The refectory at Agios Varlaam was restored as a museum in the 1960s. At the Great Metéoron you can see the simple kitchen with its bowls and ladles. In both, the churches are adorned with frescoes depicting hell and the grisly sufferings of martyrs. The deserted monastery of Agios Nikolaos has fine 16th-century frescoes by an artist from Crete named Theophanis.

BACKGROUND: *Views from Roussanou—one of the few monasteries to accept women.*

See also: Potala Palace 97

the facts

- Muhammad I al Ghalib, founder of the Nasrid dynasty, began construction work on the Alhambra in the middle of the 13th century.
- The royal apartments date from the reigns of Yusuf I and Muhammad V, in the second half of the 14th century.

The Alhambra

Externally, the Alhambra in Granada was a fortress, a defensive stronghold with 23 towers. It was built by the Moors in the 13th century at a time when Islamic power in Spain was threatened by Christian resurgence. Internally, it was an attempt to create paradise.

The Alhambra served the Nasrid dynasty of Granada as military headquarters, administrative base and royal palace. Courtyards, corridors and water conduits combine to create a remarkable sequence of vistas. The decoration is sumptuous and ubiquitous, in the form of ceramic tiles, pierced stonework, carved foliage designs and amazingly elaborate calligraphy. There is something insubstantial and other-worldly about the exuberant *muqamas* vaults—riotous honeycomb-like structures suspended from wooden frames, which are themselves supported on slim columns. Verse inscriptions speak of the stars and the heavens, water

BELOW: *Granada, framed in an arch of Palacios Nazaries.*

BELOW: *A shady corner of the Patio de la Acequia at the Generalife.*

The Generalife

The Generalife was a summer palace of the Nasrid royal family, built in the 14th century and once directly linked to the Alhambra by a covered walkway across a ravine. It sits on the summit of a hill known as El Sol (The Sun), which is a mirror image of the hill upon which the Alhambra is built.

It was built by Aben Walid Ismail in 1318. Only two buildings survive, one at each end of the rectangular Patio de la Acequia. A long, narrow pool runs through the patio, with a stone bowl at each end. Fountains, rosebushes, colonnades and pavilions adorn the garden, which is thought to be one of the oldest of its kind in the world.

runs in channels to symbolize the four rivers of the Islamic paradise, and water and light are employed by the architects as essential components in the overall design.

Heaven on Earth

The Alhambra's plan is one of gardens and courtyards, with apartments opening off each of four sides. The names are evocative: the Court of Myrtles (planted in beds beside a long pool); the Hall of the Two Sisters (white marble stones set in the floor), and the Court of the Lions (with a fountain supported by 12 stone lions). The Hall of the Ambassadors, intended for royal audiences, has a carved ceiling 18.3m (60ft) above ground, an attempt to suggest the heavens.

By the mid-13th century Granada was the last major Moorish kingdom remaining in Spain. The Nasrid dynasty ruled it for 250 years under an unbroken succession of 25 sovereigns. They were notable patrons of art and learning, and attracted the great Muslim historian Ibn Khaldun to their highly civilized court.

The Nasrids finally left Granada in 1492. The emperor Charles V built his own palace within the Alhambra walls in the 16th century, but later the buildings suffered neglect, and Napoleon's forces destroyed part of the Nasrid fortress. In the 19th century, the romance of the place captured the imagination of visitors such as Victor Hugo, Théophile Gautier and Washington Irving, whose *Tales of the Alhambra* was published in 1829. It was partly their descriptions that inspired efforts to preserve the Alhambra.

BELOW: *The Alhambra, backed by the mountains of the Sierra Nevada.*

The Moors in Spain

Muslims came from North Africa to Spain in the year 711 and conquered the Visigoth rulers, who had their capital at Toledo. Islamic power was based in Córdoba, 160km (100 miles) from Granada, which became first an emirate and later a caliphate.

Here a remarkable mosque was built, begun in the eighth century and subsequently extended and embellished. The building was later converted into a Christian cathedral, but it still displays all the fundamental elements of Moorish architecture, with horseshoe arches, polychromatic brickwork and inscriptions taken from the Koran.

The Muslims were driven out of Córdoba during the Christian reconquest in 1236. Many escaped to Granada, where the Nasrid dynasty was then established. The last Muslim ruler of Granada was driven into exile in 1492.

See also:
The Blue Mosque 72-3
Fez Medina 124-5

- Gaudí was born in Reus, Spain, the son of a coppersmith.
- The 12 towers of the façades represent the 12 Apostles, and Gaudí planned another 6 towers, representing the four Evangelists, the Virgin Mary and Jesus Christ.
- The tallest tower—that representing Christ—is 112m (367ft) high.

the facts

The Sagrada Família

Work on the Basilica of the Sagrada Família (the Church of the Holy Family) began in 1884, and it continues to this day. Intended as a symbol of the living Roman Catholic faith, the church was to be the focus of a complex of buildings, including schools and educational workshops. Even in its unfinished state, this huge and exuberant building is known throughout the world as a major work of architect Antoni Gaudí (1852–1926).

Its Nativity façade takes a familiar and conventional subject of Christian art and, with no sacrifice of respect or reverence, presents it in an original, almost surreal setting. Gaudí's work reveals a Moorish influence, and has some affinities with Art Nouveau, but his was a unique approach to architecture. He treated buildings as an organic process—stone takes on a living form, and decoration grows out of it in a way that a plant might grow.

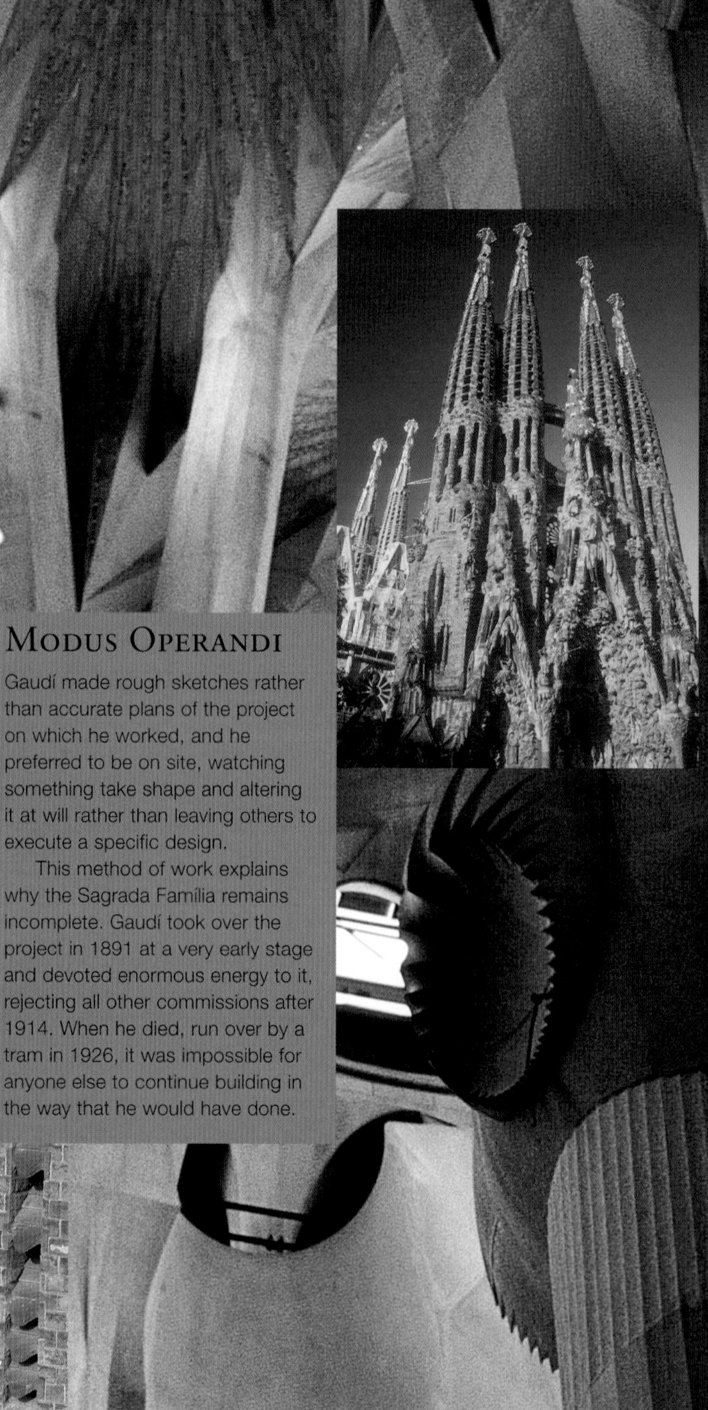

Modus Operandi

Gaudí made rough sketches rather than accurate plans of the project on which he worked, and he preferred to be on site, watching something take shape and altering it at will rather than leaving others to execute a specific design.

This method of work explains why the Sagrada Família remains incomplete. Gaudí took over the project in 1891 at a very early stage and devoted enormous energy to it, rejecting all other commissions after 1914. When he died, run over by a tram in 1926, it was impossible for anyone else to continue building in the way that he would have done.

RIGHT: *An arched bridge links the towers.*

RIGHT: *Gaudí's Guell Park is topped by a fantastic green mosaic chimney.*

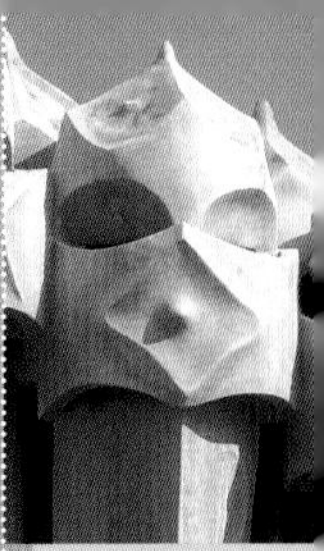

It is known that Gaudí intended the church to have three monumental façades depicting the Nativity, the Passion, and the Resurrection, and each was to have four huge towers of the type that were completed above the Nativity façade in the 1950s. Gaudí was a perfectionist. For his representation of the Flight into Egypt, for example, he is said to have found a working donkey and, with the owner's permission, to have made plaster casts of this animal because its weary appearance was exactly the image he wanted to portray in his sculpture. It is unlikely that the church would have retained the shade of the original stone if Gaudí had lived to complete it. He was inspired by the colours as well as the forms of natural things, and much of his work displays a riotous use of different tones, textures, and surfaces.

A Striking Style

The architect was an accomplished artist and craftsman. He designed furniture and fashioned iron gates and railings that astonish the eye. Among his buildings in Barcelona, the Casa Batllo (said to illustrate the triumph of St George over the dragon) and Casa Mila (Spain's most controversial apartment block, are particularly striking.

There have been arguments about the wisdom of completing Gaudí's work. Some say the concept should have been abandoned, or the Nativity façade turned into an altarpiece. An entirely new Passion façade has been built, obscuring some of Gaudí's original design. His remarkable vision is all the more striking when seen in conjunction with subsequent attempts to complete the building.

BELOW: *The ornate curved staircase and lift of Casa Batllo, another example of Gaudí's unique style of architecture.*

Guell Park

Eusebio Guell, Gaudí's patron and a rich industrialist, wanted the architect to build a whole suburb northwest of central Barcelona. The plan was never completed, but Gaudí did create a remarkable park in an area that had been without water or plants.

Here it is possible to see what Gaudí could achieve by reusing ceramic tiles. A huge curving bench is decorated with bright mosaic work, and a great dragon—looking more friendly than menacing and also created out of vivid tiles—clutches playfully at a wall near the entrance. The park also contains two very unusual entrance pavilions with mosaic-tiled roofs and a central square supported on columns that represent Gaudí's idiosyncratic version of Doric style.

See also:
Church of the Holy Sepulchre 78
Haghia Sophia 73
St Peter's Basilica 48-51

the facts

- The Kremlin is triangular in shape, and covers 28ha (69 acres) of ground beside the Moscow River.
- The belltower of Ivan the Great is 81m (266ft) high and was completed in 1600 by Czar Boris Godunov.
- The Czar Cannon, made in 1586 and tipping the scales at 40.6 tonnes (44.8 tons), has never been fired.

The **Kremlin**

ABOVE: *The evening sun strikes the colourful cupolas and towers of St Basil's Cathedral.*

Ivan the Terrible, the first man who could justly claim to be Czar of All the Russias, was crowned in the Kremlin in Moscow in 1547. There is a *kremlin*, or fortress, in many an ancient Russian city, but since that moment the citadel in Moscow has been the Kremlin. The stronghold was the nucleus around which Moscow grew after its foundation in the 12th century. Inside are the palaces of the

BELOW: *The Armoury was commissioned by Nicholas I in 1851 as an extension to the Great Kremlin Palace.*

Autocrat of All the Russias

In 1453 the city of Constantinople, or Byzantium, fell to the Turks, marking the end of the Eastern Roman Empire and the long reign of Byzantium as the Second Rome. The Grand Dukes of Muscovy proclaimed themselves Byzantium's spiritual heirs, with their capital of Moscow as the Third Rome.

Ivan IV, 'the Terrible', inherited the Grand Duchy at the age of three, and took the reins of government at 14. At 16 he was crowned *czar* (Caesar); his conquests established a Russian empire. He had a savage temper, and killed his son in a rage in 1581, three years before his own death. It is said that when St Basil's Cathedral was finished, Ivan had the architect blinded so that he could never create a rival.

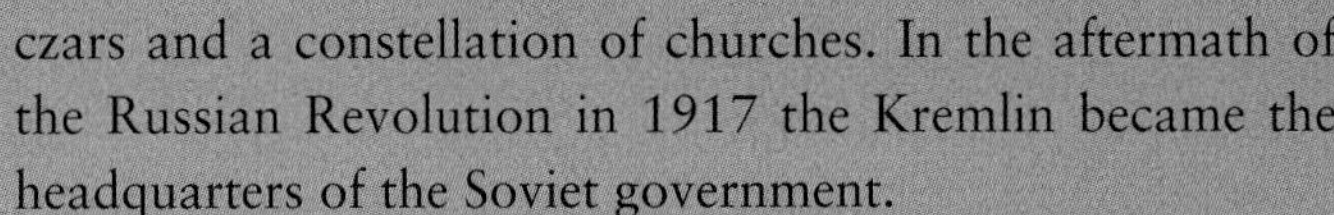

czars and a constellation of churches. In the aftermath of the Russian Revolution in 1917 the Kremlin became the headquarters of the Soviet government.

The towering walls were rebuilt in brick late in the 15th century. Standing up to 18.3m (60ft) high, they run for more than 1.6km (1 mile) and are punctuated by 20 towers, some with tent-shaped steeples above the gates. The main entrance is the Spassky Gate, which faces Red Square.

Matters of State

The Granovitaya Palata, completed in 1491, with the splendid Renaissance throne room, is still used for state occasions. The Cathedral of the Assumption, built in the 1470s, was where czars' coronations took place. The carved walnut throne of Ivan the Terrible, made in 1551, stands near the main entrance. The Cathedral of the Annunciation, rebuilt in the 1560s, was known as 'the golden-domed' because its entire roof was gilded. The Cathedral of St Michael the Archangel, the czars' burial place, is in Russian style with Italian Renaissance influence. All three churches contain impressive frescoes and icons, and there are lesser churches close by.

The Great Kremlin Palace, subsequently the meeting place of the Supreme Soviet, was completed in 1849. From here there is access to the czars' private apartments in the 17th-century Terem Palace. The treasures amassed by the imperial family are displayed in the Armory. They range from weapons and armour to crowns and regalia, thrones, jewels, vestments, carriages, snuffboxes and Fabergé Easter eggs. The Palace of the Patriarchs of the Russian Orthodox Church, which dates from the 1650s, now houses a museum of 17th-century Russian art and culture.

Also in the Kremlin is the building used for Communist Party conferences, completed in 1961 and specially sunk into the ground so as not to detract from the older buildings. Immediately outside is Red Square, with the mausoleum where the body of Lenin was displayed after his death, and the onion-domed Cathedral of St Basil, built on the orders of Ivan the Terrible in the 1550s.

BELOW LEFT: *Cast in 1586 in Moscow, the Czar Canon was designed to protect the Saviours' Gate.*
BELOW RIGHT: *The south portal of the Cathedral of the Assumption.*

Unburied Caesar

The Soviet government made its headquarters in Moscow in March 1918, and since then Russia has been ruled from the Kremlin.

Vladimir Ilyich Lenin himself moved into the 18th-century Senate building, where he lived in an austere fashion on the top floor. The clock on his study wall was kept at 8.15, the time when, desperately ill, he left the room for the last time. Lenin died on 21 January 1924, and his embalmed body was displayed for veneration in a wooden pyramid in Red Square, which in 1930 was replaced by a granite mausoleum.

Stalin also lay in state in the mausoleum from his death in 1953 until 1961.

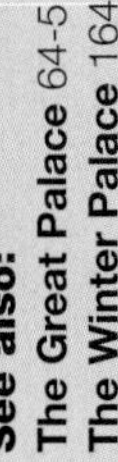

See also:
The Great Palace 64-5
The Winter Palace 164

the facts

- The palace waterworks require about 34,095L (7,500–9,000 gal) of water per second.
- House rules at Monplaisir in Peter's time included a prohibition on guests going to bed in riding boots.
- Catherine the Great was living here when she arranged the coup that overthrew her husband, Peter III.

The Great Palace

In 1703 Czar Peter the Great (1672-1725) founded his new capital city of St Petersburg (known as Leningrad during most of the 20th century). An energetic and determined Westernizer, Peter set out to create outside the city a complex to rival Versailles. He planned the layout himself and assembled an army of soldiers and serfs to dig canals and channels for the dizzying array of waterworks

In the 21ha (300-acre) park are regiments of cascades and fountains, some intended to go off unexpectedly and drench unsuspecting visitors. They cumulate in the Great

ABOVE RIGHT: *The Great Palace is fronted by a vast ornamental lake.* LEFT: *A close-up view of a dome from one of the golden pavilions flanking the Great Palace.* BELOW: *The palace's ornate ceremonial staircase, designed by Rastrelli.*

Imperial Grandeur

Pushkin, 27km (17 miles) south of St Petersburg, is better known as Tsarskoe Selo, and was mainly laid out in the 18th century for Empress Elizabeth and Catherine the Great. Rich families from St Petersburg built houses here, and it is said to have been the first town in Europe entirely lit by electricity. It was renamed Pushkin in 1937 on the centenary of the poet's birth.

The major building is the Yekaterinsky (Catherine) Palace, or Summer Palace, created in sumptuous baroque by Rastrelli for Empress Elizabeth. The interiors were redone in the Robert Adam manner for Catherine the Great by a Scottish architect, Charles Cameron. The war-damaged palace and park have been restored, including the fabulous Amber Room, whose walls were entirely covered with amber.

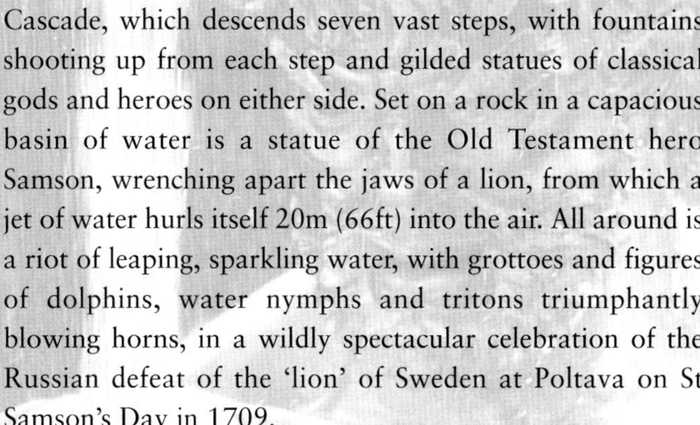

Cascade, which descends seven vast steps, with fountains shooting up from each step and gilded statues of classical gods and heroes on either side. Set on a rock in a capacious basin of water is a statue of the Old Testament hero Samson, wrenching apart the jaws of a lion, from which a jet of water hurls itself 20m (66ft) into the air. All around is a riot of leaping, sparkling water, with grottoes and figures of dolphins, water nymphs and tritons triumphantly blowing horns, in a wildly spectacular celebration of the Russian defeat of the 'lion' of Sweden at Poltava on St Samson's Day in 1709.

Post-War Restoration

The palace complex and park at Peterhof—now called Petrodvorets (Peter's Palace)—was severely damaged during World War II and has been magnificently restored since 1945. Behind the Great Cascade is the Great Palace, on a terrace looking out over the Gulf of Finland, the arm of the Baltic Sea on which St Petersburg is set. Begun in 1714 for Peter the Great, the palace was substantially enlarged and altered for his daughter, Empress Elizabeth, and later czars and czarinas have changed it in their turn.

Out in the park are smaller buildings, including Monplaisir, on the Gulf shore, where Czar Peter lived while the Great Palace was being built. It was completed in 1722 and enlarged for Empress Elizabeth. The Lacquer Room, hung with lacquered papier-mâché plates showing Chinese scenes in gold on a black background, has been superbly recreated. The Hermitage, also built for Peter, has a dining pavilion on the upper floor. Part of the table can be lowered to the ground floor to be cleared and reset by the servants.

LEFT: *The gilded Neptune Fountain was created in the 1650s to celebrate the end of the Thirty Years' War.*
BELOW: *Water jets are a feature of the extensive gardens.*

Other Homes of the Czars

The Alexandrovsky Palace, built in the 1790s, was the place considered as home by the ill-fated last czar, Nicholas II, who was murdered with his family by revolutionaries in 1918. The palace has recently been opened to the public and is furnished with a 12-room gallery space.

Just 3km (2 miles) from Pushkin is Pavlovsk, where yet another palace of astonishing grandeur is set in a breathtaking park of 607ha (1,500 acres). It was created by the designer of the Yekaterinsky, Charles Cameron.

See also:
Hofburg 37
Neuschwanstein 32-3
Versailles 24-5

the facts

- The Trans-Siberian was first built with a single track running 7,416km (4,608 miles) between Moscow and Vladivostok on the Sea of Japan. A second track was added later.
- The line was built to an unusually broad gauge of 1.5m (5ft).

The Trans-Siberian Railway

The Trans-Siberian is by far the longest railway line in the world on which a regular service operates. It was built between 1891 and 1905, primarily to exploit the gold and minerals of Siberia. Political prisoners were forced to work on the line, which was also used to transport criminals and dissidents into exile. The railroad made it possible for peasants to migrate to Siberia and it led to the industrialization of this vast and remote region.

Work began simultaneously at both the Moscow and the Vladivostok ends, and the western arm reached Irkutsk in 1898. At this point passengers had to be ferried the 65km (40 miles) across Lake Baikal—frozen during the long Siberian winter—in a 4,267-tonne (4,199-ton) icebreaker, which was built in England and transported to Siberia in sections. The rail line was subsequently constructed around the southern end of the lake to cut out the ferry passage. A three-month journey had been reduced to two weeks, and would later be cut to one week.

The Sleeping Land

Siberia covers close to 12,949,000 sq km (5 million square miles) and measures more than 6,437km (4,000 miles) across from west to east and close to 3,219km (2,000 miles) from north to south.

Its name means 'Sleeping Land' in the Tartar language, and it is full of wonders. Mammoths are preserved whole in ice, tigers prowl the remoter areas, and wolves roam the steppes. There are vast reserves of oil, coal and iron, and sinister monsters are believed to lurk in the depths of its lakes. As late as the 1940s, an unknown tribe of people was discovered by geologists.

Siberian winters last seven or eight months, and temperatures almost as low as -68°C (-90°F) have been recorded in the far north.

The timetables are in Moscow time, as are the clocks at the stations along the route, but the train passes through eight time zones, making the east coast seven hours ahead of Moscow time. Along the way it crosses rivers and negotiates mountain ranges and vast, sweeping plains blanketed with snow in winter, passing lakes, cornfields, villages and towns the railroad itself has largely created.

Most of the rolling stock today is of 1940s vintage, with sleeping cars and a dining car that is open all day; the diner doubles as a shop, used by people from the towns and villages on the route. Starting from Moscow, the train crosses the Volga River and then heads southeast to the Ural Mountains where, 1,770km (1,100 miles) out from Moscow, it crosses from Europe into Asia. From Sverdlovsk, a major industrial town in the Urals, the line continues on to Omsk and Novosibirsk, across the Ob River, busy with cargo boats and barges, to Krasnoyarsk on the mountains south of Lake Baikal, then passes over the edge of the Gobi Desert and runs beside the Shlika River to reach Khabarovsk and Vladivostok.

Two branches now extend from Moscow to Beijing—one weekly train crossing Outer Mongolia and the Gobi Desert before entering China and passing through the Great Wall, the other (also weekly) going via Manchuria. The former journey covers 7,621km (4,735 miles), the latter 8,986km (5,623 miles) and each takes six days.

BACKGROUND: *The Trans-Siberian Express passes through the rugged scenery on the shores of Lake Baikal.*
BELOW: *The emblem of the Trans-Siberian Express.*

From Beginning to End

The Trans-Siberian express trains leave Moscow from Yarolslavl Station, a remarkable Art Nouveau edifice of 1904 designed by Fedor Shekhtel. With its weird, steeply pitched roof, it looks more like the gateway to Fairyland than a train station.

At the other end of the line is Vladivostock, a lively port which was a Soviet military base and was closed to foreigners, who had to end their journeys at Nakhodka, 80km (50 miles) north. The town was opened again in 1992 and is now thriving on trade and tourism.

See also:
The Canadian Pacific Railway 148-9

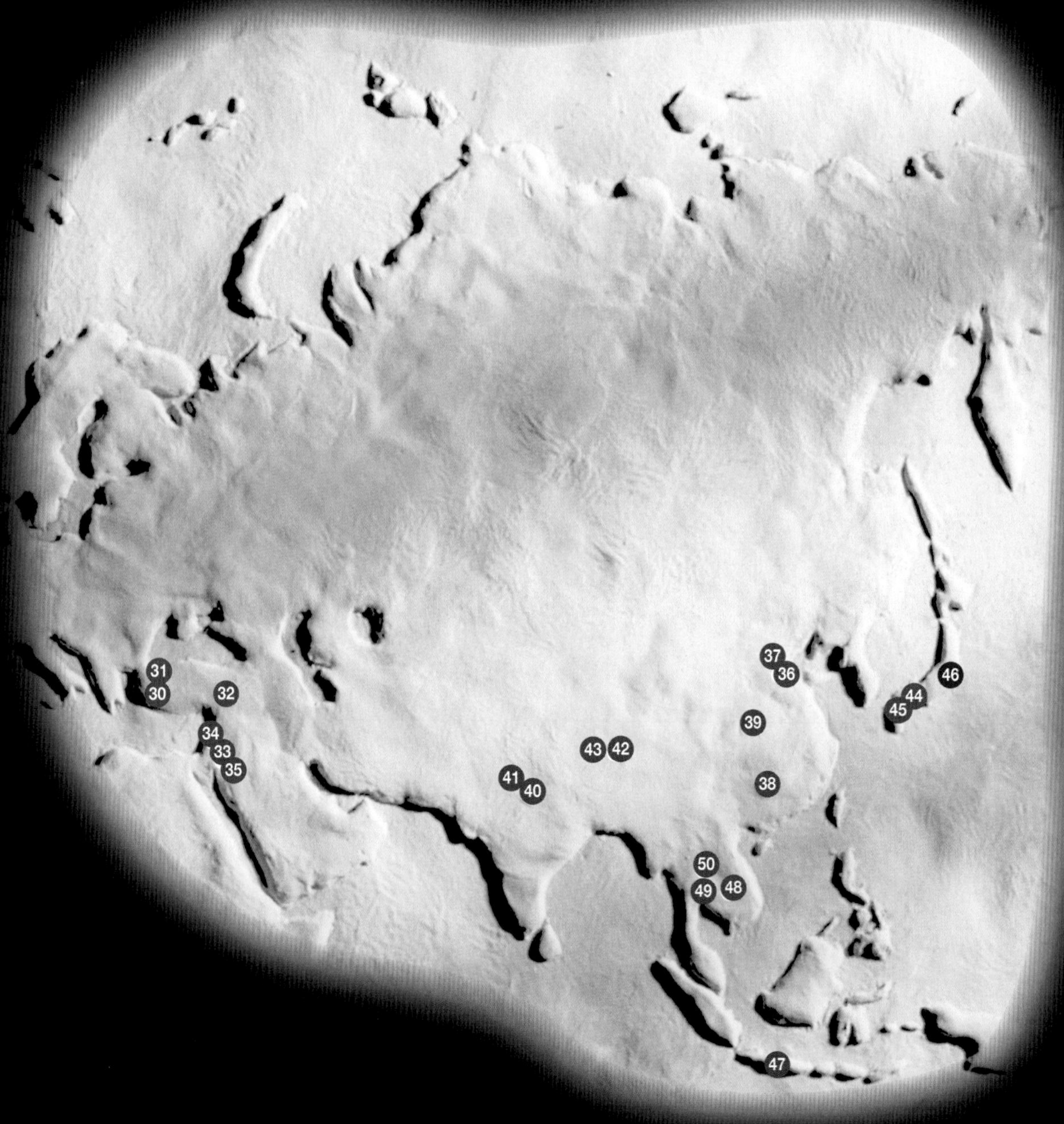

30 **Pamukkale**

31 **The Blue Mosque**

32 **Nemrut Dag**

33 **The Dead Sea**

34 **Jerusalem**

35 **Petra**

36 **The Great Wall of China**

37 **The Forbidden City**

38 **The Guilin Hills**

39 **The Three Gorges Dam**

40 **The Taj Mahal**

41 **The Red Fort**

42 **Potala Palace**

43 **The Himalayas**

44 **Itsukushima Shrine**

45 **Beppu**

46 **Mount Fuji**

47 **Borobudur**

48 **Angkor Wat**

49 **Wat Phra Keo**

50 **Ayutthaya**

Asia

Extending from the Mediterranean to the Pacific, Asia is the largest of the world's continents, covering about one-third of the globe's land surface. The first steps to civilization were taken in the Near East, where, 10,000 years ago, small groups of hunter-gatherers began to settle, clear the ground and grow crops, eventually developing into sizeable communities.

Towns grew into cities, and cities into kingdoms and mighty empires. In Mesopotamia the Babylonian and then Assyrian kings held sway, and the Persian Empire, founded in the sixth century, stretched from the Mediterranean to the Indus River.

Far to the east in the third century BC in China, a new empire was established that would endure for more than 2,000 years and undertake the biggest construction job ever known—the Great Wall of China. In the 21st century work is progressing on another Chinese wonder, the subject of intense controversy and widespread upheaval: the Three Gorges Dam. Whereas the Great Wall was a defence against hostile neighbours, the dam is designed to tame the Yangtze River as well as easing the passage of huge trading ships and providing a source of electricity.

Religion has left a visible mark all across Asia, in the form of churches, monasteries, shrines, mosques and pagodas, and Hindu and Buddhist temples replete with exuberant carvings. Islam flourished from the seventh century on, and its monuments range from the Dome of the Rock in Jerusalem—a city holy to three major faiths—to the beautiful Taj Mahal in Agra, India.

Two religions exported from India inspired some of Asia's most impressive monuments. In Japan the largest wooden building in the world was built at Nara to house an enormous image of the Buddha, and Borobudur in Java is the world's largest Buddhist temple. The immense temple complex, Angkor Wat in Cambodia, raised to celebrate the Hindu god Vishnu, has survived the ravages of time and modern war, and still has the power to take the breath away.

30 Pamukkale, Turkey

the facts

- Pamukkale means 'cotton castle' in Turkish.
- The tiers of tufa basins reach a height of around 91m (300ft).
- There is some seismic activity in this area nearly every day.

Pamukkale

The hot springs at Pamukkale, in a remote region of western Turkey, are a dazzling sight on a bright, sunny day. The effect is rather like looking at an ice fall on a glacier. People have come here to take advantage of the springs for centuries, but the extraordinary tufa basins and their cascades of water existed long before the first human visitors arrived.

The medicinal and therapeutic properties of some mineral waters have long been recognized, and the Romans built a thermal resort around the springs at Pamukkale. However, their structure was destined not to survive the ravages of time as successfully as the tufa. Some Roman ruins can still be seen, and there is now a modern spa resort built on the same site.

Formation of the Tufa

The waters of a geothermal area are invariably rich in dissolved mineral salts, but the composition of the salts

RIGHT: *The Roman theatre at Hierapolis, near Pamukkale.* BELOW: *Bathing at Pamukkale's famous thermal spa.*

Mineral Waters

Water is an essential ingredient of life in any form, but some waters with particular mineral contents are considered to be positively beneficial to health. Pamukkale has been a popular health spa for 2,000 years, since the Romans first came to bathe in the hot springs and drink the supposedly curative waters.

Tourists driven away by earthquakes in the 14th century returned in the 20th century to enjoy the water and to admire the natural beauty of the site. Now, as then, the water runs through open channels, losing heat as it goes. However, by the time it reaches the open-air swimming pools and terraces it is still warm enough to bathe in for about half of the year.

Outside the Roman temple of Apollo nearby, the fountain used water carried here by aqueducts.

varies from place to place depending on the composition of the underlying rocks through which the waters flow. Hot water is able to dissolve any number of different mineral salts, although some are more soluble than others. The water is usually saturated with salts by the time it reaches the surface and, once in the open air it starts to evaporate naturally. As the solution dries out, the salts crystallize, forming deposits on the ground. The appearance of these deposits depends on the composition of the salts, and although many salts are white, impurities can cause a range of colours.

At Pamukkale the hot springs bubble out of the ground near the top of the hillside. This water, which is rich in calcium bicarbonate, emerges at a temperature of about 43°C (109°F). The water evaporates as it flows down the hillside, leaving a spectacular veneer of snowy-white salts called travertine (a calcium carbonate rock) encrusting the ground.

These salts have accumulated over thousands of years and now the deposits are quite thick. Such deposits, known as tufa, are not uncommon, but what makes those at Pamukkale so special is their unusual formation and scale. Tier upon tier of gleaming pools adorn the surface of the hill, looking like stacks of shallow porcelain basins. No other hot spring areas around the world exhibit quite the same shapes.

BELOW: *Sunset over the travertine pools at Pamukkale.*

See also:
Beppu 103
Rotorua 228-9
Volcanic Iceland 14-15

the facts

- The Blue Mosque's official name is the Mosque of Sultan Ahmet I.
- Sultan Ahmet I died at the age of 27, shortly after the opening of his new mosque.
- Around 20,000 tiles have been used to decorate the interior.

The Blue Mosque

Work on the Blue Mosque began in 1609 on the instructions of the 19-year-old Sultan Ahmet I. The architect of the mosque was Mehmet Aga, and his masterpiece took seven years to complete. All the standard features of mosque design can be seen, but the Blue Mosque is unusual in having six minarets—one at each of the four corners, as might be expected, and another two, slightly shorter, at the outer edge of the courtyard. According to one story, the young sultan offended authorities at Mecca, the very heart of the Islamic religion, and was required to pay for the construction of a seventh minaret for the mosque, ensuring that it would have no rivals.

Exploring the Mosque

The temple courtyard can be approached from three gateways that lead into an outer colonnade of granite columns. Beyond the colonnade, which has a roof

Museums

The Blue Mosque attracts large numbers of visitors, but many overlook the Carpet and Kilim Museum in the mosque's imperial pavilion. The museum houses a fine collection of Usak, Bergama and Konya carpets dating from the 16th to the 19th century. A range of restored Turkish carpets dating from the 13th to the 20th century is displayed along the ramp which forms the entrance to the pavilion, and in the rooms where the sultans used to rest.

Haghia Sophia

Opposite the Blue Mosque is the Church of Holy Wisdom, Haghia Sophia. Built during the sixth century on the site of earlier churches, it is a vast domed basilica. It was the mother church of the Byzantine Empire until Constantinople (Istanbul) fell to the Turks in 1453. At this point it was transformed into a mosque. The mosaics inside, uncovered and restored since the building was declared a museum in the 1930s, are Christian. They depict Christ, flanked by the archangels Michael and Gabriel, with the inscription 'I am the light of the world'.

ABOVE: *An elderly man playing music outside the Blue Mosque.*
LEFT: *The distinctive six minarets of the Blue Mosque.*

composed of 30 small domes, a hexagonal fountain stands in the middle of the courtyard. Such fountains are familiar features of mosques, and enable the faithful to wash before entering the mosque. To the east of the courtyard stands the *medressah* or college.

The mosque itself presents a pleasing roofscape of domes—a large central one surrounded by four half-domes, and four more small domes beyond these. Inside, this arrangement of domes can be fully appreciated, with four huge elephant-foot columns supporting the whole structure. The dazzling effect of thousands of tiles might be overpowering if it were not for the spaciousness of the interior and the remarkable light that streams in through the 260 windows.

The *mihrab* (the niche facing towards Mecca) and the *nimber* (the pulpit) are carved from white marble, and the floor is covered in thick carpets, mostly deep red, but it is the complex of blue tiles that makes the greatest impact. There are numerous shades of blue, and many other colours can be seen on closer inspection. This elegant ceramic work is the product of the famous Iznik factories, which achieved tremendous success during the 16th century, exporting their ceramics far and wide. Insistent that this new mosque would have nothing but the best, Sultan Ahmet is said to have forbidden the potteries from producing tiles for any other building than his.

See also:
Alhambra 58-9
Fez Medina 124-5
Karouyine Mosque 124-5

the facts

- After centuries of obscurity, Nemrut Dag was rediscovered in 1881 by Karl Sester, a German engineer.
- The statues' vast heads are an amalgam of Greek facial features with Persian headdresses and hairstyling
- The tumulus (ancient burial mound) is 49m (160ft) tall and 152m (500ft) in diameter.

Nemrut Dag

Antiochus I, a king of mixed Persian and Greek descent, ruled the area known as the Commagene from 69 to 34BC. On the 2,134m (7,000ft)-high summit of Nemrut Dag, in Anatolia (now part of Turkey), he built an extraordinary monument to his own glory and that of the gods.

A tumulus, formed of heaps of loose stones, crowns the mountain peak, guarded on the east and west sides by lions, eagles and 9-m (30ft) statues of Heracles, Zeus-Oromasdes, Tyche, Apollo-Mithras and Antiochus himself. The seated figures have by now lost their heads, which lie near by. Bas-relief figures, on stone slabs that once formed a long frieze, show Antiochus' ancestors, with incense-burning altars before them.

Antiochus had no doubt that he belonged with the gods, as he is shown shaking the hands of Apollo, Zeus, and Hercules in bas-reliefs on the west terrace. Another slab depicts a lion and the planets Jupiter, Mercury and Mars, arranged in an astronomical conjunction that occurred on 7 July 62BC—possibly when building began.

Arsameia on Nymphaios

The arrangement of statues, altars, and tumulus on Nemrut Dag is known by the technical term *heirotheseion.* A similar complex, but with no surviving colossal statues, has been discovered near by at Arsameia on Nymphaios—the heirotheseion of Antiochus's father, Mithridates I. Again, there are inscriptions and Antiochus is featured in a bas-relief, shaking hands with a god. Particularly intriguing is a long, manmade tunnel that descends 152m (500ft) into the rock before coming to a dead end. A long inscription by the entrance reveals nothing about the tunnel.

A relief in the same area shows a Commagene king, presumably Mithridates, elaborately dressed and shaking hands with a naked god who carries a club and a lion skin, the hallmarks of Heracles.

33 The Dead Sea, Israel

the facts

- The River Jordan and other small streams discharge up to 7,112,329 tonnes (7,000,000 tons) of water into the Dead Sea each day.
- The Dead Sea's mineral content is about ten times as high as that in most other oceans.
- The Dead Sea is 396m (1,300ft) below sea level.

The Dead Sea

The Dead Sea is not really a sea at all, but a lake made up of two basins that together are around 72km (45 miles) long and 14km (9 miles) wide. Water flowing into them is evaporated by the Jordan Valley's intense heat, leaving a deposit of minerals and salts. While the high salinity ensures that buoyancy is no problem, actually swimming in the Dead Sea is tricky. It is simpler just to sit comfortably, supported by the water. No fish can survive the extreme saltiness, but the Dead Sea supports a number of salt-loving bacteria.

At the southern part of the lake there are hot springs and pools of rich black mud which have long been held to have healing powers. Hotels here allow guests to enjoy their mud-baths in air-conditioned bathrooms, rather than face the searing heat of the Dead Sea's shimmering shores.

Looking Back

The shores of the Dead Sea are as remarkable as the lake itself. Great pancakes of salt have been left by the evaporating water, and pillars of salt stand at the southern extremes of the lake. One of these salt pillars is embedded in legend.

A Biblical story recalls the cities of Sodom and Gomorrah, which were rife with sin. Lot, a righteous man, was warned that the cities would be destroyed as a punishment, and that he should flee with his family. Lot and his relations were warned that they should not look back. Unfortunately, Lot's wife took one last look, and she was turned into the large salt pillar near the modern town of Sedom.

ABOVE: *Beauty treatment, Dead-Sea style.*

See also:
Camargue 22-3
Lake Nakuru 130-1

Jerusalem

For 5,000 years people have made their homes in this area between the Mount of Olives and the Judean Hills. Today Jerusalem is divided into the New City and the walled Old City, where seven gates lead into the historic heart, sacred to the Jewish, Christian and Islamic faiths. Among its cobbled streets, markets, houses and courtyards are three particularly significant monuments: the Wailing Wall, the Dome of the Rock and the Church of the Holy Sepulchre.

King David captured Jerusalem at the beginning of the first century BC and built an altar on the summit of Mount Moriah, where Abraham had prepared to sacrifice his son Isaac. This rock was considered by many to be the centre of the world. It was here that David's son Solomon later built the great Temple which housed the Ark of the Covenant, and a small part of the platform on which it stood still exists. The Temple was rebuilt after the destruction of the city by Nebuchadnezzar, and both platform and Temple were extended by King Herod during the first century BC. In the seventh century AD a mosque was built near by, marking the spot where Muhammad ascended to receive the Islamic commandments from Allah. Pilgrims can still see his footprint and three hairs from his beard.

The Wailing Wall, properly known as the Western Wall (*Kotel Maaravi* in Hebrew), is one of Judaism's most poignant symbols. After the Roman army had destroyed Jerusalem in AD70, killing or enslaving its inhabitants, survivors were forbidden to return to the site of the Temple of Solomon. Later, the faithful were permitted to return once a year to the scene of devastation to weep over the stones, and the tradition continues to this day. The wall, which remained in Jordanian hands from 1948 until the Six-Day War of 1967, is part of the platform of the enlarged Temple dating from the time of King Herod.

the facts

- Jerusalem Old City covers 1sq km (0.4 square mile).
- Its walls are about 12m (39ft) high and 4km (2.5 miles) long.
- The gates leading into the city were built in the second century and reconstructed in the 16th century.
- Until the late 19th century the city gates were still locked every night.
- There are over 300 holy buildings and monuments in Jerusalem.

The dome of the rock

The Dome of the Rock is one of Islam's holiest shrines and is in the world's oldest Islamic building. The dome, said to have been made originally of gold, is an outward symbol of the sacred rock that it shelters and is 20m (65ft) in diameter and 34m (110ft) high.

An outer arcade has an octagonal plan echoed by the outer walls of the building. The rock sits at the centre of the building and the arcades around it allow processions of pilgrims to move freely around the object of veneration. Inside there is sumptuous mosaic work showing clear Byzantine influence.

RIGHT: *A group reading the Koran inside the Dome of the Rock.*
ABOVE: *Colourful goods for sale in the market in the Old City of Jerusalem.*
LEFT: *The octagonal structure of the Dome of the Rock has a gilded aluminium dome.*

the **history**

3000-2000BC
Jerusalem founded by Canaanites.

960BC
Solomon builds the First Temple.

586BC
Nebuchadnezzar destroys Jerusalem and takes captives to Babylon.

525BC
Jewish exiles return to build the Second Temple.

AD70
Temple destroyed after Jewish revolt against Rome.

688-692
Arab conqueror, Umar ibn-Khatib, uncovers temple rock and builds mosque nearby.

1228
Christian Crusaders capture Jerusalem.

1517-1917
Ottoman Empire rules the city.

1917
British troops capture Jerusalem. British declare support for Jewish homeland in Palestine.

1948
First Arab-Israeli war ends in partition of city between Israel and Jordan.

1967
Israel takes control of whole city.

2003
Scientists use carbon dating to show when Jerusalem's Siloam Tunnel, described in the Bible, was excavated.

Built of huge dressed stone blocks over 1.2m (4ft) high, it gives a memorable indication of the vast scale of the Temple.

The Church of the Holy Sepulchre, which is in the northwestern quarter of the Old City, stands at the end of the Via Dolorosa, the route along which Christ carried his cross from the headquarters of the Roman procurator to the place of his crucifixion. The first church to stand here, built in AD326 by Helena, mother of Emperor Constantine, was destroyed by Persians in 614. A rebuilt version was razed by the Egyptian caliph El-Hakim in 1009 and a series of shrines was built in its place. When the Crusaders entered the city in the 12th century, they brought the shrines under one vast, cruciform roof, an arrangement that largely survives to this day.

BROAD WALL

Archaeologists had to revise their ideas about the Old City after a team led by Professor Nahman Avigad discovered part of the city wall in the 1970s. Known as the Broad Wall, it indicated that Jerusalem had extended much further than experts had previously believed during the eighth century BC, reaching as far as the slopes of Mount Zion.

The unearthed section, which is 7m (23ft) thick and up to 3m (10ft) high, dates from 701BC when King Hezekiah of Judah built defences against Assyrian invasion, having refused to pay tribute to the Assyrian king, Sennacherib. The Biblical account given by Isaiah—a contemporary of Hezekiah's—tells of Hezekiah noting 'the breaches of the city of David', numbering the houses of Jerusalem and breaking them down to fortify a new wall.

Excavations revealed that residences on the site had been demolished and that their stones had been re-used. Isaiah goes on to describe a ditch being constructed between the two walls for the 'water of the old pool'—namely the Pools of Siloam. In the end, Sennacherib overran most of Judah but did not take the city of Jerusalem.

LEFT: *Detail of a sculpture in the Holocaust memorial, Yad Vashem.*

ABOVE: *The Dome of the Rock.*
LEFT: *Hasidic Jews praying at the Wailing Wall.*
RIGHT: *Floodlit walls surround the Old City of Jerusalem.*

See also:
Ayutthaya 110-11
Carthage 122-3
Fez Medina 124-5

35 Petra, Jordan

the facts

- The façade of the Treasury is 27m (90ft) wide and 40m (130ft) tall.
- Its design is classical rather than Nabataean.
- The urn that tops the Treasury's façade is believed to have contained treasure belonging to a pharaoh. Early visitors took pot shots at it in the hope of dislodging its riches.

Petra

Mention Petra and chances are that someone will respond with the familiar quotation: 'A rose-red city, half as old as time'. These words are from a poem by the 19th-century Englishman JW Burgon. Unfortunately, the description is not completely accurate, as Burgon himself conceded when he visited the place some years later. Petra is not so much rose-red as salmon-pink and is not really a city either. It's more of a monumental cemetery—any houses here were probably made of mud and have long since disappeared. Petra is a place that poses many unanswered questions, and this air of mystery makes an already spectacular site all the more fascinating.

A Monumental Legacy

In the sixth century BC a nomadic tribe, the Nabataeans, gained control of a rift valley area between Aqaba and the Dead Sea on the eastern side of Wadi Arabah in Jordan. (A *wadi* is a ravine or dry river valley that may flood at certain times of the year.) Gaining control over important existing

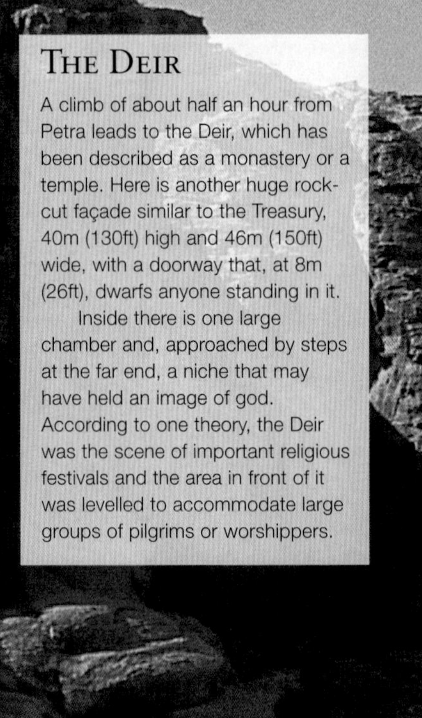

BELOW: *The elaborate rock-cut façades cover surprisingly spartan chambers.*

The Deir

A climb of about half an hour from Petra leads to the Deir, which has been described as a monastery or a temple. Here is another huge rock-cut façade similar to the Treasury, 40m (130ft) high and 46m (150ft) wide, with a doorway that, at 8m (26ft), dwarfs anyone standing in it.

Inside there is one large chamber and, approached by steps at the far end, a niche that may have held an image of god. According to one theory, the Deir was the scene of important religious festivals and the area in front of it was levelled to accommodate large groups of pilgrims or worshippers.

trade routes, the Nabataeans became powerful and wealthy and Petra is their legacy. It's a complex of monuments once believed to be houses but now recognized as tombs, cut into the rock in an inaccessible area 914m (3,000ft) above sea level. Some have remarkable classical detailing while others have a distinctive Nabataean 'crow-step' decoration and reveal the influence of Egyptian and Assyrian building styles. All the emphasis is on the façades because inside, the bare chambers are completely free of ornament.

Petra became part of the Roman Empire in AD106, acquiring a forum, baths, a theatre and all the usual elements associated with Roman civilization. Trade patterns changed with the rise of Palmyra and obscurity followed. For centuries Petra was known only to local tribesman, who had little difficulty in warding off inquisitive strangers until rediscovery came in 1812. Swiss explorer Johan Burckhardt, fluent in Arabic, persuaded a local guide that he wished to sacrifice a goat at a tomb, near which there was said to be a buried city. Burckhardt was escorted along the Siq—the deep, narrow cleft in the rocks through which visitors approach the site today—and he came upon the dramatic view of the Treasury, or el-Kasneh, perhaps Petra's most famous monument.

Beyond the Treasury the valley opens out, revealing numerous rock-cut tombs in pink sandstone. The carving that has been exposed to the wind has eroded, although enough archaeological evidence has been found to suggest that originally Petra was clad in stucco decoration.

BELOW LEFT: *The pillared façade of the Monastery.*
BELOW: *Bedouin guards outside the Treasury at Petra.*

THE HIGH PLACE

A steep climb leads to the Attuf Ridge, where two obelisks sit, one on a manmade plateau and another, a little farther up, on a flattened area measuring around 61m by 18m (200ft by 60 ft).

This 'High Place' has been interpreted as a setting for ritual sacrifice with a high altar on which offerings were made, perhaps to the two gods that the Nabataeans are believed to have worshipped, Dusares and Al Uzza.

The altar is equipped with drainage channels, presumably for blood, and there is some evidence to suggest that the some sacrifices that the Nabataeans performed were human.

See also:
Ayutthaya 110-11
Carthage 122-3
Jerusalem 76-9

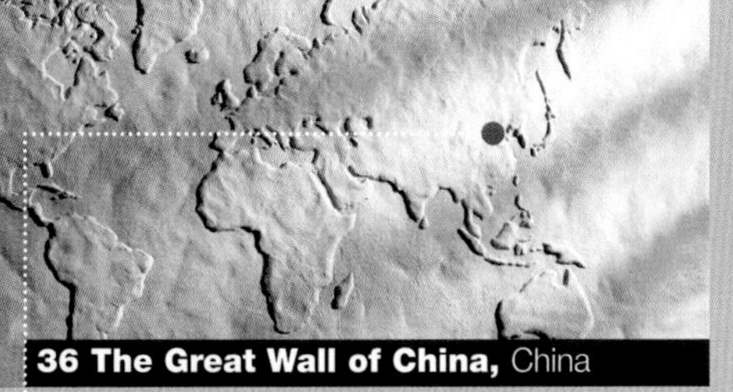

36 **The Great Wall of China,** China

The Great Wall of China

*The Great Wall of China is one of the most remarkable feats of engineering of all time, and one of the most brutal. It was constructed in about 10 years after 220*BC *by the first man to rule a united China, the savagely formidable despot Qin Shihuangdi. The wall was a bulwark against the warlike nomadic horsemen of the Mongolian plains to the north and probably also a titanic assertion of the Emperor's own power and glory.*

Sections of defensive wall had been built earlier by the various rival minor kingdoms of northern China, but nothing on the scale of the Great Wall. Qin Shihuangdi conscripted an army of peasants, soldiers, convicts and political prisoners, and put his most successful general, Meng Tian, in charge of rebuilding and connecting the earlier sections in a single barrier through the mountains on his northern frontier. The wall snaked its way up and down the mountains, through desert country and through marshes, and was built of earth faced with brick on stone foundations. From the watchtowers, smoke signals during the day and bonfires at night sent information cross-country with unprecedented speed.

It is said that 300,000 people toiled to build the wall, and the organization and supply of such an enormous work force was itself an astonishing achievement. Legend says that Qin Shihuangdi was told by a wizard that the wall would not stand unless *wan*—or 10,000—were buried in it. The Emperor found a man named Wan and had him killed and interred in the wall. It seems that thousands who worked on the wall died in the process, and that their bodies did go to cement the wall. It has been called the world's longest graveyard: the Wall of Tears.

BELOW: *A Ming Guard on duty at the Great Wall.*

the facts

- At the top the wall was 5.5m (18ft) wide, enough to allow infantry to march along it ten abreast or cavalrymen to ride five abreast.
- It still stands an average 9m (30ft) high.
- The watchtowers rise to 12m (40ft).
- During the Ming dynasty (1368-1644) the wall was renovated 18 times.

Qin shihuangdi

Qin Shihuangdi, of the Qin dynasty, was one of the most ruthless and effective tyrants in history, a Chinese version of Russia's Ivan the Terrible.

He was born in 259BC and succeeded to his father's kingdom as a boy of 13, though it was rumoured that his real father was a merchant. A terrifying autocrat, he mastered the various warring kingdoms along the Yellow River and to the south to create an empire in 221BC.

He was a great builder and used forced labour to construct roads and canals as well as the Great Wall. He also standardized Chinese script and coins, weights and measures.

Qin Shihuangdi left his mark on China, as his imperial system lasted through recurrent changes of dynasty from 221BC until 1911, when it was finally toppled after more than 2,000 years, the longest surviving political regime in history. A few years after his death in 210BC, the Han dynasty took power.

770-476BC
Ducal states extend existing defence works.

220-210BC
Qin Shihuangdi, ruler of unified China, orders the building of the Wall.

127-119BC
Wall extended westward into Hexi corridor and Xinjiang region by Emperor Wu of the Han dynasty.

AD607
Reconstruction work begun under Sui dynasty.

1368–1644
Further building takes place under Ming dynasty, using bricks and granite.

Sustaining the Wall

The Great Wall was effective when properly manned, but over subsequent centuries it was neglected, abandoned and rebuilt many times over. When the Sui dynasty rulers ordered reconstruction in the seventh century, it is said that no fewer than a million people were forced to work on it and that half of them perished. The wall took its final shape under the Ming dynasty, and sections of it have been restored for tourists.

The wall runs from near Bo Hai Sea northeast of Beijing across China and into the Gobi Desert. Figures for its total length vary by hundreds of miles, because of the numerous rebuildings. The wall twists and turns on itself, there are parallel walls in some places and numerous offshoots that may or may not be counted. A recent official figure is 6,350km (3,946 miles), but in 1990 a Chinese walker was reported to have covered the entire length and his pedometer indicated a distance of 6,700km (4,163 miles).

THE MING TOMBS

The Ming dynasty ruled China from 1368 to 1644, and 13 of their emperors rest in the Badaling Valley, near the Great Wall. Their tombs were positioned according to the principles of Chinese geomancy, which ensured that they would be surrounded by positive supernatural influences.

A succession of great gates marks the Spirit Way, which each emperor's funeral procession followed. At the Great Red Gate, everyone had to dismount and proceed on foot, as the central arch of the gate was to be used only by the emperor's coffin. Just beyond the arch is a stele (an upright slab of stone) 9m (30ft) high, which rests on the back of a huge stone tortoise, a symbol of the universe and immortality. The road passes between 15th-century statues of lions, horses, camels and other animals which are believed to bring good fortune, with human figures providing a guard of honour.

The Dragon and the Phoenix gates lead to the tombs. The largest and best-preserved one belongs to Emperor Yongle, who died in 1424. It is believed that 16 concubines were buried alive in his tomb.

LEFT: *The wall featured in Beijing's bid for the 2008 Olympic Games.*

See also:
Forbidden City 86-7
Three Gorges Dam 90-1

the facts

- The Forbidden City is square in shape, on an axis running north to south, and is surrounded by a broad moat and a 9m (30ft) wall.
- All the major buildings face south, turning away from hostile supernatural forces and the Siberian winds.
- There are 9,999 rooms altogether.

The Forbidden City

Cut off by its moat and purple wall, banned to all ordinary mortals, roofed in the yellow tiles allowed only to emperors, the Forbidden City was a city within a city at the heart of Beijing. The Ming and Qing dynasties lived and ruled here until the fall of the empire in 1911.

Beijing's history goes back much farther, but the Forbidden City itself was created by Emperor Yongle of the Ming dynasty, who moved his capital here from Nanking in 1421. It was pillaged when the Manchus toppled the Ming dynasty in 1644, but the Manchu emperors, who installed themselves on the Dragon Throne as the Qing dynasty, restored it to its former glory. New temples and palaces were built and lakes and gardens were laid out. By the 18th century the city had reached the height of its glory.

Inside, arranged symmetrically, are palaces, gates, courtyards, streams and gardens. The emperor, his mother,

BELOW INSET: *The colourful Gate of Supreme Harmony which leads to the largest hall in the Forbidden City.*

Outside the City

South of the Forbidden City is the vast expanse of Tiananmen Square. The name, which means 'Square of the Gate of Heavenly Peace', is inextricably linked with the atrocities of 1989. Mao Zedong proclaimed the People's Republic of China here in 1949 and the People's Culture Palace occupies the former Temple of the Imperial Ancestors.

Not far away, in its 220-ha (540 acre) park, is the Temple of Heaven, where emperors carried out the rituals believed to preserve the order and harmony of the universe, offering sacrifices at the circular three-tiered Altar of Heaven.

In the northwest outskirts of Beijing is the Summer Palace. This was looted in 1860, but a new palace was built in 1888.

his wives and his concubines lived here, along with an army of eunuchs and servants. Life was regulated by an elaborate code of rules, etiquette and taboos.

Accessing the Forbidden City

The main gate is the massive southern Meridian (*Wumen*) Gate, from which the emperor formally reviewed his troops. Beyond it is a courtyard crossed by a stream, known as the River of Gold, which is itself crossed by five marble bridges, which represent the five virtues and lead to the elegant Gate of the Supreme Harmony. Beyond this gate is a vast courtyard, said to have been designed to hold 90,000 people. At the far side, raised on a high marble terrace, is the largest building in the Fordidden City, the Hall of Supreme Harmony, where the emperor sat enthroned on great state occasions.

Beyond this lie two more grand ceremonial chambers, the Hall of Perfect Harmony and the Hall of Preserving Harmony. Further north is the warren of rooms where the emperor and his family lived. In various rooms are displays of the impressive and beautiful treasures that the emperors accumulated, including a notable collection of clocks and automata—yet these are only a fraction of the original treasures. The Japanese looted the Forbidden City in the 1930s and the Nationalists took many items away with them to Taiwan in 1949. The imperial gardens are beautifully landscaped with trees and rock gardens, statues and pavilions, and pools and waterfalls.

LEFT AND BELOW: *Rooftops in the Forbidden City are ornately carved and colourfully painted.*

Imperial Capital

Beijing was given its present name, which simply means northern capital, by Emperor Yongle in the 15th century. He built the Forbidden City inside the Imperial City, which was also square in shape and surrounded by its own walls. It had been an important town long before that, but in the 13th century it was sacked by Genghis Khan's Mongol hordes.

The oldest buildings in Beijing today date from the subsequent rebuilding, from 1267, by Kublai Khan, the Mongol emperor who made it his winter capital.

In 1648 the new Qing emperor ordered the Chinese inhabitants to leave, to make room for his Manchu and Mongol supporters. The Chinese inhabitants moved to the south, and this area was later named the Chinese City.

See also:
Great Wall of China 82-5

the facts

- The limestone region, of which the Guilin Hills are a part, stretches across south-central China to northern Vietnam.
- In Chinese, Guilin means 'forest of cassia trees'.
- The Guilin Hills reach average heights of 99m (325ft).
- Fubo Hill gives panoramic views of Guilin City.

The Guilin Hills

RIGHT: *A road winds between a patchwork of intensively cultivated fields in Guangxi province near the city of Guilin.*

Pinnacles of rock cluster together on the shores of the River Li, in the Guangxi Zhuang Autonomous Region of southern China. The thick layers of limestone that form the Guilin Hills were laid down under an ancient sea. Millions of years later the land was uplifted and acidic rain began to dissolve those rocks, which were already weakened by cracks and fractures. When the land was uplifted a second time some weakened rocks collapsed, leaving free-standing conical towers made of a limestone more resistant to erosion. These towers are good examples of what is known as tower karst scenery.

Secret Places

The Guilin Hills are riddled with caves and passageways created by the erosive rain, and during World War II many people hid here to escape Japanese bombing. It was also the site of fierce fighting in the late 1960s when clashing Red Army factions turned the region into a battlefield. The people of Guilin once again fled to the caves in the hills to hide from the fighting.

One well-known cave is the Reed Flute Cave, one of a series of caverns and channels full of delicate stalactites and stalagmites. It is named for the reeds that grow outside it, which are used to make the flutes that produce the haunting melodies evocative of China.

A Unique Landscape

The steep-sided hills rise abruptly from bright green valley floors and disappear into the distance as row upon row of jagged summits and peaks. Many are draped with vines and small trees that maintain a tenuous hold on their rocky sides. Others explode with colour when orchids come into bloom. Sometimes shrouded in a soft mist and reflected in the sluggish waters of the River Li, these hills emanate a mystical quality which has been an inspiration for artists and poets over centuries.

This ageless landscape was for many years closed to Western visitors. The Ming court, which retreated to Guilin when the Manchus took over Beijing in 1664, included some Jesuit priests, who were attempting to convert the royal household to Christianity. Apart from a small group of imprisoned Portuguese seamen in 1550, these Jesuits were the first Westerners to see the Guilin Hills. When Communist forces took over Guilin in 1949, they closed the city to most foreigners. The city was only reopened in 1973, and the area has quickly become one of China's most visited beauty spots.

The Guilin region contains rich agricultural land, and the underground water is often pumped to the surface for irrigation. Some of the underground rivers that flow through the tropical karst are used as sources of hydroelectric power. Karst landscapes get their name from an area of caves and sinkholes covering 80km (50 miles) in northwestern Slovenia. Formed of limestone, such landscapes usually have dry and arid surfaces, which are drained of water by underground channels and streams. This kind of landscape makes up about 10 percent of the earth's land surface.

LEFT: *Traditional farming methods are still used in Guangxi province.*
BELOW: *Rafts on the busy Li Jiang river.*

Land and Water

Limestone consists almost entirely of calcium carbonate. Groundwater and rain can both contain carbon dioxide, forming a mild acid which is capable of dissolving limestone, especially where the rock is already weakened by cracks and crevices. Thus water which moves across the surface of harder rocks may suddenly disappear underground when it reaches the softer limestone, often into geological formations known as sinkholes, sometimes reappearing elsewhere as springs.

As the water flows underground, caves are eroded, and the dissolved minerals are deposited on the walls of caves or drip from the ceiling to form stalactites and stalagmites. Some of the best caves formed in this way include the Frasassi Caves in Italy and Réseau Jean-Bernard in the foothills of the French Alps, the deepest known cave in the world.

See also:
Table Mountain 144-5
Tierra del Fuego 208-9

the facts

- Three Gorges is the collective name given to the Qutang, Wuxia and Xiling gorges.
- The Three Gorges area begins at Baidicheng in Fengjie County, Sichuan Province and ends at Nanjinguan in Yichang County, Hubei province, 193km (121 m) away.
- This is the world's biggest hydroelectric scheme.

The Three **Gorges Dam**

China's massive hydroelectric dam project, begun in 1994 and scheduled for completion in 2009, is a task of staggering proportions. The project, which was conceived to control calamitous floods and provide irrigation and electricity, has been condemned by environmentalists and human rights groups across the world.

The Yangtze, Asia's longest river, has always been prone to flooding, often on a devastating scale. In the 20th century alone over a million people were killed by floodwaters and millions more have perished over the centuries. Production of electricity, the dam's other main purpose, is also an urgent need in this vast country. The power produced by damming the Yangtze's waters will be the equivalent of that produced by more than 12 new nuclear power plants. Another aim is to enhance trade and industry by improving navigation for large ships, which could not previously pass into the upper reaches of the river. Ships of up to 3,000 tonnes (2,952 tons) will be lifted over the dam in the biggest container ever built—120m (394ft) long and 18m (59ft) wide.

Ambition and Opposition

Among the many concerns expressed by opponents of the dam are the submerging of hundreds of historical and cultural sites, farms, orchards, villages and cities. The dam will lead to the extinction of many endangered species, the destruction of commercial fish stocks and the displacement of between one and two million people.

Whatever the pros and cons of the project, there is no denying its breathtaking ambition. Proposals for a dam were first mooted in 1919, the first designs were planned in the 1950s and the go-ahead was given in 1970. In order to make construction work possible engineers have had to divert the Yangtze, using coffer dams to shift the river away from the site itself in the biggest such project ever undertaken. The main dam is designed to flush out any sediment through 23 gates, which will be opened every year as the flood season starts and then closed as it ends. At the centre of the dam 22 gates act as an overflow, a failsafe element designed to deal with four times the Yangtze's average flow and prevent the floodwaters from overwhelming the dam. Problems reported during construction include the appearance of cracks, leading to fears of trapped pollutants affecting the river water.

TOP LEFT: *An aerial view of the permanent ship lock on the Yangtze river.*
LEFT: *The first boat sails through the five-stair canal, part of the Three Gorges Dam project.*

Threatened Species

Endangered wildlife species that are threatened by the Three Gorges Dam include the giant panda, the Chinese tiger, the Chinese alligator, the Chinese sturgeon and the Siberian crane. There are only about 200 Yangtze dolphins left in the world, which the World Wildlife Fund for Nature considers one of the most endangered creatures.

Environmentalists and conservationists have suggested that an alternative scheme involving a number of smaller dams would have had a less devastating ecological impact. The government's argument is that although such a scheme would succeed in monitoring floodwaters and irrigating crops, it would be unable to generate the vast quantity of power that the Three Gorges project expects to produce.

See also:
Aswan High Dam 121
Hoover Dam 168-9
Itaipú Dam 224

40 The Taj Mahal, India

The Taj Mahal

In 1631 the wife of the Moghul Emperor of India died at the age of 36, giving birth to her 14th child. Her husband, Shah Jehan, had lost a beloved wife and a shrewd political advisor and, according to one account, his hair turned white with grief. He vowed to build a tomb worthy of his wife's memory, something utterly without equal anywhere in the world, and few would deny that in the Taj Mahal, he succeeded.

So many superlatives have been used to describe the Taj Mahal that many visitors approach it wondering if they will be disappointed. The silhouette, familiar from countless photographs, crops up again and again, wherever one instantly recognizable emblem of India is needed. And yet disappointment is rare. The Taj can be seen again and again and still surprise, such is its ability to take on a different character according to the time of day and the nature of the light. Although a tomb, the building lacks the cold monumentality one might expect; instead, it seems to float between heaven and earth. The proportions, the remarkable symmetry, the surrounding gardens, and the reflections in water all combine to create a place of indescribable beauty.

A Frenchman and a Venetian are said to have had some part in its construction, but no single architect's name is recorded with any certainty, as befits a building intended to be associated with the name of its occupant only. It is made of marble brought from quarries 322km (200 miles) away, but is by no means the pure white building that some photographs suggest. Thousands of precious and stones are inlaid in the marble surfaces, and black marble is used

BELOW: *Even on a cheap souvenir, the Taj Mahal looks graceful and sublime.*

the facts

- Arjuman Banu Begam, Shah Jehan's wife, was known as Mumtaz Mahal (Chosen One of the Palace). Taj Mahal is an abbreviation of her name.
- The Taj Mahal was built by an estimated 20,000 workers and took 22 years to complete.
- The pearl-shaped dome is an Islamic symbol representing both womanhood and paradise.

the history

1612
Arjuman Banu Begam marries Prince Khurram.

1631
Death of Arjuman Banu Begam.

1648
Taj Mahal completed.

1657
Prince Khurram becomes the fifth Moghul Emperor and is named Shah Jehan.

1810
Cracks discovered in underground vaults.

1830s
Lord William Bentinck, the Governor General of Bengal, proposes to dismantle the Taj Mahal and sell off the marble.

for calligraphic decoration. There is also remarkable craftsmanship in the pierced marble screens, which cast dramatic shadows when struck by the sun. Once there were silver doors and, inside, a gold railing and a cloth of pearls over the queen's cenotaph (this stands directly above the actual burial place). Thieves stole these precious items, and many have tried to extract inlaid jewels from their settings, but the magnificence still remains overwhelming.

The building is set in landscaped gardens and is approached through a massive and magnificent gateway, symbolically an entrance to paradise. Surmounted by domed pavilions, it originally had a door of solid silver studded with hundreds of silver nails. This was plundered and the present door is of brass.

In 1658, Shah Jehan's son Aurangzeb proclaimed himself emperor and held his father under house arrest in the fort at Agra for nine years until his death. From the fort, Shah Jehan had a view of the Taj Mahal in the distance and later, he too was buried there.

TOP: *Emperor Shah Jehan, builder of the Taj Mahal.*
ABOVE: *The gateway is intricately inlaid with coloured stones.*

MOGHUL ARCHITECTURE

The Taj Mahal represents the high point of Moghul architectural achievement. The style of the monumental tomb—standing on a plinth, furnished with minarets, and approached with the same reverence as a mosque—can be seen developing and declining in Northern India. Humayun's Tomb, begun in Delhi in 1564, is an ancestor of the Taj, solid and imposing rather than delicate and ethereal. In the late 1670s Aurangzeb built an imitation of the Taj Mahal for his wife at Aurangabad, but it lacks the grace and proportion of the original.

Another tomb in Delhi, that of Safdar Jang, begun in 1753, has been called 'the last flicker of the lamp of Moghul architecture'. There is a standard pattern for these monuments: a large, onion-shaped dome, water channels, a garden divided into four sections, a plinth and minarets. The builders of the Taj managed to combine these in a way that created something unique. Some say Shah Jehan intended to build himself a black marble monument across the Jumna River, but in the event the Taj Mahal remained in solitary splendour.

LEFT: *Sunset over the Taj Mahal.*

ROBBERS AND RESTORATION

The activities of the thieves who made off with the precious metals of the Taj look negligible when compared with a scheme hatched by Lord William Bentinck, who was a Governor General of Bengal in the 19th century. In the 1830s he put forward a money-making proposal to dismantle the Taj Mahal (which was neglected and overgrown), and ship the marble to London where it could be sold. The idea was abandoned when a similar plan for marble stripped from the Red Fort at Delhi failed due to a lack of buyers.

In the 20th century, Lord Curzon, who became Viceroy of India in 1900, had the Taj Mahal restored to its former glory. He also retrieved some marble panels from the Red Fort which had previously found their way to London and had them restored to their original position. As well as the buildings he attended to the neglected ornamental gardens.

See also: Red Fort 96

Shah Jehan ordered the 'peacock throne' to be built for the fort's private audience chamber. The throne took seven years to build and was studded with jewels.

The Diwan-i-khas was a chamber for private consultations between the emperor and foreign ambassadors. It had a spacious courtyard, marble pavement and silver ceiling.

the **facts**

The **Red Fort**

The Red Fort, or Lal Qila, takes its name from the red sandstone used to build its vast walls. Its palaces and audience chambers were celebrated for their opulent marble, silver, gold and jewels, but inevitably, much of this wealth has disappeared over the years, along with some of the buildings. The fort was built for Moghul Emperor Shah Jehan between 1638 and 1648, when he transferred his capital from Agra to Delhi, or rather to a new city called Shajehanabad. The fort's audience chambers—the public Diwan-i-am and the private Diwan-i-khas—still survive, as do some of the royal palaces (there were originally six), including the Mumtaz Mahal, which is now a museum and the Rang Mahal ('painted palace'), but without its paintings and silver ceiling. The Khas Mahal is a set of three private imperial apartments designed for eating, sleeping and for worship. An arcade of shops leads into the fort from the impressive Lahore Gate, and the royal baths also survive.

Lord Curzon

Lord Curzon, Viceroy of India at the beginning of the 20th century, arranged for restoration work to take place at the Red Fort.

After the Indian army's uprising in 1857, the British had removed some inlaid marble panels from the Diwan-i-am and sent them to London. One of the subjects depicted was the Greek myth of Orpheus, which suggested that this was the work of a European. These marble panels, which had suffered the indignity of being used as table tops, were eventually exhibited in the Victoria and Albert Museum. Lord Curzon retrieved them and put them back in their rightful position. He also found gardeners for the Red Fort's ornamental gardens, which had been neglected.

42 **Potala Palace,** China (Tibet)

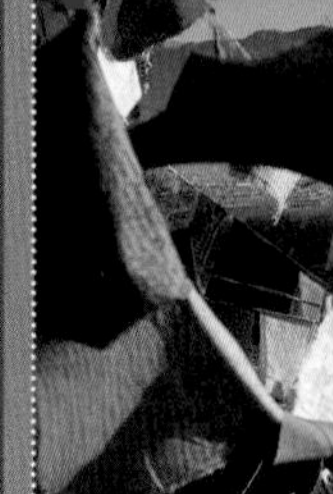

the facts

- Potala Palace is on a rocky outcrop called Marpori (The Red Hill), about 91m (300ft) above Lhasa.
- The name of the palace derives from a Sanskrit word meaning 'Buddha's mountain'.
- The solid-silver stupa (tomb chest) of the 13th Dalai Lama, who died in 1933, stands over 21m (70ft) high.

Potala Palace

Ocean of Wisdom

Tibetan Buddhism developed from a combination of the Buddhism of northern India and Nepal and the native Tibetan nature religion, Bon. The title Dalai Lama, conferred on the head of the sect that eventually came to power in Tibet, means 'ocean of wisdom'. A feature of Tibetan Buddhism is succession by reincarnation which means that when a Dalai Lama dies, the search begins for the child in whom he is reborn. This may take several years, and the child is often revealed by his ability to pick out from a selection of objects, those that were his as the previous Dalai Lama.

Once found, the new Dalai Lama is taken to Lhasa where he is trained, before taking up his duties at the age of 18.

The palace of the Dalai Lama dominates Tibet's holy city of Lhasa, towering 13 floors high, with white walls, regiments of windows, and serried roofs. Songsten Gampo, Buddhist king of Tibet in the seventh century AD, built a palace on this spot, and in 1645 the fifth Dalai Lama, ruler of Tibet, ordered work to begin on a new palace on the site. When he died in 1682 the building was not yet finished, so his death was kept secret until its completion in 1694. Now a museum, it was the winter residence of the Dalai Lamas until the 14th escaped to India in 1959.

In the 1,000-plus rooms, there are 10,000 shrines and 20,000 statues. In addition to government offices, staff living quarters and a monastic training school, there were meditation halls, libraries, armouries, granaries, torture chambers and even a dungeon known as the Cave of Scorpions. The fifth Dalai Lama and seven successors are laid to rest here.

LEFT: *Prayer wheels outside the palace in Lhasa.*
BELOW: *Potala Palace seen through prayer flags on Chokpuri Hill.*

See also:
Ayutthaya 110-11
Metéora Monasteries 56-7
Wat Phra Keo 108-9

The concept of sacred sites is probably as old as humanity itself, and almost as old is the practice of marking such sites with shrines, monuments or buildings. Over the centuries these houses of one god or many have ranged from simple places of meditation to grandiose spaces where the faithful can congregate.

the facts

- The Hall of the Great Buddha at Nara is 57m by 51m (187ft by 166ft) long and 49m (160ft) high. The Great Buddha here was cast from 444 metric tonnes (489 tons) of bronze and the ears are 2.4m (8ft) long.
- The 14th-century Protestant cathedral in Ulm in Germany has the tallest spire in the world. It was completed in 1890 and stands 161m (528ft) high.

Houses of Worship

CHURCHES AND SYNAGOGUES

Early synagogues and churches were based on Roman basilicas, with a recess at the eastern end for the holy scriptures or altar. Later churches developed a cruciform structure, with four equal arms (in Eastern Europe) or one long western arm housing the nave (in the West). From the 12th century the western Gothic style introduced pointed arches and spires.

The Renaissance brought a revival of classical architecture, and decoration became increasingly lavish. More recent buildings combine several styles—as in Gaudí's Sagrada Família church in Barcelona, which mixes Gothic with swirling Art Nouveau.

CLOCKWISE FROM RIGHT: *The 16th-century Dome of the Rock, Jerusalem; incense burning outside a temple; the Xuankong Si monastery nestles against the rockface at Datong, Inner Mongolia; playing music outside a Hindu temple, southern India.*

MOSQUES

Mosque design flourished under Islamic dynasties between the 11th and 19th centuries. Ottoman buildings emphasise the large central dome, guarded by minarets, and during the Moghuls' reign elements of Hindu architecture were introduced. Local influences were sometimes incorporated—as in West Africa's mud-built mosques—but most designs feature a courtyard, a fountain and a colonnaded hall housing the *minbar* (pulpit) and the *mihrab*, a prayer niche set into the wall facing Mecca. Abstract decoration (depictions of living beings is forbidden) includes mosaics, fretwork and calligraphy.

Muslims from over 70 nations undertake the hajj, or pilgrimage, to Mecca, in present-day Saudi Arabia, every year. Once there they must make seven circuits of the Ka'ba (Islam's holiest shrine) and touch the Black Stone.

CLOCKWISE FROM BELOW: *A 13th-century bronze Buddha at the Kotukin Temple, Kamakura, Japan; the freshly-gilded dome of a synagogue in Berlin, Germany; a constant stream of pilgrims make their way to the ghats, on the banks of the River Ganges, India; Roman Catholic pilgrims outside the cathedral at Lourdes, France.*

TEMPLES

Hindu temples are approached through a series of towered gates. A complex of halls surrounds the square shrine, marked by a tower, and walls are exuberantly carved.

In Buddhist shrines the *stupa* (covering the Buddha's relics or form) is the ultimate goal. The Chinese equivalent—brought to Japan with Chinese Buddhism—is the tiered pagoda. Japan's indigenous religion, Shinto, is observed in plain, temple halls on stilts with steep, over-hanging roofs, approached via a *torii* or gate.

43 **The Himalayas,** Nepal/China (Tibet)

- The Himalayas contain 96 of the 109 peaks in the world that are over 7,315m (24,000ft) high.
- The highest mountain in the world is Chomolungma (Mount Everest), which is 8,840m (29,002ft) high.
- The longest glacier outside the polar regions is Siachen in the Himalayas, measuring 76km (47 miles).

the **facts**

The Himalayas

The Himalayas are the greatest mountain range on earth, containing 96 of the 109 peaks in the world over 7,315m (24,000ft). The South American Andes form a longer chain, but are not as high. Facts and figures are one thing, but the awesome sight of the Himalayas is quite another. Although the highest mountain in the world is known across the world as Mount Everest, perhaps its Nepalese name conveys an image that might be applied to the whole range: Chomolungma, Goddess Mother of the Snows.

The Himalayan mountain range, including the Karakoram Mountains, stretches for more than 1,500 miles (2,414km) across the northern edge of the Indian subcontinent, separating it from Asia to the north. From the northwest, in northernmost Pakistan, the Karakorams extend to the southeast through Kashmir in northern India. The Himalayas sweep round to the east, taking in the mountain kingdoms of Nepal, Sikkim and Bhutan and continue into the Arunachal Pradesh province of northeastern Assam. The northern boundaries of these countries lie along the

ABOVE: *Lamjung Himal in the Annapurna mountain range.*
BELOW: *The Bhotia Busti monastery in the Darjeeling region of the Himalayas.*

Himalayan Mountaineering

WW Graham was the first European to tackle the Himalayan mountains, in 1883. Ten years later the Royal Society and the Royal Geographical Society sent an expedition from England under Martin Conway, to explore and climb the Karakoram Mountains. Then, in 1895, AF Mummery set out to climb Nanga Parbat, a peak in the Karakoram Mountains which is 8,126m (26,660ft). Many expeditions followed, often climbing subsidiary peaks while reconnoitring routes on major peaks. Between the two World Wars, the major effort focused on Mount Everest, approaching it from Tibet because Nepal was closed to expeditions.

After World War II Nepal opened its borders to Everest expeditions and explorations from the south side began. Mountaineers now seek greater challenges by making solo or ascents without oxygen tanks.

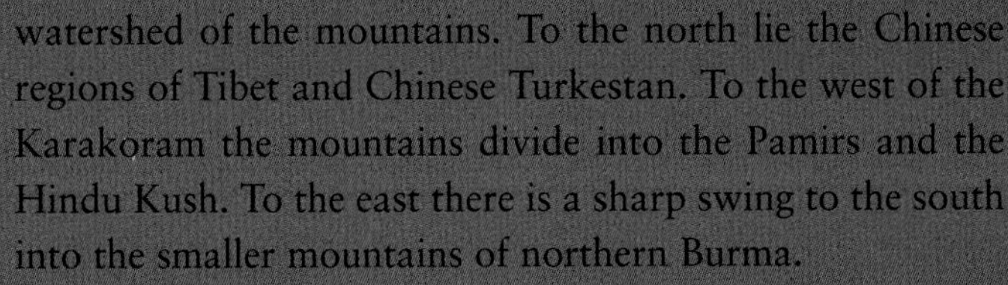

watershed of the mountains. To the north lie the Chinese regions of Tibet and Chinese Turkestan. To the west of the Karakoram the mountains divide into the Pamirs and the Hindu Kush. To the east there is a sharp swing to the south into the smaller mountains of northern Burma.

Conquering the Peaks

The native peoples of the Himalayas didn't feel the need to explore their mountains beyond their own immediate needs. This was left largely to the more restless Europeans. In the 19th century, while pioneering climbers were conquering peaks in the Alps, the Department of Survey of the Government of India had triangulated the position of a peak that seemed higher than the others. In 1856, the final calculations showed that the height of Peak XV on the Tibet-Nepal border was 8,840m (29,002ft), the highest in the world. It was named after Colonel Sir George Everest (pronounced Eve-rest), the former Surveyor-General of India. Now there was a new target for the mountaineers. It was not until 29 May 1953 that the summit was conquered by the New Zealander Edmund Hillary and the Nepalese Sherpa, Tenzing Norgay.

In 2004, a 26-year-old Nepalese Sherpa, Pemba Darji, set a new world record by repeating the journey to the top which had taken Hillary seven weeks. It took Darji eight hours and ten minutes.

Evolving Mountains

More than 200 million years ago the former single continental mass of Pangaea broke into two super-continents, Laurasia and Gondwana. Laurasia was made up of the present continents of North America, Greenland, Europe and Asia, while Gondwana comprised South America, Africa, India, Australia and Antarctica.

When Gondwana began to fragment, South America and Australia started to move towards the ocean and their present positions, but Africa and India continued their northward drift until they finally collided with Eurasia. Over a period of millions of years, and still continuing today, these collisions buckled the rocks of southern Eurasia and produced the mountains we know as the Alps and the Himalayas.

LEFT: *Annapurna Machhapuchhre Base, Nepal.*

See also:
The Alps 40-1
The Andes Mountains 100, 185, 208
The Matterhorn 40-1

the facts

- Dogs are not allowed on the island of Miyajima where the shrine stands, lest they disturb the resident deer.
- Mount Misen, the island's highest point at 530m (1,740ft), has wonderful views.
- Offshore on a separate platform is the oldest Noh theatre in Japan, built in 1568 and later restored.

Itsukushima Shrine

Japan's most famous gateway is the red wooden *torii*, or portal, of the Itsukushima Shrine on Miyajima island, near Hiroshima. Built in 1875, it stands in a small bay, its two main pillars rising 16m (53ft) and supporting a curved lintel 23m (76ft) long. Beyond it are the shrine buildings, constructed on wooden piles so that at high tide they seem to float on the water. The principal shrine is dedicated to three Shinto goddesses, daughters of the storm god Susano, one of the major native Japanese deities. Other buildings include halls of prayer, purification and offerings, a stage for traditional Shinto dances and shrines for the god Okinonushi, a son of Susano, and another for the god Tenjin. The buildings in the bay are linked to each other by covered gangways and to the shore by a red wooden bridge. At night, when the stone lanterns are lit, the scene is enchanting.

Miyajima island is so sacred that for centuries no one could be born or die there, and pregnant women and the elderly or ill had to cross to the mainland. The dead are still buried on the mainland and their relatives are ritually cleansed before they can return to the island.

Phoenix From the Ashes

At 8.15am on 6 August 1945, an area of Hiroshima, 6.5km (4 miles) in diameter was laid flat by the first atom bomb. Estimates of the numbers killed start at 250,000 and go up from there.

Since 1949 Hiroshima, which is near Miyajima island, has been rebuilt and is now a thriving city with a population of about a million. Only the skeleton of the Chamber of Commerce building, which somehow remained standing at the heart of the destruction, has been left as it was. It is now known as the Atom Dome. The Park of Peace in the former city centre contains the Peace Memorial Museum.

45 Beppu, Japan

the facts

- Beppu is one of the world's largest thermal regions.
- Its hot springs and geysers emit more than 56,600 cu m (2 million cu ft) of water each day.
- There are about 3,500 fumeroles (vents which allow gases to escape), hot springs and geysers in the Beppu area.

Beppu

In the bitter cold of winter in Beppu, in southern Japan, small monkeys head for the warmth of volcanically heated waters, occasionally sitting up to their necks in warm water while the snow settles on their heads. They even have a rota system, sending one or two delegates to fetch food while the others wait in the warm water.

The city of Beppu is at the bottom of a slope of volcanic debris hurled from one of the several nearby volcanoes in the recent past. Its hot springs and geysers emit huge quantities of water each day, and the area is a major tourist attraction, where visitors immerse themselves in hot sand baths and the healing, mineral-laden waters.

For those who don't want to get into the water there is plenty to admire, including boiling ponds, called *jigokus*, which occur in a fantastic range of sizes and shades. Chinoike Jigoku, for example, is bright red because the water has oxidized some of the underlying rocks, whereas the larger Umi Jigoku is deep blue, reflecting the colour of the sky. The geyser Tatsu-maki Jigoku erupts every 20 minutes or so and a great spray of steam is forced high into the air with an ear-splitting hiss.

ABOVE: *Local monkeys keep warm by bathing in the thermal pools.*

Volcanoes and Thermal Springs

Japan has been described as sitting on 'Mother Earth's Cradle', and with more than 500 volcanoes on the main islands, the description is apt. Many volcanoes are extinct but some remain active, including Fuji, Asama and Aso. As well as volcanoes there are hundreds of areas of thermal activity, the best known being Noboribetsu, Beppu and Kusatsu.

Noboribetsu, on Hokkaido, Japan's largest island, is home to the Jigokudani Hot Springs. Geysers, boiling springs and bubbling mud, as well as vents that give off rather unpleasant sulphurous gas, occupy a volcanic crater 2km (1.25 miles) across.

See also:
Pamukkale 70-1
Rotorua 228-9
Volcanic Iceland 14-15

Mount Fuji rises to 3,776m (12,388ft) at its peak.

Japan is part of a string of volcanic islands on the Pacific rim, known together as 'The Ring of Fire'.

60 of Japan's 65 volcanoes are classified as active.

the facts

Mount Fuji

All along the Pacific margin of Japan there is evidence of the country's dramatic volcanic history—long-dead lava fields, hot spring areas and volcanoes, several of which are still active. Many Japanese volcanoes exhibit the classic cone-shape, and the most famous of these is Mount Fuji.

Fuji-san (the Japanese name may be translated as Fuji-mountain or simply as a respectful form of address) lies on the main Japanese island of Honshu, about 97km (60 miles) southwest of the capital, Tokyo. It is the highest mountain in Japan and has for centuries provided an important focus in Japanese culture. Seen from the south, the mountain stands majestic and isolated, its symmetrical sides leading steeply to the truncated summit, which hides the central crater. On the southeastern flank is the explosion crater of Hoei-zan that was formed during the volcano's last eruption in 1707. The oldest lavas on Mount Fuji have been dated as only 8,000 years old, making it a very young volcano.

Careful geological survey and the examination of drill cores from the mountain have shown that Mount Fuji is

Volcanic Sources

As the crust of the Pacific Ocean floor expands in one area, it must be accommodated elsewhere. This happens around the margins of the ocean, where the oceanic crust slides beneath the adjacent continental crust. As the oceanic crust descends into the earth's mantle it is heated by friction against the overlying rocks, causing melting and expansion. The resulting increase in pressure is reduced by volcanic activity, and the accompanying tension in the rocks is relieved by earthquakes.

The younger rocks of Japan are largely volcanic in origin and earthquakes are common. Japan is not unique in this respect, as all the lands and islands surrounding the Pacific Ocean experience some form of volcanic activity. Geologists call the Pacific Rim 'The Ring of Fire'.

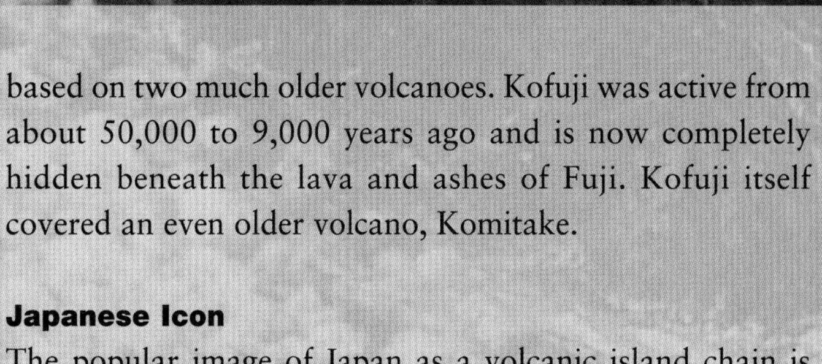

based on two much older volcanoes. Kofuji was active from about 50,000 to 9,000 years ago and is now completely hidden beneath the lava and ashes of Fuji. Kofuji itself covered an even older volcano, Komitake.

Japanese Icon

The popular image of Japan as a volcanic island chain is only partly true. Ancient Precambrian rocks and the sedimentary rocks that lie over them have been folded over during a slow sequence of mountain-building events. These upheavals of the earth have given rise to Alpine-style ranges of mountains. Japan's volcanic activity—known to geologists as island-arc type volcanism—has been predominant only during the last 60 million years, which in geological terms makes this a new kid on the block.

The beauty of Mount Fuji lies in its near-perfect shape, with the top of the cone permanently covered in snow. On a fine day it is a magnificent sight, and at sunrise and sunset the mountain assumes an ethereal quality, suffused with a rose-pink light. Fuji is regarded by the Japanese as an icon of peace and serenity, the home of the gods. Followers of the Shinto religion worship the beauty of nature, so for them, the sight of Mount Fuji in spring with flowering cherry trees in front, is a moving and spiritual experience.

LEFT: *Mount Fuji seen from the Space Shuttle Columbia.*
BELOW: *Japan's famous bullet train speeds past Mount Fuji at sunset.*

See also:
Mount Erebus 232-3
Mount Kilimanjaro 134-5

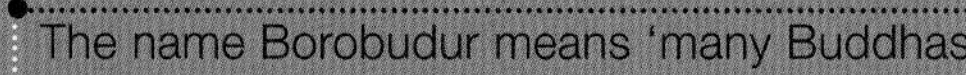

the facts

- The name Borobudur means 'many Buddhas'.
- The monument is said to contain more than 56,634 cu m (2 million cu ft) of stone.
- The monument has 1,500 panels carved in relief with scenes of the Buddha's life. Hundreds of other panels depict scenes from everyday life.

Borobudur

Borobudur, the largest monument in the southern hemisphere, is Java's version of Mount Meru, the giant golden peak of Indian mythology on which the universe rests. Built on and over a hill, Borobudur is a step pyramid of receding terraces, rising to about 400m (1,310ft). The five lower, square terraces represent the material world, while above them, three circular terraces represent the spiritual realm.

BELOW: *Detail of a stone relief on Borobudur, the largest Buddhist shrine in the world.*
BELOW INSET: *Stupas on the upper terrace with the lush valley beyond.*

On the upper terraces are rows of *stupas* (bell-shaped shrines), each of which contains a Buddha. At the top, at the centre of the highest terrace and commanding a wonderful view of the surrounding mountains, is a single shrine 15m (50ft) in diameter, which represents *nirvana*, spiritual freedom or heaven.

Borobudur was built by the Saliendra dynasty of kings around the year AD800. It probably took an enormous workforce several decades to construct. The site was abandoned 200 years later and was rediscovered by an English army officer in the 19th century.

Ancient Kingdoms

The area of central Java in which Borobudur stands is historically and culturally the island's heartland. Among its mountains and volcanoes there is a wealth of archaeological remains. There are Buddhist and Hindu temples, ancient mosques, Portuguese castles and the palaces of Muslim sultans. With Indian influences powerful in Indonesia from the eighth century on, there were Buddhist and Hindu kingdoms whose rulers claimed to be earthly incarnations of Indian gods.

The temple complex of Prambaa was built in the ninth and tenth centuries and, like Borobudur, is covered with bas-reliefs in stone. These vividly depict mythical beasts, frolicking monkeys and the cosmic dance of the Hindu god Shiva.

48 Angkor Wat, Cambodia

the facts

- There may be as many as 200 temples on the site, an area of 260sq km (100 square miles).
- The whole temple complex was virtually lost in the jungle for 600 years.
- In 1973 the complex of temples became a Khmer Rouge hideout.

Angkor Wat

The world's most stunning example of Hindu architecture is in Cambodia, where the 12th-century god-king Suyarvarman II built the huge temple of Angkor Wat. Dedicated to the Hindu god Vishnu, it doubled as a sanctuary and funeral monument for Suyarvarman himself. Cambodia's Khmer rulers (10th–13th century AD), considered themselves to be earthly incarnations of Vishnu, and Angkor Wat was a sort of heavenly palace where the spirit of the king might roam.

The temple is surrounded by a moat, and large reservoirs lie outside the walls. The plan, geometrical and elegant, is on an enormous scale. An outer wall encloses an area of 83,610sq m (100,000 square yards) and visitors approaching through a gate in the outer wall see the whole building rising steadily up on a succession of platforms. The temple has vivid stone carvings depicting scenes from Hindu epics, exuberant gods and goddesses cavorting in erotic poses and real figures from Khmer history marching in friezes that stretch for hundreds of metres.

Angkor Thom

Khmer art shows both Hindu and Buddhist influences, and both religions appear to have been treated with equal respect. Angkor Thom, a Khmer city built for Jayarvarman VII at the beginning of the 13th century near Angkor Wat, has at its heart a Buddhist monument, the Bayon. Again, the king was honoured in conjunction with a god and there were towers, rectangular galleries and a central, elevated shrine.

Bas-reliefs depict rulers riding on elephants surrounded by crowds of people. The deity here is Lokesvara, the Buddha who has attained the state of nirvana. The towers of the city are crowned with massive, smiling faces, which represent this state of blissful serenity.

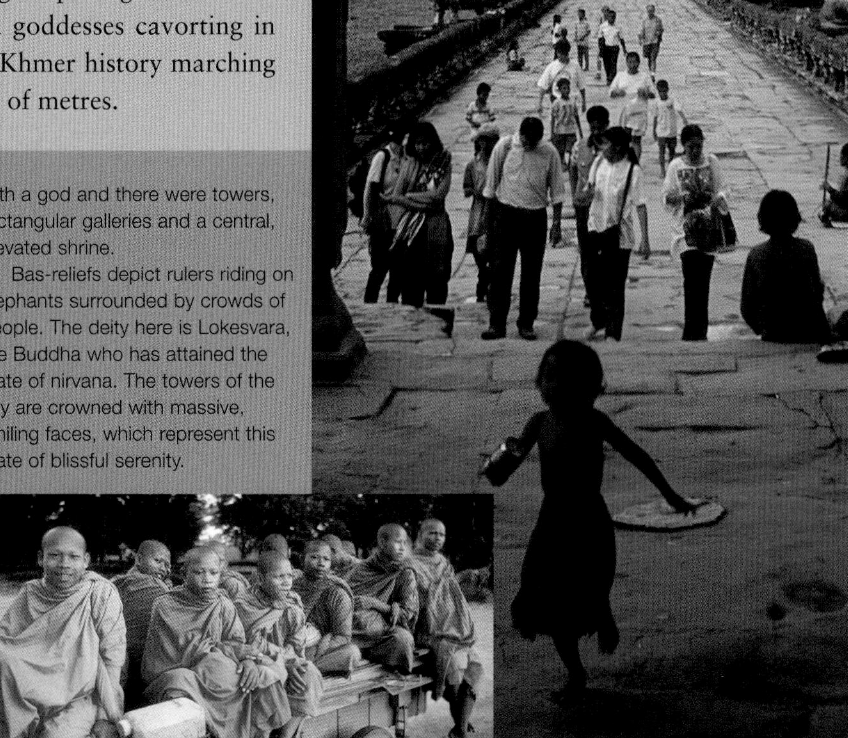

RIGHT: *Crowds follow the walkway into the monumental temple complex.*
INSET RIGHT: *Young Buddhist monks at Angkor Wat.*

See also:
Parthenon 54-5
Temple of Karnak 114-15
Wat Phra Keo 108-9

the facts

- The Grand Palace covers an area of 218,400sq m (2,350,838 square feet) and has over 100 buildings, including the Temple of the Emerald Buddha.
- The palace walls are 1,900m (6,233ft) long.
- The stone used to build the palace is believed to be inhabited by a guardian spirit that protects Bangkok.

BELOW: *The golden stupa—erected as a Buddhist shrine—beside the rest pavilion in the grounds of the Grand Palace.*

Wat Phra Keo

When Rama I ascended to the Thai throne in 1782 he moved the centre of administration from the west to the east bank of the Cha Phraya River. Here, on the site of present-day Bangkok, he had fortifications and monasteries built and established his residence and offices in a huge complex of buildings now known as the Grand Palace. In 1784 the Wat Phra Keo, or Temple of the Emerald Buddha, was completed and consecrated on the upper terrace of the Grand Palace, connected to the royal residence by a gate. This most sacred of Thai temples houses the country's most revered image: a small statue of Buddha, carved from a block of jade and seated high on a golden altar which represents the flying chariot of the Hindu gods. From outside, the temple is a dazzling visual and aural experience with the sun

Other Palace Buildings

There are other sacred buildings near the Wat Phra Keo on the upper terrace. The Royal Pantheon is surrounded by gilded *Kinaree*, half-human figures, holding Buddhist sculptures, and the golden Phra si Rattana Chedi contains the Buddha's ashes. North of the terrace, at ground level, are the Scripture Library, which has a fine western façade, the gabled Wiharn, which is adorned with tiles and porcelain, and the Royal Mausoleum, the last resting place of several members of the royal family.

Two small chapels behind the Assembly Hall to the west contain effigies of Buddha, one of which is decorated with murals attributed to a well-known Thai painter, Khrua In Khong. He was renowned for the mural work he produced during the reign of Rama IV (1851–68).

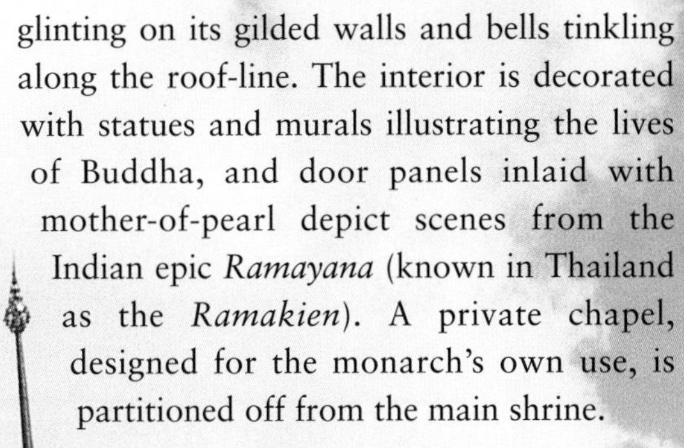

glinting on its gilded walls and bells tinkling along the roof-line. The interior is decorated with statues and murals illustrating the lives of Buddha, and door panels inlaid with mother-of-pearl depict scenes from the Indian epic *Ramayana* (known in Thailand as the *Ramakien*). A private chapel, designed for the monarch's own use, is partitioned off from the main shrine.

The Emerald Buddha

The 79-cm (31in) Emerald Buddha has had an eventful life. Its origin is unknown, but it is first recorded in 1434, when it was covered in stucco, which subsequently crumbled away. King Tilok of Lannathai acquired the figure and took it to his capital, Chiang Mai, to be enshrined. When a new capital, Viang Chan, was built the Buddha was moved there, where it stayed until its eventually seizure by the king of Thonburi. When King Rama I built Bangkok, he had the Emerald Buddha installed with great ceremony.

Rama III had two standing images of Buddha cast and set in front of the high altar, dedicating them to his royal predecessors. One more statue of Buddha—the Samphutthapanni Buddha—was added before the altar by King Mongkut, Rama IV (all kings were known as Rama); this too is held in high veneration.

The Wat Phra Keo Museum in the palace compound contains the seasonal costumes worn by the Emerald Buddha, offerings made to him by those attending the temple and architectural fragments from the temple picked up during restoration work.

ABOVE LEFT: *Statues with blue-painted faces and mosaic armour support part of the wat.*
BELOW INSET: *A young child is helped with his incense offering at the temple.*

Temple Murals

Above the window frames of the Wat Phra Keo are murals depicting the life of Buddha. The series starts in the southwest corner to the right of the high altar, with illustrations of Buddha's birth, childhood and youth, and his renunciation of wealth and material gain in favour of the search for Truth. On the east wall facing the high altar, more paintings show the temptation of Buddha and his subsequent enlightenment. Underneath his seat is a figure representing Mother Earth.

From here the story progresses along the northern wall with depictions of Buddha's mission and his death. The cycle ends in the northwest corner of the wall. Painted at the back of the temple is a representation of the universe.

See also:
Ayutthaya 110-11
Potala Palace 97

- During Ayutthaya's ascendancy as the Thai capital, 33 kings of different dynasties ruled the kingdom.
- The research institute on Rochana Road studies the city and has a museum with reconstructions of the city.
- Ayutthaya's Elephant Kraal, an enclosure made of teak logs, was used to pen wild elephants.

the **facts**

Ayutthaya

Between 1350 and 1767 Ayutthaya was the capital of the Thai—then the Siamese—kingdom. Founded by King U-Thong, it replaced Sukhothai, which had served as the capital until northern forces pushed the Thai people southward. For 417 years the city flourished, until its destruction by the Burmese in 1767. Today its ruins are a tranquil tourist sight, just a day's trip from Bangkok, and the *prang* (pagodas or reliquary towers) and 400-plus Buddhist monasteries only hint at the glory of its heyday.

At the heart of the city is the Ancient Palace, originally built by King U-Thong but extended during later reigns. Among the new additions were Wat Phra Si Sanphet, the most significant temple within the complex, of equivalent status to the Wat Phra Keo (Temple of the Emerald Buddha) in Bangkok's Grand Palace (see pages 108–109). This housed a 16-m (52.6ft) gilded Buddha cast by King Ramathipodi II in 1500, which weighed about 170kg (625lb). When the Burmese sacked Ayutthaya, they set fire to the image to melt off the gold, destroying both the image and its temple in the process.

Significant Buildings

Other buildings that suffered during the assault of 1767 included several pavilions, which were reduced to their brick foundations, porticoes and walls. Further monuments and buildings that fell victim to the Burmese have since been renovated in their original style. The Tri Muk Building, a wooden structure with a brick foundation, was rebuilt during the reign of King Chulalongkorn in 1907, and in 1956 the Thai government undertook to rebuild all of the historic city's ruins. In that year various buildings were restored, including three 15th-century *chedis* (bell-shaped towers), which were constructed to house the ashes of Ayutthayan kings, and the Wihan Phra Mongkhon Bophit, which contains one of Thailand's largest bronze images of Buddha.

Chankasem Palace was added to the city during the reign of King Maha Thammaraja, the 17th Ayutthayan monarch, and served as the residence of his son, King Naresuan. After lying in ruins for many years it was reconstructed for King Mongkut of the present Chakri dynasty, who used it as a residence for his visits to Ayutthaya. Chao Sam Phraya National Museum, on Rochana Road, opposite the city wall, has displays of ancient bronze Buddha images and carved panels, along with relics associated with the Buddha and works of art dating back more than 500 years.

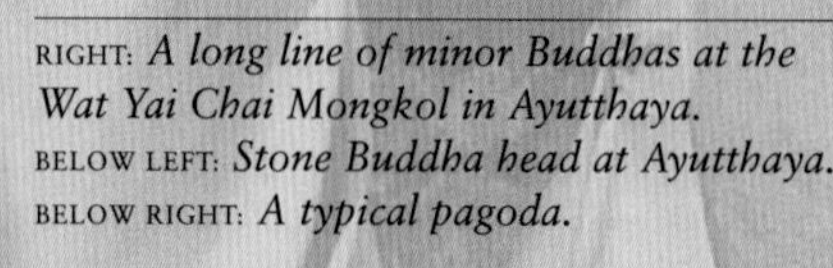

RIGHT: *A long line of minor Buddhas at the Wat Yai Chai Mongkol in Ayutthaya.*
BELOW LEFT: *Stone Buddha head at Ayutthaya.*
BELOW RIGHT: *A typical pagoda.*

Ancient Rivalries

Chedi Phu Khao Thong, a temple usually known as Golden Mount Pagoda, soars 80m (263ft) high on the northern outskirts of Ayutthaya. It was originally built in Burmese style by King Burengnong of Burma to mark his successful invasion of Ayutthaya in 1569. However, after the city's independence had been restored by King Naresuan in 1584, the pagoda was reworked in a more obviously Thai style.

A short distance outside the city is Wat Yai Chai Mongkhon, built for King U-Thong in 1357. In 1592 King Naresuan killed the Burmese Crown Prince in combat on elephant-back. He promptly had the temple's pagoda added to match the high pagoda at Chedi Phu Khao Thong. Though it's in a delapidated state, this pagoda can still be seen from miles away.

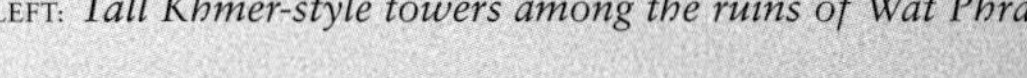

LEFT: *Tall Khmer-style towers among the ruins of Wat Phra Mahathat.*

Twin Temples

Wat Phra Mahathat, on the corner of Chi Kun Road and Naresuan Road, was built by King Ramesuan in 1384 and had a high pagoda, or *prang*, which was destroyed by the Burmese. When major restoration work was begun in 1956, the pagoda was excavated and a treasure chest was unearthed containing valuables, including a relic of Buddha inside a golden casket, several golden Buddha images and other objects in gold, ruby and crystal. All are now housed in Bangkok's National Museum.

Opposite the temple is its twin, the Wat Ratburana, built by King Boromraja II, the seventh Ayutthayan king, at the site of his brother's cremation. Items unearthed during its restoration in 1958 include royal regalia, exquisitely worked gold pieces and images of Buddha.

See also:
Wat Phra Keo 108-9

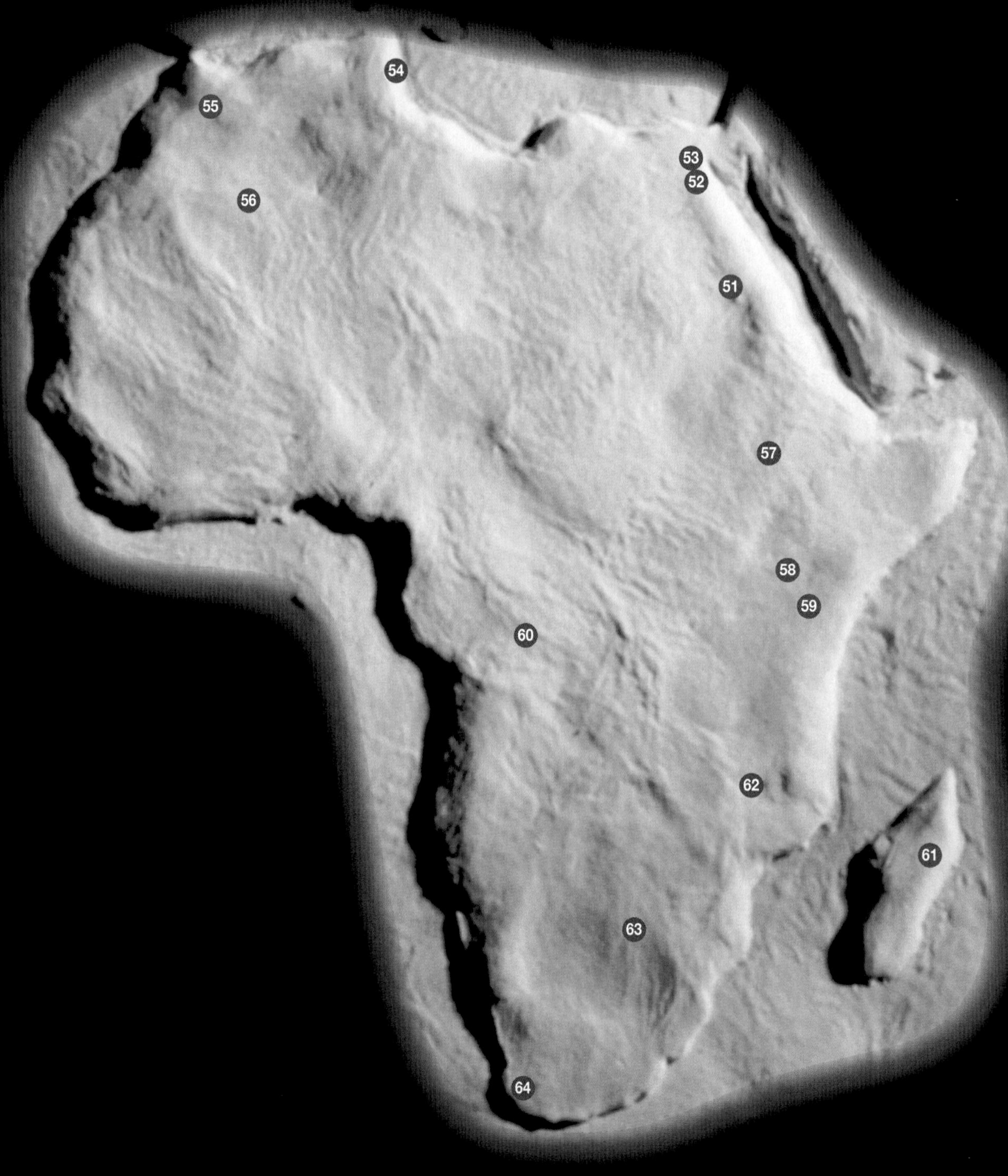

51 **The Temple of Karnak**

52 **The Great Pyramid**

53 **The River Nile**

54 **Carthage**

55 **Fez Medina**

56 **The Great Sahara**

57 **The East African Rift Valley**

58 **Lake Nakuru**

59 **Mount Kilimanjaro**

60 **The Zaire River**

61 **Madagascar**

62 **Victoria Falls**

63 **The Okavango Delta**

64 **Table Mountain**

Africa

Africa is the second largest of the continents, occupying about a fifth of the world's land surface, and is also the probable cradle of the human species. The earliest known human beings lived here millions of years ago and ventured out to other parts of the earth. By 5000BC there were farming communities in the fertile valley of the Nile. To the west the Sahara was not yet a desert, and there is evidence of cattle-breeding in what is now a great wilderness. By about 3000BC there was a unified kingdom of Egypt, from which a major empire developed. It survived for 2,000 years and more, until the land of the pharaohs was conquered by Assyrians in the seventh century BC and Persians in the sixth. Meanwhile, the Phoenicians established a colony at Carthage, in modern Tunisia, which would become a formidable power in its own right until its destruction by Rome in 146BC.

The Arabs conquered Egypt in 641 and swept in a torrent across North Africa. Mosques were raised in walled cities like Fez in Morocco, which was the seat of a university founded as far back as 859. To this day Fez retains its ancient battlements, its venerable mosque and its narrow, crowded, clamorous streets. From the 15th century on, Africa was a magnet for European powers, who exploited its mineral wealth and its people. In the 19th century the continent was carved up between them, and not until the 20th century did African states win their independence one by one.

Today the continent is home to a rich diversity of peoples—Africa's 797 million people speak over 1,000 languages. Landscapes range from desert to great lakes and from rainforest and swamps to snow-covered mountains. In Madagascar, the island that broke away from the mainland about 165 million years ago, there is a staggering array of plants and animals which were left to evolve in a unique habitat, free from outside interference.

The New Kingdom in Egypt dates from about 1560 to 1085BC.

In Egyptian mythology the pillars symbolized palm trees from the island where life began.

The Great Pillared Hall covers an area one third the size of St Peter's in Rome.

the facts

The Temple of Karnak

The city that the Greeks called Thebes, the capital of Egypt for some 1,500 years, stood approximately where the town of Luxor is today, on the east bank of the Nile. Nothing is left of the city itself, but the mighty ruins of the Temple of Karnak still overawe today's visitors. With its imposing gates, its courts and halls, its forests of pillars, its carvings and statues and obelisks, it was the largest temple complex in ancient Egypt.

The principal temple here was sacred to Amun, god of the winds and the air. He was represented as a human figure with a double feather crown and his special animal was the ram. Originally a minor local god, he was made Egypt's national god by the New Kingdom pharaohs, from the 16th century BC on, and he was identified with Re, the sun god. He was worshipped here with his consort, the goddess Mut, and their son the moon god Khons.

The little temple to Amun at Karnak was enlarged by Thutmose I at the beginning of the New Kingdom and his successors expanded it again and again. Different areas are entered through huge portals known as pylons, each consisting of a doorway flanked by massive towers. There

BELOW: *Relief carvings on a sarcophagus at Karnak.*
BELOW RIGHT: *Ram-headed sphinx at the Temple of Amun at Karnak.*

The Valley of the Kings

With their capital at Thebes, most of the New Kingdom pharaohs were buried in the desert to the west of the Nile, in the Valley of the Kings, where more than 60 tombs have so far been discovered. By far the most famous is the tomb of Tutankhamen which was opened in 1923, revealing a coffin of solid gold, golden diadems and masks, jewels, statues, chariots, weapons, ornaments and paintings. There was such a profusion of treasures that it took three years to clear.

The pharaoh, who died when he was only 18 in 1352BC, still rests inside his sarcophagus in the tomb, but the treasures are in the Egyptian Museum in Cairo. The tombs are particularly interesting for their murals with scenes of the afterlife.

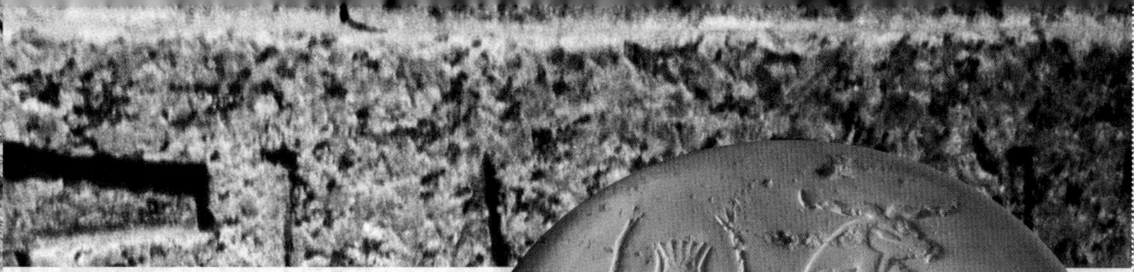

FAR LEFT: *Tomb entrances in The Valley of the Kings*
CENTRE: *The immense decorative columns of the Hypostyle Hall in Karnak.*
LEFT: *Relief carving in the 100-m (328ft) long tomb of Seti I.*

are ten of these at Karnak. As the worshipper penetrated the temple, he passed from the bright sunlight of the outside world into the deepening darkness of the great halls toward the mystery of the innermost shrine, which contained the image of the god. This shrine was barred to all except the king and the priests.

The complex was approached along two avenues of ram-headed sphinxes, one leading from the Nile and the other from Luxor. The vast front pylon of the main temple still stands and beyond it is the Great Court, surrounded by a colonnade with subsidiary temples opening off it. The second pylon opens into the Great Pillared Hall and a third leads to the central court. Beyond, there are three more pylons which lead to the inner sanctuary, where the golden statue of the god stood in his sacred boat. To the south lies the Temple of Mut, surrounded on three sides by the sacred lake. The complex also contains temples of Khons and other gods. The gardens in which the buildings were set vanished long ago, but there is a fine view of the complex from across the sacred lake.

BELOW INSET: *The remains of a statue at Hypostyle Hall at Karnak.*

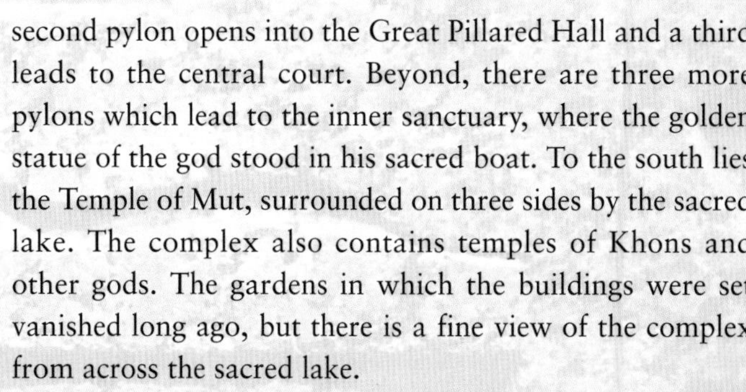

The Colossi of Memnon

Not far from Luxor, on the west side of the Nile, two enormous seated figures of Pharaoh Amenhotep III stand alone in a field. These are the Colossi of Memnon, made from carved blocks of quartzite, which tower more than 15m (50ft) high and which once stood at the entrance to the pharaoh's temple. The northern statue depicts the pharaoh with his mother, Mutemwia, and the southern statue shows him with his wife, Tiy, and one of his daughters.

After an earthquake in 27BC a strange bell-like ringing was sometimes heard from the statues. The Roman Emperor Septimius Severus tried to repair the statues in AD199 and somehow put an end to their magical song.

See also:
The Great Pyramid 116-19

52 The Great Pyramid, Egypt

The Great Pyramid

The Great Pyramid at Giza has stood at the edge of the desert, to the west of the River Nile, since the 26th century BC, when it was built for Pharaoh Khufu (Cheops). Two later kings of the 4th dynasty—Khafre (Chefren) and Menkaure (Mycerinus)—built pyramids of their own close by, and together these three monuments form one of the world's most familiar groups of buildings, regarded for centuries with fascination and awe.

The fascinating aspect of the Great Pyramid, which weighs over six million metric tonnes (nearly seven million tons), is that its massive stone blocks were probably moved without the use of modern machinery, by huge armies of conscripted workers and slaves, using ramps, levers, rollers, ox-drawn sledges and brute force. Despite the difficulties involved, the pyramid was constructed with uncanny accuracy. For example, it stands on an artificially flattened site that deviates from a level plane by less than 2cm (0.5in). The base of the pyramid is remarkably close to being a perfect square which means that the four corners are almost perfect right angles. The building was carefully aligned with the cardinal points of the compass, with the four sides facing due north, east, south and west, again with only a tiny deviation from pinpoint accuracy.

No one knows for certain why the Great Pyramid was built in the first place. The generally accepted theory is that it was the Pharaoh's tomb, which may well be true, but strangely enough no corpse was ever found. When an official party broke into the pyramid in the ninth century AD and with great difficulty forced their way into the King's Chamber, they found the great stone coffin empty, but with no obvious sign of previous disturbance by robbers.

BELOW: *Environmentally-friendly transport at the Pyramids of Giza.*

the facts

- The Great Pyramid stands 137m (450ft) high.
- It is constructed of more than 2.25 million blocks of limestone, which weigh more than 2.5 tonnes (2.75 tons) each.
- The largest blocks weigh over 15.25 tonnes (16.25 tons).
- The granite roof slabs over the King's Chamber weigh up to 50.75 tonnes (56 tons).

the **history**

2589-2566BC
Great Pyramid is built for Pharaoh Khufu.

2558-2532BC
Khufu's son Khafre has a second pyramid built.

2490-2472BC
Menkaure, possibly Khafre's son, rules as pharaoh and adds the third and smallest of the pyramids.

820AD
Abdullah Al Mamun has a tunnel bored into the pyramid to search for treasure.

1954
Khufu's 'sun boat' excavated on the south side of pyramid.

1982
Five more boat pits are discovered at the base of the south face.

LEFT: *Photographing the Sphinx circa 1910.*

There is an entrance to the north side from which a low, narrow passage leads the cramped and crouching visitor to a long passage called the Grand Gallery, 46.6m (153ft) long. This leads to what is usually called the King's Chamber, 42.7m (140ft) above ground level, containing an empty granite sarcophagus. The two other chambers inside the pyramid are both empty. In 1954 a cedar boat was found in a long pit just outside the pyramid. Partly dismantled, it was 43.6m (143ft) long and it can be seen today in the Solar Barque Museum on the site. Other boats were buried close by, perhaps for the dead ruler's voyages in the afterlife.

The three pyramids are part of a complex that includes temples, miniature pyramids thought to have been provided for the pharaoh's wives, and the tombs of priests and officials. This city of the dead is guarded by the watchful Sphinx, which gazes out over the desert sands.

LEFT: *The Egyptians believed that the solar boat carried the Sun God through the underworld until he reappeared at dawn.*

RIGHT: *The mortuary temple at the entrance to the Great Pyramid.*

RIDDLE OF THE SPHINX

The Sphinx was built by Pharaoh Khafre (the head was apparently a portrait of him), although it seems a mere kitten in proportion to the vast bulk of the pyramids looming behind it. It is a recumbent lion with a human head and is 20m (66ft) high and 73m (240ft) long, and was made out of a knoll of rock left in place when the stone was quarried for the Great Pyramid.

Presumably the Sphinx is a guardian of the necropolis behind it, but no one knows for sure. It wears a royal headdress and has the symbol of a cobra on its forehead. Its nose is partly missing and the beard has gone completely. It was also plastered over and painted red.

In front of the Sphinx there is a *stela*, an upright slab of granite on which is recorded the curious experience of a pharaoh of the 15th century BC, Thutmose IV. He sat down to rest in the shade of the Sphinx during a hunt and dreamed that he would win Egypt's throne if he cleared the sand from the monument. He did, and the prediction was fulfilled.

ABOVE: *The Pyramid of Menkaure, the smallest of the group, is partly built from Aswan granite.*

See also:
Borobudur 106
Teotihuacán 186-7
Tikal 192-3

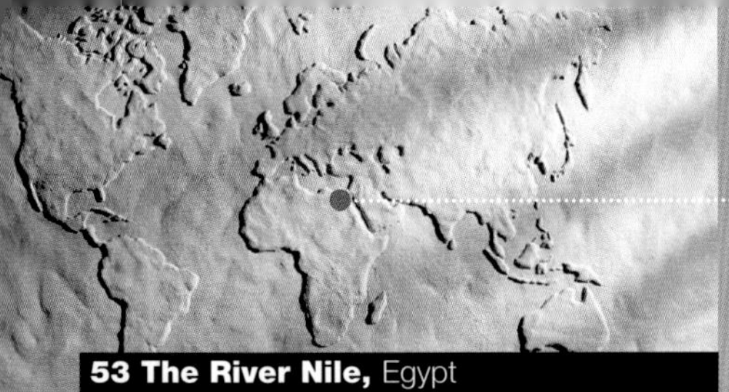

53 The River Nile, Egypt

the facts

- The Nile is the longest river in the world at 6,695km (4,160 miles) long.
- The Nile Delta is one of the most fertile places on earth.
- In 1,609km (1,000 miles) between Juba and Khartoum the White Nile falls only about 73m (240ft).

The River Nile

The world's longest river originates in the great lakes of Africa and winds its way for thousands of miles through deserts and swamps, sometimes meandering gently and sometimes plunging down cataracts and rapids. South and east of Khartoum two rivers converge to become the Nile: they are the Blue Nile to the east and the White Nile to the south.

The Blue Nile rises in Lake Tana in the Ethiopian highlands. From here the river flows southeast over the magnificent Tisisat Falls, and then more than 644km (400 miles) in a grand arc, cutting through the Ethiopian plateau, before pouring down into the hot plains of southern Sudan. On its way, the river slashes a huge gorge through the middle of the plateau, reaching 1.6km (1 mile) deep and 24km (15 miles) wide in some places.

Although the difficulty of crossing the desert southeast of Khartoum and following the river through the untamed

ABOVE: *Herons are one of the many species of bird which come to feed from the river.*

BELOW: *Feluccas on the river at Aswan.*

The Nile Crocodile

The ancient Egyptians revered the Nile crocodile. The god Sebek had the head of a crocodile, and crocodiles were kept in temples and given gold bracelets to wear. Even a city, the Crocodilopolis, was named after the creature. Archaeologists have discovered thousands of crocodile graves, where the animals were buried with great care and sometimes with expensive jewels.

The Nile crocodile no longer abounds on the shores of the Egyptian Nile and is in fact quite rare in Africa today. There are some conservation programmes and small populations are being monitored and protected in places such as Lake Turkana in northern Kenya.

BELOW: *Rowing across the Nile to feed the livestock with fresh greenery.*

gorge prevented an exact mapping of the Blue Nile until Colonel RE Cheesman's efforts in the 1920s and 1930s, Europeans had reached its sources hundreds of years before. The first to make the discovery was Pedro Paez, a Portuguese priest who journeyed to Tisisat Falls in 1618, but the best known was a Scotsman, James 'Abyssinian' Bruce, who reached the falls in 1770.

In contrast to the fast-paced Blue Nile between Juba in the southern Sudan and Khartoum, the White Nile is slow and sluggish. In the Sudd, a region of seasonal swamp, the river degenerates into a series of constantly shifting channels choked with underwater reeds and roots. Until 1899, when a permanent channel was finally carved out of it, the Sudd halted almost all boats trying to sail upriver.

The Nile Delta

At the north end of the river the Nile Delta is still as vital to Egypt's economy now as it was in the past. The building of the Aswan High Dam, 965km (600 miles) from Cairo has threatened the delta area, preventing the deposit of valuable silt from upstream. The water control however, has meant that year-round irrigation can be achieved and as many as three crops a year can be harvested in some areas. Sub-saharan countries which suffer from periods of severe drought are eager to exploit the Nile's waters themselves, and are in dispute with Egypt about the control and use of this great river.

Search for the Source

By the middle of the 19th century the discovery of the White Nile's sources had become the world's greatest geographical challenge. In 1858 John Hanning Speke, on a diversionary journey from an expedition led by Richard Francis Burton, was the first European to reach Lake Victoria, which he proclaimed as the source. Burton, meanwhile, insisted that Lake Tanganyika was the source. A number of explorers, including Scottish missionary David Livingstone, attempted to resolve the question.

In the 1870s Henry Morton Stanley circumnavigated Lake Victoria, proving that it did not have a major river running into it and that it had only one major outlet, Ripon Falls, where the Nile actually starts. Speke had been right all along.

- The name Carthage is derived from the Phoenician words for 'new city'.
- The centre of Carthage appears to have been on the Byrsa Hill, which means 'ox hide'.
- An island in the city's naval dock had dry-dock space, according to Greek historian Appian, for 220 vessels.

the **facts**

Carthage

BELOW: *Cypress trees punctuate the ruined villas on Byrsa Hill.*
BELOW RIGHT: *An anxious stone face in the museum at Carthage.*

Dido was the sister of the king of the ancient capital of Phoenicia, Tyre. When the king murdered her husband for his money, Dido gathered a band of supporters and set sail in search of a new kingdom. She built a magnificent city on the coast of North Africa and it was here that the Trojan prince Aeneas arrived with his fleet during his long journey to Italy after fleeing from defeated Troy. Dido's city was Carthage and the story of her love for Aeneas and her suicide when he left her, poignantly told by the Roman poet Virgil in his epic poem *The Aeneid*, inspired many later writers, artists and composers.

Where Carthage is concerned, it is almost impossible to separate legend from fact and despite much archaeological work, clues remain elusive. Even the date of the city's founding is uncertain. Literary evidence suggests a time at the end of the ninth century BC, but no archaeological

Hannibal and the Punic Wars

Hannibal, the young Carthaginian general who led an army of 38,000 foot soldiers, 8,000 cavalry and 37 elephants over the Alps to take Rome totally by surprise, has captured the imagination of generations.

Between 264 and 241BC the Romans and the Carthaginians fought the First Punic War—the inevitable consequence of increasing rivalry between the two powers. Carthage was ultimately forced to surrender her hold on Sicily and made to pay a huge indemnity.

In 218BC Hannibal seized the initiative by overrunning Etruria. Then in 216 he defeated the Roman army at the battle of Cannae. Hannibal fought on until recalled to Carthage in 203. The Second Punic War finally ended in 201 when Rome invaded Carthage.

evidence has been found to indicate occupation before the eighth century BC.

During the sixth century BC Carthage grew increasingly powerful, building up a fleet and acquiring a number of colonies. Signs of her naval power can been seen in two manmade ports near Topheth. One was a circular naval dock connected to a large merchant port, whose silted-up entrance has been traced.

Exploring the Ruins

If Carthage is a prominent feature in European artistic tradition, it is less prominent on the ground. In the middle of the second century BC the Roman senate resounded with the words of Cato the Elder, who repeatedly declared that Carthage must be destroyed. In 149BC, after a long period of intermittent conflict, Rome declared war again. Carthage, the one-time ally of Rome, was besieged and reduced to ruins in a fire that was said to have raged for ten days

The heart of the city appears to have been on the Byrsa Hill and there is now an archaeological museum here. Excavations on the side of the hill have revealed some houses and shops belonging to the late third or early second century BC. However, most of the remaining ruins which can be seen today—an amphitheatre, the ground plans of the Antonine Baths and a number of villas—bear the stamp of the city's triumphant rival Rome, whose force Carthage was unable to withstand.

BELOW: *A bacchanalian satyr, vividly depicted in a mosaic which is now in the site's museum.*

BELOW: *The Antonine Baths, the biggest bath complex outside Rome.*

BELOW: *Stone balls, probably for use in a giant catapult, litter the ground.*

The Dark Side of Carthage

The oldest finds in Carthage are sinister ones. An area known as the Topheth, apparently a sanctuary of the goddess Tanit, has produced evidence of child sacrifice on a large scale. The theory is that in moonlit ceremonies, young children were sacrificed to the city's principal deity, Baal Hammon.

There seems to have been a tradition of sacrificing members of prominent and ruling families, whose bodies were sent to the next world along with goods for the afterlife. The story of Dido's death may be connected with a primitive idea that the death of a king or queen could benefit the country.

See also:
Pont du Gard 30
Colosseum 42

The old city at Fez, Fez el Bali, was divided into almost 200 different districts, each one a community with its own mosque, *hamman* (Turkish bath) and bakery.

The city is the home of one of the oldest universities in the world and was a key centre of academic debate in the Middle Ages.

the facts

Fez Medina

Fez is a large, modern city with over half a million inhabitants, where it is possible to leave behind cars, wide streets and high-rise buildings and enter a medieval metropolis. Medina was the city to which the Prophet Muhammed escaped in AD622 when he came under threat in Mecca, and the name has since been applied to the old quarter of any Islamic city. The Medina at Fez is the old city (Fez el Bali) established in the ninth century, where narrow, winding streets, fountains in elegant courtyards, traditional houses and the noise and bustle of the bazaar combine to offer a window onto a different world. Many of the goods on sale may be modern and much may be aimed specifically at tourists, but the atmosphere and the scale of the old city survive.

Mosques and Koran Schools

With nearly 800 mosques (usually with schools attached), thousands of shops, and enough houses for a population of around 125,000, by the 13th century Fez had become one of the world's most important cities. The principal mosque, the Karaouyine, was founded in the ninth century and rebuilt in the thirteenth. It is the largest mosque in North Africa (it can accommodate 20,000 people), and connected with it are the university of Fez and an outstanding library.

Fez also has a large number of *medressahs* (Koran schools), which usually consist of three rooms—school, prayer hall and library—arranged around a courtyard with a central fountain. The Bou Inania Medressah is particularly impressive, with decoration that manages to be lavish without being overpowering and that has similarities to the Moorish architecture of Spain (see The Alhambra on pages 58-59) . A curious arrangement of windows, wooden blocks and brass bowls has been described as a water clock dating from the 13th century, but no one has been able to say how it works. The brass bowls may have been shaped by distant ancestors of the men who can be seen today beating various metals into shape in the Place Seffarine.

Dyeing and tanning are two other traditional activities, unchanged for hundreds of years, that can be seen at Fez. At the dyers' *soukh* (marketplace) by the river, a watermill is used to crush the seeds that provide vegetable dyes. Further downriver there are tanners hard at work.

Volubilis

Fez was founded by a descendant of Muhammad called Moulay Idriss, who chose to create his new city rather than expand the existing Moroccan metropolis at Volubilis.

Volubilis was originally a Roman city and the ruins that can be seen today give a good idea of Roman civilization in Africa during the third century AD. The remains of a basilica, a capitoline temple (dedicated to three deities—Jupiter, Juno and Minerva), and a forum are at the heart of the site, and there are also a triumphal arch, the remains of some public baths and a number of houses.

This region supplied Rome with large quantities of olive oil and you can still see ancient oil presses here. Some of the treasures found at Volubilis are housed in the Museum of Antiquities at Rabat.

BELOW: *Dyeing, like tanning, is one of the industries on which modern Fez was built, and is still carried out in traditional clay pits lined with tiles.*

ABOVE: *Wicker screens provide some welcome shade for stallholders and shoppers in the soukh.*

LEFT: *The green-tiled roofs and long courtyard of the Karaouyine Mosque, in the old quarter of the city.*

See also:
Alhambra 58-9
The Blue Mosque 72-3

56 The Great Sahara, North Africa

the **facts**

- The Sahara is the biggest desert in the world, covering an area of 9,269,594sq km (3,579,000 square miles).
- Dunes in parts of the Sahara roll forward at a rate of 11m (36ft) per year.
- One of the hottest places is Kebili, where temperatures can reach 55°C (131°F).

The **Great Sahara**

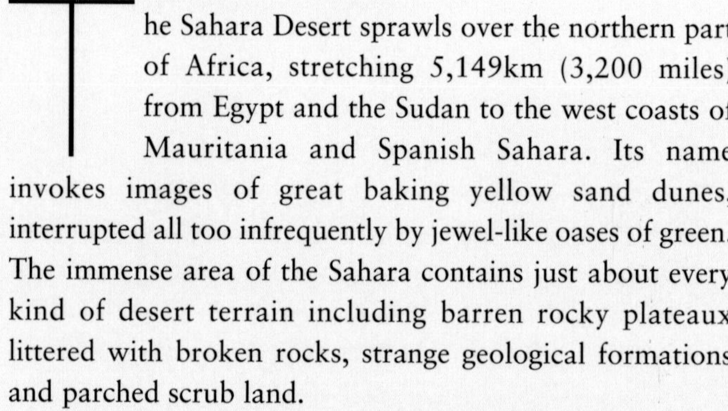

The Sahara Desert sprawls over the northern part of Africa, stretching 5,149km (3,200 miles) from Egypt and the Sudan to the west coasts of Mauritania and Spanish Sahara. Its name invokes images of great baking yellow sand dunes, interrupted all too infrequently by jewel-like oases of green. The immense area of the Sahara contains just about every kind of desert terrain including barren rocky plateaux littered with broken rocks, strange geological formations and parched scrub land.

The bulk of the desert is far inland, and the prevailing winds dry any moisture from the air before it can reach the interior. Mountain ranges between the desert and the sea cause clouds to drop their rain long before they reach the interior. With few clouds in the sky, days in the desert are ferociously hot. Cloudless skies also allow the heat to escape easily into the atmosphere once the sun has gone

BELOW: *Date palms flourish around the oases.*
BOTTOM: *Robes dyed blue with indigo are a distinctive feature of tribes from the western and central Sahara.*

Discovery of Lake Chad

Before the 19th century Europeans had very little knowledge of the interior of the Sahara. Their first accurate information came from attempts to solve the mysteries surrounding the source of the River Niger. The first significant exploration was by an expedition involving three British explorers—Dixon Denham, Hugh Clapperton and Walter Oudney.

The small party left Tripoli in 1822, spent 68 days going through the uncharted desert and on 4 February 1823, they became the first Europeans to see Lake Chad. Denham went on to explore the area to the south, while Clapperton and Oudney turned west toward the Niger. Not long afterwards Oudney died, but Clapperton reached the great walled town of Kano and Sokoto, both of which are in Nigeria.

down, and temperatures at night can drop below freezing. One of the hottest places in the desert is Kebili, where high temperatures are due not only to the burning hot sun, but also to the Sirocco. This wind originates in the scorching interior of the desert and blows hot air northwards like a blast from a furnace.

The best-known areas of the Sahara are the sand dunes associated with the battles in North Africa during World War II. These tracts of rolling waves of sand cover vast areas as large as 101,010sq km (39,000 square miles). In places, these great dunes are highly mobile, driven by the wind, and oases such as Faja are under constant threat from this ever-advancing tide of smothering sand. In other areas the dunes appear not to have moved for thousands of years. This has resulted in the formation of trenches between them, which have become permanent paths for caravans crossing the desert.

Because the Sahara is arid it cannot be cultivated, and nomadic tribes still wander with their small herds of animals. There is mixed farming around a few oases, but most of the desert is economically unproductive.

Concern has grown recently about a process known as desertification which has been taking place around the edges of the Sahara Desert. Inappropriate agricultural methods combined with natural factors such as drought and wind storms have resulted in the advance of the desert across what was once productive arable land. The removal of native plants has led to the loosening of fertile soil which is then baked by drought. Winds blow this soil away like dust, leaving behind desert where once there were crops.

Oases: Green Eyes in the Sand

Oases are fertile areas in the desert—sometimes just a few trees around a small spring, sometimes the banks of a river, such as the River Abiod, which flows through Algeria towards the Sahara. Seen from the air, the river is a ribbon of dark green palms, with groves of date palms, apricots, pomegranates and figs.

A different kind of oasis is found at Nefta in Tunisia. This is an important watering station for caravans crossing the northern fringes of the Sahara, and was known and used in Roman times. Each year the water table under the Nefta area rises, saturating the porous rocks and forming underground wells. Water is forced out of the wells as springs, nourishing fruit trees and palms.

See also:
Atacama Desert 234

the facts

- Lake Tanganyika is the second deepest lake in the world.
- The Ngorongoro crater measures 20km (12.5 miles) across.
- As the Rift Valley widens its crust thins from about 40km (25 miles) to about 6km (3.8 miles).

The East African **Rift Valley**

The East African Rift Valley is a vast split in the earth's crust and one of the great geological features of the planet. The view from the top of the steep slope on one side is of a sweeping panorama across a deep, flat-bottomed valley, in places too wide to see the opposite side. The western arm of the rift extends for about 3,057km (1,900 miles) from Lake Malawi in the south, close to the Mozambique coast, then northward along the line of the great African lakes to the west of Lake Victoria.

The eastern arm starts to the east of Lake Victoria and continues northward for about 2,574km (1,600 miles). It goes from Tanzania through Kenya and into Ethiopia and the complex area known as the Afar Triangle, an area of volcanic rocks and frequent earthquakes. Here the rift divides, with one part continuing north towards the Red Sea, while the other strikes eastward into the Gulf of Aden.

ABOVE: *Grevy's zebras, found in northern Kenya, rarely stray more than 32km (20 miles) from a source of fresh water.*
BELOW: *Looking over the Rift Valley from the Nyambeni Hills in Kenya.*

Life in the Valley

The sheer scale of the Rift Valley is difficult to grasp. Most visitors to the area concentrate on the abundant wildlife that typifies this part of Africa.

The crater of Ngorongoro is a large volcanic crater, that formed in a titanic explosion about three million years ago. It is the site of Africa's finest game reserve, where elephants, Cape buffalo, lions and hyenas are among the inhabitants.

North of Lengai is Lake Natron, a very shallow lake partly fed by soda-rich hot springs that support a rich growth of algae. The springs provide ideal breeding grounds for thousands of pink flamingoes.

Near Ngorongoro is Olduvai Gorge, where hominid fossils were discovered, and regarded by some as the birthplace of the human race.

Understanding the Rift Valley

The German meteorologist Alfred Wegener, who developed the Theory of Continental Drift at the end of the 19th century, noticed that the opposing shores of the Red Sea formed a perfect match, and that the sea could be closed by sliding Africa against Arabia—except that the Yemen would overlap the Afar Triangle. Geologists now recognize that the volcanic rocks in both these areas are younger than the Red Sea, and so could not have existed before the Red Sea opened; thus the match would have been perfect.

Active rifts are characterized by earthquakes and volcanic activity, and in the African rift, the Afar Triangle is currently the most active part. Earthquakes are frequent here, but the shape of the rift is less spectacular because volcanic activity, with huge outpourings of lava over thousands of years, has tended to fill the valley. Volcanism currently occurs around Lake Victoria, in the Virunga Mountains of southwestern Uganda to the west and in northern Tanzania to the east. Lengai, in Tanzania, is the only active carbonatite volcano in the world, where the lava is like a volcanic limestone that turns to the colour of dirty snow within 24 hours of erupting.

The other main feature of the African rift is the intermittent line of lakes along the valley floor. Lake Tanganyika has 5,029m (16,500ft) of sediment beneath it, indicating a long or very fast history of rifting.

BELOW: *Reticulated giraffes are native to northeastern Kenya.*

ABOVE: *The dormant volcano, Mount Longonot, in the Rift Valley.*

Formation of a Rift Valley

A rift valley is formed by tension in the earth's crust where the opposite sides of the valley are slowly moving apart. As the valley widens, the floor of the valley drops between two roughly parallel escarpments.

The fault systems along the valley margins are complex, but generally result in wedge-shaped slices of crust that slip downward to jam in the widening gap.

Over millions of years the valley gradually widens and deepens, but continued erosion blurs the sharp lines of the escarpments and sediments accumulate on the valley floor. When the crust grows too thin, a new crust is formed by magma erupting from the underlying mantle. The bed of the Atlantic Ocean was formed in this way.

See also:
Grand Canyon 176-7
Zion National Park 166-7

Lake Nakuru lies south of the equator at an altitude of 1,759m (5,770ft).

It has a catchment area of about 1,800sq km (695 square miles).

Most of the lake's water flows into it from two main rivers, the Njoro and the Nderit.

the **facts**

Lake Nakuru

Lake Nakuru forms the heart of the national park which bears its name, and is truly one of the great wildlife spectacles of the world. It is, however, only one of a series of important bodies of water that lie in a string down the east side of Africa in the Rift Valley from Lebanon to Mozambique. These lakes are found at different altitudes, and vary in saltiness from freshwater through those of moderate salinity to others which are hypersaline or soda lakes.

There is no major outflow from Lake Nakuru, but its surface area varies with the level of inflow (dependent on rainfall), the amount of water taken for human use, the input from other intermittent springs and the rate of loss by evaporation.

This is a hypersaline lake, the result of very high levels of carbonates and bicarbonates—not chlorides, as is the case with sea water. Such an alkaline environment is very harsh. Living things require a very high level of specialization to be able to survive these conditions, and so the diversity of aquatic species is very low. The waters do not support any large plants, but six species of phytoplankton have been recorded. By far the most numerous of these is the tiny blue-green alga *Spirulina platensis*, which occurs in such vast numbers that it turns the water dark green with a thick, slimy consistency. This tiny species forms the basis of the entire food web in the lake. It is unusually high in protein and contains large amounts of beta-carotene. The alga is the main prey of the five species of zooplankton, four species of water boatmen, two midge larvae and a calanoid copepod, which together make up the entire natural aquatic invertebrate fauna. There is also one fish species which was introduced to the lake in 1953 and again in 1962, after the lake had entirely dried up and then reflooded.

The combination of these different species make Lake Nakuru a wildlife spectacular, providing a vast food resource for countless numbers of birds. Most notable are the flamingoes, which cometothe lake to feed, forming a brilliant pink carpet around the margins of the lake. The beta-carotenes in the *Spirulina* give the flamingoes their brilliant pink hue. More species of birds have appeared on the lake since the fish were introduced.

Lake of Many Birds

As well as the lesser flamingo there are also extensive numbers of the greater flamingo, a bigger bird which feeds on the midge larvae and the copepod.

More than 100 other bird species are represented at Nakuru, including the fish-eating cormorants, anhingas, several types of heron, great white pelicans, yellow-billed storks, spoonbills and African fish eagles.

Most birds use the lake for feeding on the way to their nest sites. The great white pelicans have a relatively short journey to their nests on nearby Lake Elementeita, 10km (6 miles) away. The lesser flamingoes, however, breed on Lake Natron, to the south across the border in Tanzania, which involves marathon flights of 193km (120 miles) or more.

Filtering Machines

Lesser flamingoes feed on the protein-rich, blue-green alga *Spirulina platensis*, and on some lakes more than 60 tonnes (59 tons) of alga can be consumed per day.

A floating bill helps the lesser flamingo concentrate its feeding effort in the surface waters. Its close relative, the greater flamingo, has a heavier bill to enable it to feed on the copepods and midge larvae in the lake's depths.

Lesser flamingoes feed with their head upside down, filtering food from the water with their tongue, which acts as a piston, pumping the water through fine filters in the bill and trapping most of the *Spirulina*. The greater flamingo has a coarser filter that allows most of the *Spirulina* to pass through.

See also:
The Camargue 22-3
The Dead Sea 75
East African Rift Valley 128-9

Our planet is constantly in flux. Land rises, folds in on itself, cracks open, melts away in the rain and the winds. Rivers alter their course, sculpt gorges and caves. Glaciers become lakes, lakes become valleys, oceans become deserts. Every change leaves its mark on landscapes that, to the human eye, seem permanent.

the facts

- Mount Etna, the biggest volcano in Europe, is 600,000 years old and emerges from the sea bed to tower 3,322m (10,900ft) above Sicily's eastern coast.
- Siberia, the largest of the former Soviet regions, covers 10.4 million sq km (4 million square miles) of coniferous forest, mountains and plains.

Great Landscapes

THE LIVING LAND

There are many places where the Earth can be seen in the course of change. The eastern Hawaiian Islands spew magma from their mountain vents as the crust of the Pacific moves westward.

Iceland's spouting geysers, bubbling mud and volcanic eruptions are evidence of mid-Atlantic forces pulling the land apart. The island forms one of the world's newest land masses.

In New Zealand recent eruptions have created new lakes and geysers, and even in the icy Antarctic volcanoes continue to steam and blow, often unseen by human eyes.

CLOCKWISE FROM RIGHT: *Sunset in Monument Valley, Arizona, USA; rice terraces in Bali, Indonesia; fish on the coral reef of Kohala, Hawaii; Derwent Water, in Cumbria, in northern England; Milford Sound, in the heart of New Zealand's fjordland.*

USING THE LANDSCAPE

People have exploited some of the most bizarre landscapes. The Göreme Valley in Turkey is a region of weirdly eroded rock fingers and cliffs, where hundreds of churches and living spaces have been carved. Also in Turkey, Pamukkale's rock basins of mineral water have made bathing pools for 2,000 years.

AT THE EXTREMES

Some landscapes are almost beyond comprehension. The vast complexity of the Grand Canyon; the Great Sahara, smothering most of northern Africa; the long journeys of the Amazon and the Nile, which confounded explorers for so many years. We feel dwarfed by the stupendous power of Niagara Falls or the soaring Himalayan peaks.

But some of the most amazing landscapes have a less immediate drama: the Great Glen, a line of lochs virtually splitting Scotland in two; the massive sweep of the East African Rift Valley; or California's small but outstandingly beautiful Yosemite Valley.

CLOCKWISE FROM LEFT: *The Perito Moreno Glacier, Argentina; morning mist on the calderas (large volcanic craters) of Mount Bromo on Java, Indonesia; the baking desert of Death Valley, California, USA.*

See also:
East African Rift Valley 128-9
The Grand Canyon 176-7
The Great Sahara 126-7

the facts

- Kilimanjaro covers an area 97km (60 miles) long and 64km (40 miles) wide.
- In Swahili its name means 'The Mountain that Glitters'.
- Tropical rainforest grows on its slopes.
- It is 5,899m (19,350ft) high.

Mount Kilimanjaro

This towering volcano with its spectacular snow-covered cap looms over the semi-desert of northern Tanzania. At 5,899m (19,350ft), it is the tallest mountain in Africa, and it can be seen for many miles across the plains of Tanzania and Kenya. Its profile is very distinctive: gently rising slopes lead to an elongated, flattened summit—really a volcanic caldera. On very hot days and from great distances the blue mountain base is sometimes indistinguishable from the savannah.

Creating a Microcosm

Kilimanjaro is so large that it can influence its own weather. As moisture-laden winds blow in from the Indian Ocean they are forced upward when they meet Kilimanjaro, and drop their water as rain or snow. The increased rainfall makes the slopes of the mountain more fertile than the scrub land that surrounds it.

At the very peak of the mountain are Kilimanjaro's permanent glaciers—an unusual feature since the mountain lies only three degrees south of the equator. Recent evidence suggests that these glaciers are retreating. The rainfall on top of the mountain is only 20cm (8in) a year, and this is insufficient to keep pace with the amount of water lost through melting.

Some scientists believe that the volcano is warming up again, which is speeding up the melting process; others blame global warming. Whatever the cause, it is clear that Kilimanjaro's glaciers are smaller than they were in the 19th century. If the situation remains constant, Kilimanjaro's icy cap will be gone by the year 2200.

A Volcanic Past

Kilimanjaro is really three volcanoes linked together by a complex history of eruptions. The oldest volcano, Shira, lies to the west of the main mountain. It was once much taller, and is thought to have collapsed following a violent eruption, which left only a plateau of 3,810m (12,500ft).

The second oldest volcano is Mawenzi, a distinct peak attached to the east side of the largest mountain. Even though it appears insignificant next to Kilimanjaro's summit, it rises to a height of 5,334m (17,500ft).

The youngest and largest of the three volcanoes, Kibo, was formed during a series of eruptions, and is topped by a caldera about 2km (1.25 miles) across. A second volcanic cone with a crater developed inside the caldera during a subsequent eruption and a cinder cone formed during a third eruption. The caldera of Kibo forms the distinctive flattened summit of the mountain.

BELOW: *Giant lobelia grow in the moorland zone of the mountain.*

Ol Doinyo Lengai Volcano

Ol Doinyo Lengai volcano is in a state of high activity, erupting frequently and spewing ash and sodium carbonate dust into the air. The volcano lies in a region of the Rift Valley in Tanzania called Sykes Grid, where the earth's crust is thought to be particularly thin.

This volcano is unusual because its contents are rich in sodium but low in silica. From a distance, Lengai appears snow-capped, like Mount Kenya and Mount Kilimanjaro. On closer inspection however, it becomes apparent that the whitish substance on its peak is not snow, but the alkaline sodium carbonates deposited from its recent eruptions.

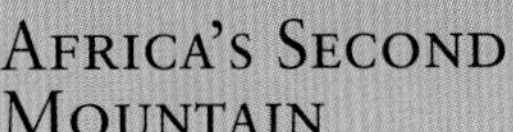

Africa's Second Mountain

Mount Kenya (Kirinyaga) lies north of Nairobi, rising 5,182m (17,000ft) above the rolling plains. It is second in Africa only to Kilimanjaro.

Like Kilimanjaro, Mount Kenya's origins are volcanic, and it is estimated to be between two and a half and three million years old. While Kilimanjaro appears as a smooth, snow-capped dome, Mount Kenya's peak is a craggy splinter of rock. This is actually a volcanic plug—a core of very hard rock that formed in the vent of the volcano. When softer rocks surrounding the plug eroded, the core was left standing like a broken tooth.

Like Kilimanjaro, Mount Kenya also has glaciers at its summit, and scientific evidence suggests that they too are melting.

BELOW LEFT: *Trekkers on the mountain take a break at Horombo Hut.*
BELOW RIGHT: *On the trail towards Kibo Peak, the summit of Kilimanjaro.*
RIGHT: *Giant groundsel among the rocks on Kilimanjaro.*

See also:
Mount Erebus 232-3
Mount Fuji 104-5
Mount Everest 100

- The Zaire River rises more than 1,524m (5,000ft) above sea level.
- Until joining the Lualaba and taking the name Zaire River, it is known as the Chamber River.
- The Stanley Falls drop the river to an elevation of 457m (1,500ft) for a course of 97km (60 miles).

the **facts**

The Zaire River

Although this river has been officially called the Zaire since 1971, its savage image is inextricably tied to its mysterious history. In the past it was known as the Congo, a name deriving from the Portuguese misinterpretation of a West African word meaning 'the river that swallows all rivers'. Indeed, it is an awe-inspiring natural force: more than 4,344km (2,700 miles) long, with a basin that is 3.9 million sq km (1.5 million square miles), and a flow that is second only to the mighty Amazon of South America, pouring almost 42,450 cu m (1.5 million cu ft) of water into the Atlantic every second.

Stanley and the Congo

By the 1870s the Congo was still shrouded in mystery to Westerners. Was it connected to the Nile, the Niger, the mysterious Lualaba in the heart of Africa, or was it a totally separate river? No one knew for sure—not even the Arab slavers who went to places in central Africa where no Europeans had ever been.

All the major questions about the African watershed were resolved by Welsh journalist and explorer Henry Morton Stanley (1841-1904) between 1874 and 1877. With the backing of *The New York Herald* and *The Daily Telegraph* of London, he made a remarkable transafrican expedition from Zanzibar to the mouth of the Congo, sailing along the river to reach the Atlantic after 999 days.

A River's Progress

The river rises in the highland savannah of northern Zambia and meanders through Zambia into the Democratic Republic of Congo (formerly Zaire), where it joins the Lualaba. Under that name, it begins its slow descent toward the tropical rainforests of West Africa, which it reaches some 805km (500 miles) later. The river flows north more than 1,609km (1,000 miles) before crossing the equator, becoming the Zaire and then turning westward in a magnificent arc that recrosses the equator going south.

In the northeast of the great arc are the Stanley (or Boyoma) Falls, a series of cataracts and rapids. This is followed by a 1,609km (1,000-mile) stretch of navigable river, culminating in Malebo Pool (once called Stanley Pool), a 24-km (15 mile) wide expanse that separates Kinshasa, the capital of the Democratic Republic of Congo, from Brazzaville, the capital of the Congo. In the 19th century explorer Henry Morton Stanley built a road around the cataracts and falls up to Malebo Pool.

Beyond Malebo Pool are the Livingstone Falls, a 354-km (220 mile) stretch that includes an entire series of rapids and 32 cataracts. The last of these, the Cauldron of Hell, takes the river out from the Crystal Mountains and down to sea level. Even after rushing the final 161km (100 miles) down to the Atlantic, the Zaire is not drained of power. Moving with a current of nine knots (10 miles) it sweeps its huge volume of water through a submarine canyon 1,219m (4,000ft) deep for another 161km (100 miles) out to sea. There, in the waves of the Atlantic Ocean, it is still possible to see both the muddy red-brown stain of the rainforest and the bits of lighter vegetation that have been carried all the way down from the plains.

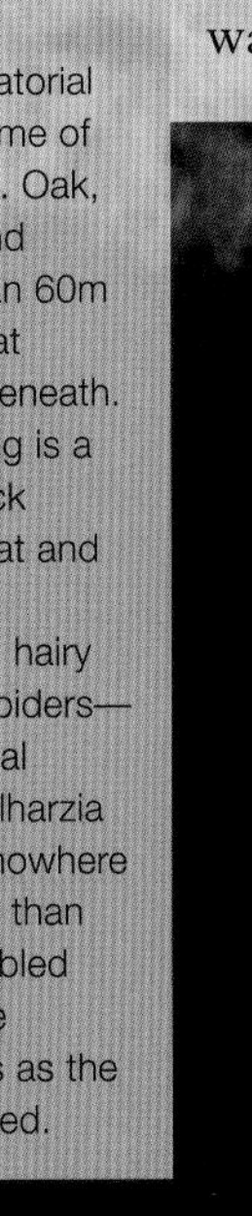

The River in the Rainforest

The Zaire flows through equatorial rainforest that is home to some of the densest growth on earth. Oak, mahogany, rubber, ebony and walnut trees grow higher than 60m (200ft), forming a canopy that creates a perpetual gloom beneath.

Below this colossal ceiling is a nether world of intensely thick undergrowth, oppressive heat and humidity, deadly animals—crocodiles, pythons, cobras, hairy forest pigs and poisonous spiders—and debilitating and even fatal diseases such as malaria, bilharzia and black water fever. And nowhere is it more a maze of mystery than between the river and the fabled Mountains of the Moon—the Ruwenzori range that serves as the Zaire's easternmost watershed.

See also:
Colorado River 176-7
River Nile 120-1
Yangtze River 90-1

61 **Madagascar,** Indian Ocean

- Madagascar is 1,609km (1,000 miles) long.
- About 10,000 species of plant exist only in Madagascar, along with half of the world's chameleons.
- The brookesia, a species of chameleon so tiny that it sits easily on the tip of a human thumb, lives only in Madagascar. Islanders believe it brings bad luck.

the facts

Rare Wildlife

Lemurs are the best known of Madagascar's primates, and species include the ring-tailed, sifaka, black, sportive, ruffed and gentle lemurs.

Primates are characterized by large brains, slender limbs, and hands and feet adapted for climbing. Lemurs are lower primates, and are less well adapted for walking on two legs.

Like apes and monkeys, lemurs have manual dexterity, and they have developed certain monkey-like traits, although there is considerable variation between the different species. For example, the rare and elusive Coquerel's lemur is monogamous, small and golden-brown in colour, while the more common ring-tailed lemur tends to live in groups.

ABOVE: *Parson's chameleons live in the rainforests of eastern Madagascar, catching insects with a tongue half as long again as their body.*

Madagascar

Madagascar is an island of staggering biological diversity. When the island ripped away from Africa 165 million years ago, animals and plants continued to evolve without interference from outside. Madagascar became, in effect, a huge natural laboratory, and the plants and animals there are often unlike any others on earth.

On the west of the island lies the forbidding Tsingy National Reserve of Bemaraha, where sharp fingers of limestone point 30m (100ft) into the air over an area of 155sq km (60 square miles). The local people say that there is barely enough flat land in the area on which to place a foot. This factor helps to protect at least some of Madagascar's plants and animals from human destruction.

South of Tsingy is Morondava, where rain falls for only four months of the year. Six species of baobab trees grow in this unique habitat—that is, five more than survive today on mainland Africa. The trees are specially adapted to Madagascar's climate: they gorge themselves on water during the rainy season and then survive on the reserves for eight months until the rains come again. Like other areas in Madagascar, the baobab forests are under threat from human expansion, but baobab forests are particularly difficult to repair once the damage has been done. The trees live for hundreds of years, and often do not fruit annually; an extended period of drought might kill an entire year's seedlings. Animals also pose problems: the giant jumping rat, for example, lives exclusively in a very small area in west Madagascar and eats baobab seedlings.

The small Berenty Reserve lies in the south of the island, where some of the largest fruit bats in the world roost in the giant tamarind trees. The colony, numbering several thousand, is believed to be one of the largest to co-exist so near human habitation. Ring-tailed lemurs also thrive at

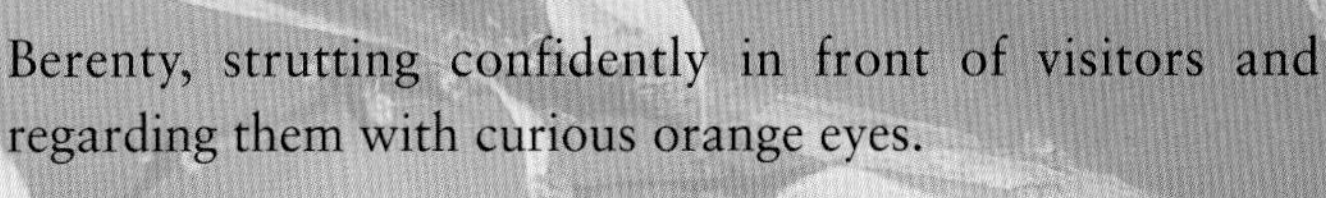

Berenty, strutting confidently in front of visitors and regarding them with curious orange eyes.

Erosion threat

Many of Madagascar's 1,000 unique species of orchid grow in the Montagne d'Ambre National Park on the northern tip of the island, but not all of Madagascar is rich and green, and years of deforestation and burning have taken their toll. On the island's east coast in particular, rivers run red with the clay that is being swept off hills once richly carpeted with vegetation.

ABOVE LEFT: *A waterfall in the Ranomafana National Park.*
LEFT: *Bulging baobab trees near Ifaty, each with its own built-in water reserve.*
BELOW: *The weathered sandstone cliffs of the Isalo ridge.*

Madagascar's Primates

Primates are a biologically similar animal group that includes apes—gorillas, chimpanzees, orangutans and humans, as well as gibbons and siamangs—and monkeys.

Fifty million years ago a squirrel-sized ancestor of all primates inhabited the subtropical forests of Africa. Through time, different species evolved from this creature: some became the ancestors of humans, apes, and monkeys, and others became lemurs, pottos, lorises and bushbabies. Lorises can be found in Asia, and pottos and bushbabies in Africa, while lemurs live exclusively in Madagascar and the nearby Comores Islands.

Another primate unique to Madagascar is the aye-aye, a small, dark brown animal that lives in a nest of leaves, emerging only at night to feed.

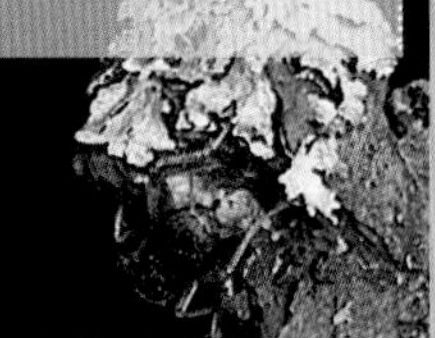

See also:
Galapagos Islands 204-5
Great Barrier Reef 220-3

the facts

- When the Zambezi River is in full flood, 7,560cu m (270,000cu ft) of water surge over the falls every second.
- The resulting spume of spray can be seen up to 40km (25 miles) away.
- The local name for the Victoria Falls is Mosi-oa-tunya, which translates as 'the smoke that thunders'.

Victoria Falls

The mighty Victoria Falls are on the Zambezi River, forming part of the Zambia–Zimbabwe border. The spray can rise to a height of 305m (1,000ft), and rainbows often shimmer above the water, adding to the beauty and drama of the scene.

The waterfall is only the start of an impressive water course, for the spray-shrouded river immediately churns its way through a narrow chasm, which zig-zags back and forth for almost 72km (45 miles). These hairpin bends were caused by faults in the rock that have been eroded by the sheer force of the water over thousands of years. The

Southern Africa's Waterfalls

In South Africa, the Orange River takes a 146-m (480ft) plunge over the edge of a plateau at the Aughrabies Falls, before ripping its way through a gorge of granite. In the dry season the Orange River is little more than a stream but, swollen with spring rain, the waterfalls are appropriately known as Aughrabies, a term which comes from the Hottentot word meaning 'the place of great noise'.

South Africa also has the Tugela Falls, Africa's highest falls, really a series of five cascades, where the water thunders down a staggering 945m (3,100ft).

Other falls which vary seasonally are the Lofoi Falls in the Democratic Republic of Congo. The 335m (1,000ft) drop is always impressive.

Waterfalls of West Africa

Dr David Livingstone described the Victoria Falls as providing 'scenes so lovely [they] must have been gazed upon by angels in their flight'. But West Africa also has its share of stunning waterfalls. The Tagbaladougou Falls in Burkina Faso are really three separate falls, including an elongated curtain of water flowing over a hard ridge, and a slender plume.

The picturesque Tannogou Falls in Benin pour off a plateau into a large pool. In Guinea, the Tinkisso River tumbles across erosion-resistant rocks in a series of rapids, culminating in the Tinkisso Falls.

Zambezi River roams across a plateau formed of layers of sandstone and basalt, and it is at the points where these different rocks meet that the faults occur.

Discovery of the Falls

In November 1855, the Scottish missionary and explorer David Livingstone (1813-73) was the first European to reach Victoria Falls. He had first heard about the waterfall four years earlier when, with his companion William Cotton Oswell, he reached the banks of the Zambezi River 129km (80 miles) to the west. Between 1853 and 1856 Livingstone crossed Africa. Hoping to open the heart of the continent to Christian missionaries, he journeyed north from southern Africa, through Bechuanaland (modern Botswana) to the Zambezi. He then headed west to the coast at Luanda in Angola. Deciding that this route to the interior was too difficult, he headed back east, following the Zambezi most of the way, and reached Quelimane on the Mozambique coast in May 1856.

Surprisingly, the explorer was not happy with his discovery of the spectacular falls. To Livingstone this virtually unbroken wall of water some 1,676m (5,500ft) long and plunging 107m (350ft) were simply an impediment to Christian missionaries attempting to reach the people of the interior. To him the highlight of his journey was the discovery of the Batoka Plateau east of the falls, a place that he saw as a potential settlement site if the Zambezi proved to be fully navigable (which it did not). Livingstone stated that such a magnificent natural wonder should be named after the British queen, Victoria.

See also:
Angel Falls 194
Iguaçu Falls 202-3
Niagara Falls 150-1

the facts

- The Okavango Delta covers a core area of 15,993sq km (6,175 square miles).
- During periods of flood after the rains this can increase to 22,015sq km (8,500 square miles).
- The Delta is home to the largest remaining number of red lechwe antelope. At least 20,000 live on the grasslands.

The Okavango Delta

The Okavango River rises in the highlands of Angola and flows to the southeast. Before it can reach the sea it disappears in the arid wastes of the Kalahari Desert in Botswana, one of the driest countries in southern Africa. The slow-moving water passes through an intricate maze of channels where more than 95 percent of it evaporates. The remainder travels either farther south by way of the Boteti River for another 161km (100 miles) before reaching the Makgadikgadi Pans, or to the southwest, where it finally enters Lake Ngami.

The Okavango Delta represents not only one of the largest inland delta systems in the world, but also an area of unique character because of the juxtaposition of the highly productive wetlands and the extremely arid land of the Kalahari Desert. Even in this vast continent the Okavango Delta is one of the largest remaining wilderness areas.

Inhabitants of the Delta

The delta is a haven for a wide variety of both plants and animals. The upper reaches of the delta are covered by extensive dense reed beds dominated by papyrus. These are interspersed with areas of permanent water which support large stands of water lilies—popular with the pygmy goose, which feeds almost exclusively on lily fruit. This wetland habitat is ideal for the hippopotamus, the crocodile and a number of species of antelope. Most notable is the sitatunga, which is very specifically adapted to an aquatic lifestyle and is largely confined to the most impenetrable areas of the delta and other similar areas in Africa. The kobs, which include the waterbuck, the puku and the lechwe, are antelope species adapted for this aquatic lifestyle and and found only in southern Africa.

The reed beds and open water areas are also home to a large number of different birds, including some of Africa's rarest species. The spectacular African fish eagle with its evocative, piercing cry hunts in these areas, along with other species such as the little bee-eater, malacite kingfisher, a number of species of heron and egret, and the African fishing owl.

In the lower reaches of the delta the reed beds give way to acacia thorn scrub and grassy flood plains, which act as a magnet to the migrating herds of plains animals, including zebra, buffalo, elephant and antelope. The predators which follow these herds into the area include lion, leopard and hyena.

BELOW: *Poling through a shallow lagoon in the flooded delta.*

Change and Management

The delta's grassy plains are inhabited by the cattle-herding Tswana and Herero tribes. In the past their livestock were confined to the margins of the delta because of attacks by tsetse flies, carriers of sleeping sickness. Aerial spraying has all but eradicated the fly, allowing cattle and herdsmen to penetrate into the swamps. The unfortunate side effect of this success has been to reduce the range available to the antelope, by disturbing its habitats and making it compete with cattle for grazing. The numbers of antelope are thus in decline and the fragile integrity of this wilderness is threatened.

This threat has been recognized by the local people and the Moremi Wildlife Reserve, covering 3,885sq km (1,500 square miles), is the first wildlife sanctuary in southern Africa to be created and managed by the local people.

See also:
The Camargue 22-3
Danube Delta 36
The Waddenzee 21

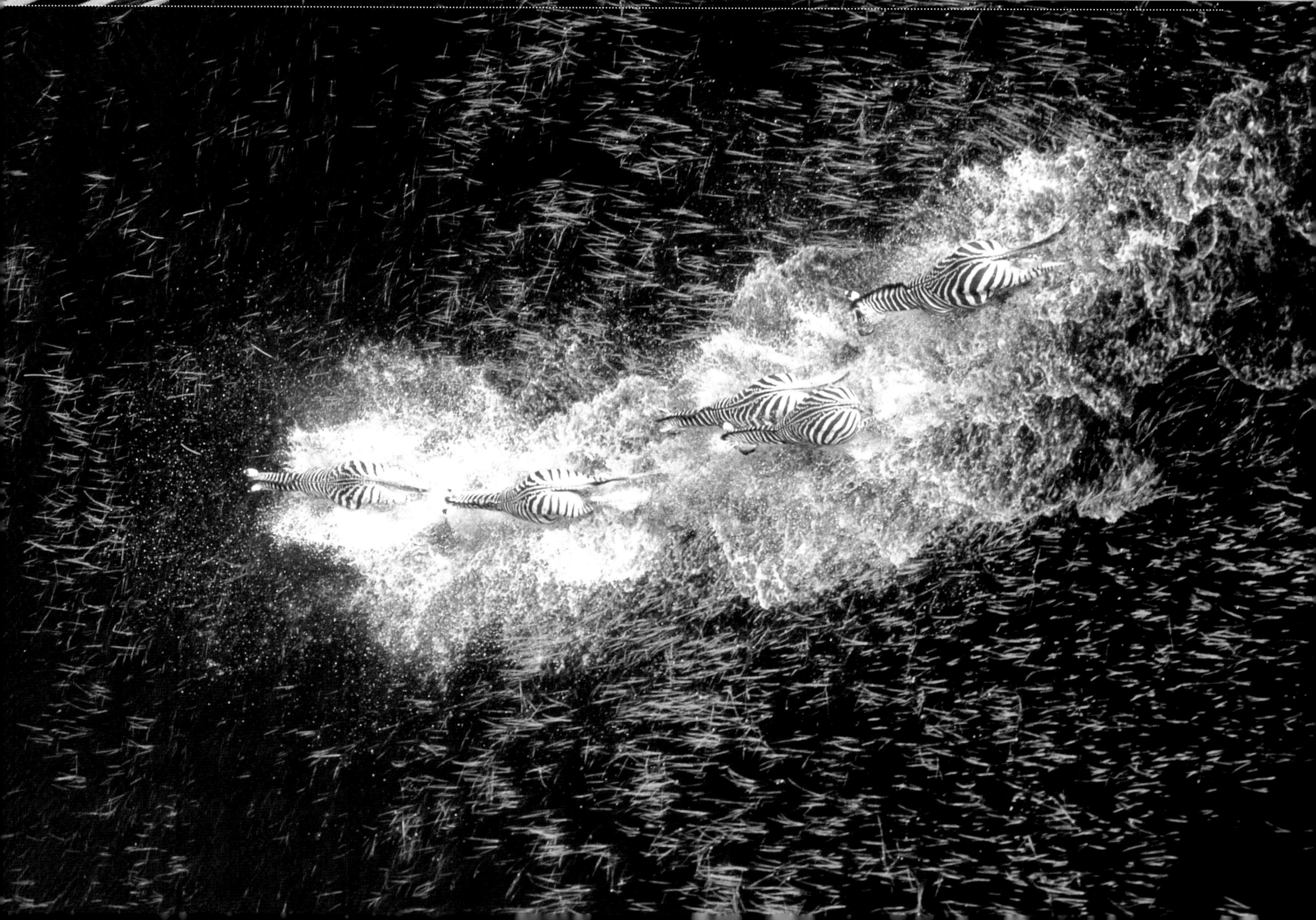

the facts

- Table Mountain's apparently flat top stretches 3.2km (2 miles) from one end to the other.
- Its cliffs rise 1,067m (3,500ft) from sea level.
- Cape Town's annual rainfall is 65cm (25.5in), while precipitation on Table Mountain's summit averages 183cm (72in) per year.

Famous Tablelands

Tablelands are formed in several different ways. The Jugurtha Tableland in Tunisia is an example of inverted relief. It developed when softer rocks formed hills (upfold), and harder rocks formed the valley bottom (downfold). As the softer rocks eroded, the hard rocks of the valley floor became a tableland. In the case of Jugurtha, the table is a natural fortress, with steep-sided cliffs of 610m (2,000ft) to protect it.

Mesa Verde, in Colorado, is formed of sandstone, with layers of shale and coal. Successive uplifting of the land, combined with erosion of softer rocks by rivers formed the tableland, which is now covered with forests of juniper and pine.

Table Mountain

Towering over the bustling city of Cape Town, Table Mountain is often shrouded in white clouds. When the clouds do lift, or resettle so that only the 'tablecloth' of mist remains draped over one end, a splendid sight is revealed. Viewed from the bay below, Table Mountain appears to have a perfectly flat top, and its cliffsides rise abruptly.

From Cape Town's bay the mountain is a great, blue-green monolith shimmering slightly in the heat, and doubtless a welcome sight to many sailors braving the stormy Atlantic seas around the Cape of Good Hope.

Table Mountain forms the northern end of a range of hills that lie between Cape Town and the Cape of Good Hope. The range is made up of sandstone and quartzite resting on shale and older rocks of granite. The broken skyline of the escarpment is known as the Twelve Apostles. East of Table Mountain is Devils' Peak, 975m (3,200ft) high, while to the west are the smaller hills of Lion's Head and Signal Hill, which reach altitudes of 640m (2,100ft) and 335m (1,100ft) respectively.

The tablecloth drapes itself over the summit of Table Mountain but never reaches the lower slopes. The clouds that form are blown in by southeast winds, constantly forced northwards down the slopes towards Cape Town, but they tend not to stay. On the summit, clouds can form very suddenly, making the weather there unpredictable.

Climbing the Heights

Heavy rainfall on the summit has eroded a number of deep ravines running down the cliff face. The deepest of these, the Gorge, is also the shortest route to the top. Today visitors have a range of options for climbing to the top of Table Mountain. The easiest way up is on the cableway, but there are also hundreds of tracks of varying difficulty leading to the summit. The mountain is a popular venue for pursuers of adventure, and it's now possible to abseil off the top or to go paragliding from Lion's Head.

On clear days the views from Table Mountain are breathtaking. Three great oceans meet at the tip of southern Africa—the Atlantic, the Indian and the Southern. Cold currents from the south meeting the warmer waters of the Indian Ocean are responsible for some of the violent storms that pummel the region around the Cape of Good Hope.

BOTTOM LEFT: *Hikers on the flank of Table Mountain, with the Devil's Peak behind.*

BELOW RIGHT: *A spectacular view over Table Bay from the crag.*

Settling Cape Town

The first European to reach the Cape Town area was Portuguese explorer Bartholomew Diaz in 1488. He named this the Cape of Storms, and its turbulent reputation was not due only to the rough sailing conditions. Two decades after Diaz' visit Portuguese sailors were massacred by the native Hottentots, and for many years afterwards ships avoided the area altogether.

It was not until 1652 that a settlement was established by the Dutch beside Table Bay, which they used to supply passing East India Company ships with fresh vegetables. These early settlers built the fortress that can still be seen in Cape Town. Still operational as a military base, today its five imposing stone walls also house a museum with artefacts dating back to the 17th century, and troops dressed in historic uniform parade on its cobbled grounds.

See also: **Guilin Hills** 88-9

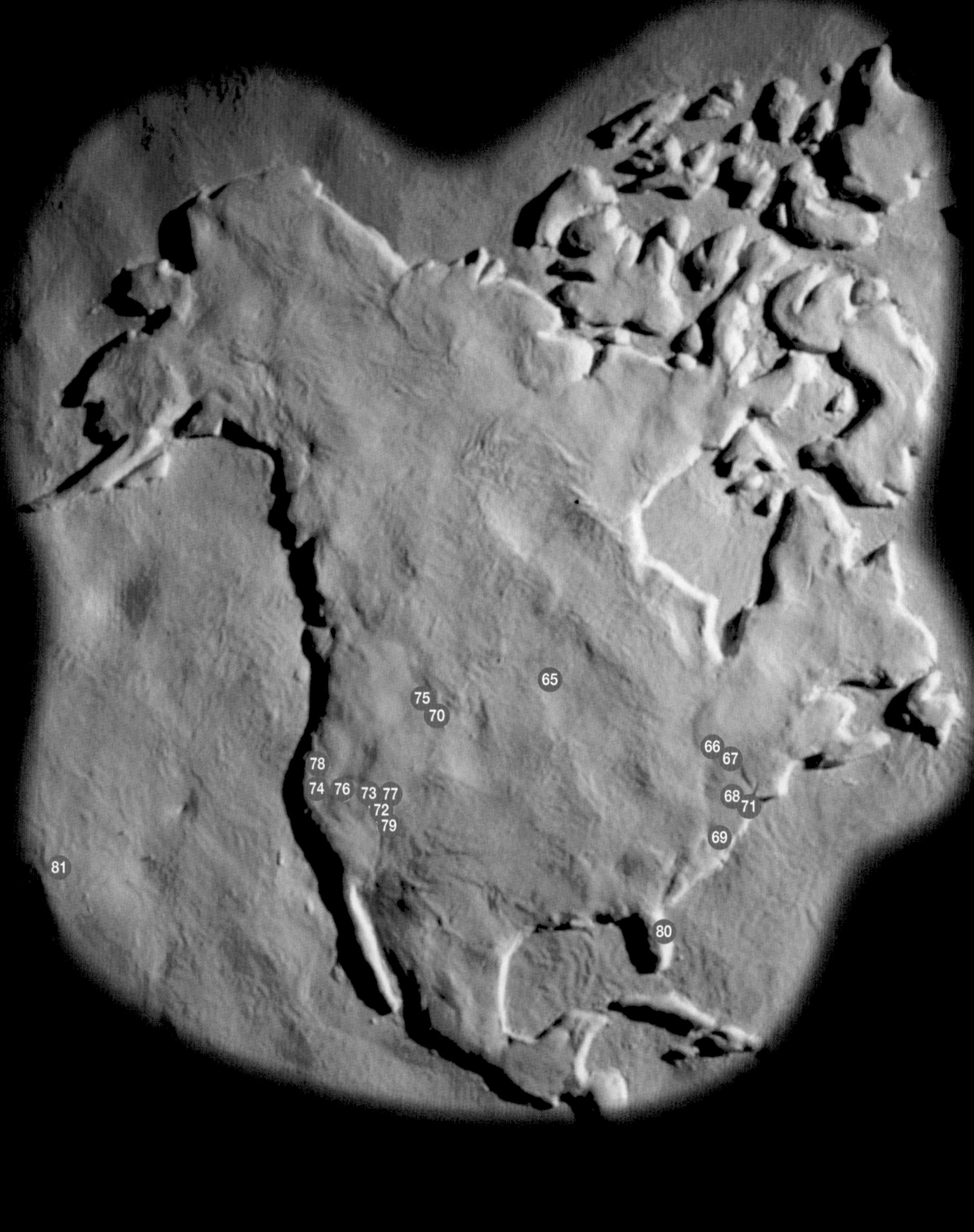

65 **The Canadian Pacific Railway**

66 **Niagara Falls**

67 **The CN Tower**

68 **The Statue of Liberty**

69 **The Lincoln Memorial**

70 **Mount Rushmore**

71 **The Empire State Building**

72 **Zion National Park**

73 **The Hoover Dam**

74 **The Golden Gate Bridge**

75 **The Devil's Tower**

76 **Yosemite National Park**

77 **The Grand Canyon**

78 **Redwoods and Giant Sequoias**

79 **Meteor Crater**

80 **The Everglades**

81 **Hawaiian Islands**

North America

North America's first human inhabitants arrived from Siberia over 20,000 years ago, journeying on foot across the Bering Strait (which at that time was dry land), moving into Alaska and then onward south. Early Americans learned how to grow crops, how to make pottery and how to work copper and gold, and they developed a way of life tied intimately to their natural surroundings.

By the early 16th century European explorers were sailing along the eastern and southern shores of the continent and venturing into the interior. They were amazed by the diversity and immensity of the landscapes that greeted them, and charting the land became a vital part of the race for power. The French explored the St Lawrence River and the Great Lakes, headed south to present-day New York, and sailed the length of the Mississippi River. The Spanish made it into the central Rockies and the British pushed inland from New England and Virginia and laid trails across the Appalachian mountains. Control of territories and trade led to bitter conflicts, particularly between British and French colonists, which the British won. Native Americans were overwhelmed and driven from their homelands.

In the 18th century 13 American colonies threw off the yoke of British rule and declared their independence. The following century saw a frenzied drive to settle the West, and the building of the Canadian Pacific Railroad brought the east and west coasts of North America closer together.

Immigrants poured into both Canada and the United States, lands of opportunity, to be greeted in the USA, by the Statue of Liberty at the entrance to the harbour in New York. North American architects and engineers invented the highrise building, establishing a tradition symbolized by New York's Empire State Building and developed in Toronto's CN Tower. The continent's rich natural resources and pioneering spirit encouraged industrial growth, expressed in such engineering wonders as the Golden Gate Bridge across the entrance to San Francisco Bay and the Hoover Dam which spans the Colorado River.

HERE WAS DRIVEN THE LAST SPIKE COMPLETING CANADIAN PACIFIC RAILWAY FROM OCEAN TO OCEAN NOVEMBER 7. 1885

the facts

- On one stretch of the line beyond Calgary, a length of 183m (600ft) was laid in a record time of 4.75 minutes.
- The highest bridge in North America (built to carry trains over Stoney Creek), is on wooden towers 61m (200ft) tall.
- Engineer Van Horne began as a telegraph operator with the Illinois Central Railroad and was later knighted.

The Canadian Pacific Railway

The single track between Montréal and Vancouver, 4,696km (2,918 miles) long, was one of the most heroic feats of engineering history and a vital factor in the development of modern Canada.

In 1867 the country's eastern provinces formed the Canadian Confederation, to the west of which lay a vast emptiness of prairies and mountains. On the Pacific coast was British Columbia, uncertain whether or not to link up with the United States. In 1871 British Columbia joined the Canadian Confederation, on condition that a railway crossing the continent be built within ten years.

All Aboard

The last spike of the Canadian Pacific Railway was driven in a simple ceremony amid the mountains at Eagle Pass on 7 November 1885, at a spot that William Van Horne named Craigellachie. In his book *The Impossible Railway*, Pierre Berton describes how the line's directors arrived at the scene, drawn by locomotive No. 148, with its diamond-shaped smokestack and gleaming brass boiler. The oldest of the directors, Donald A. Smith, drove the final spike in total silence, followed by a tremendous cheer as it went home, and the shrill whistling of the locomotive. Van Horne, not given to great speeches, simply remarked that the work had been well done, and a voice cried: 'All aboard for the Pacific!'

RIGHT: *Posing on the cow-catcher of a CPR steam locomotive, 1895.*

Building the Dream

In the event, work did not begin until 1881, with a formidable American of Dutch descent, William Van Horne, in charge. The line across the prairies was built rapidly in 15 months. From the supply base in Winnipeg construction trains moved west with clockwork regularity, each one carrying exactly the quantity of material needed for 1.6km (1 mile) of track: rail and ties, telegraph poles, bridging material. Getting the track through the Rocky Mountains presented a particular challenge. Beyond the little settlement at Calgary, the line had moved swiftly along the Bow River, but an army of 12,000 men was needed to drive over Kicking Horse Pass, 1,628m (5,340ft) up among the towering peaks, and down a dizzying descent on the other side.

The original plan was to follow the Columbia River, but a surveyor named A. B. Rogers discovered a pass, now named after him, through the Selkirk Mountains, saving 241km (150 miles). Because of avalanches the line had to be protected with miles of snowsheds, and later a tunnel was driven through the worst section.

Beyond Shuswap Lake the track threaded through the Coast Mountains by way of the wild Fraser Canyon, which Van Horne described as one of the worst places in the world. The line was intended to end at Port Moody on Burrard Inlet, but Van Horne pushed it down the inlet to the site of what is now Vancouver.

The railway line opened central and western Canada to settlers, who came swarming in by the thousands. Winnipeg thrived on its rail yards and the tide of immigrants pouring through to the prairies. Regina was created by the railroad and was named in tribute to Queen Victoria when the first train arrived in 1882. Banff, the first major Rocky Mountain tourist resort, was named by the president of the Canadian Pacific Railway, a Scotsman originally from Banffshire.

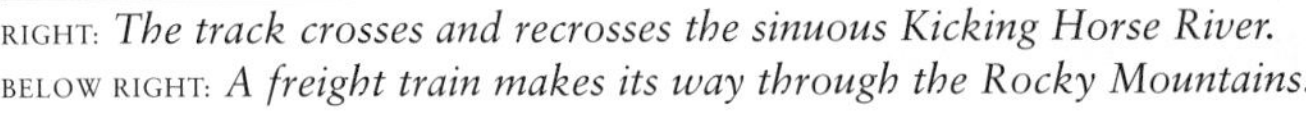

RIGHT: *The track crosses and recrosses the sinuous Kicking Horse River.*
BELOW RIGHT: *A freight train makes its way through the Rocky Mountains.*

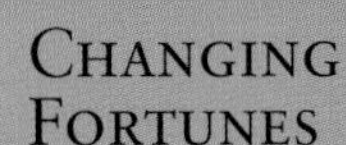

Changing Fortunes

The completion of North America's oldest transcontinental rail line marked a spectacular engineering feat, and trains continued to run between Montréal and Vancouver for over 100 years. The service was discontinued in 1990, and the line given over to commercial traffic.

However, since 2000 the CPR-owned *Royal Canadian Pacific* has run tours along sections of the route every year between May and November, using cars from the vintage fleet that date from between 1916 and 1931. The Canadian Railway Museum at St Constant, in the southern suburbs of Montréal, has a collection of items relevant to the line.

See also:
The Trans-Siberian Railway 66-7

66 **Niagara Falls,** Canada/USA

the facts

- The Horseshoe Falls in Canada form an arc about 792m (2,600ft) long.
- The American Falls in the USA form a straight line about 305m (1,000ft) long.
- Lake Erie's outflow pours into Lake Ontario via the 56-km (35 mile) Niagara River down a drop of 100m (330ft).

Niagara Falls

A spume of spray lifts high into the air as the dark green waters of the Niagara River thunder into the frothing cauldron at the base of the falls. There are two parts to this famous waterfall: the American Falls and the Horseshoe Falls. Between them is Goat Island, a tree-covered islet that sits in the middle of the river.

The Horseshoe Falls, on the Canadian side of the border, are perhaps the better known of the two. A road beside the river gives a good view of the falls at very close range, where the surface of the water has the appearance of dark green glass, turning to foaming white as it slides over the cliffs. The American Falls are smaller and have piles of broken rocks at their base, as opposed to the sheer plunge of the Horseshoe Falls. Both waterfalls are about 50m (165ft) high.

The Niagara Falls have been in existence only for around 10,000 years—a relatively short time in geological terms. Above the falls the river bedrock is hard dolomite, but underneath the dolomite are layers of softer rocks such as shale and sandstone. Originally the river dropped over an escarpment about 11km (7 miles) north of the present falls, but as the softer rocks underneath the dolomite were eroded by the fast-flowing water, the dolomite collapsed. Bit by bit the waterfall retreated, so that the falls today are a long way from where they were 10,000 years ago, and in their retreat they have left behind a deep gorge. The falls moved back at a rate of about 1m (3ft) per year, and are about 305m (1,000ft) farther upstream than they were when Louis Hennepin, the French explorer, saw them in 1678. However, Goat Island has divided the river in two, and this, coupled with the fact that at least half the water of the Niagara is channelled away from the waterfalls to generate electricity, means that the falls are much more stable now than they were in the past.

Bridges and parks on both sides of the river provide good vantage points. One of the most popular is Rainbow Bridge, named after the rainbows that shimmer in the spray above the falls. The sheer power and size of Niagara is best seen from the boats that brave the churning waters beneath the falls.

ABOVE AND BELOW: *The little* Maid of the Mist *carries plastic-wrapped thrill-seekers into the Niagara Falls spray.*

Canada's Other Waterfalls

Canada is the world's second largest country, so it is no surprise that it has many other spectacular waterfalls. At Virginia Falls in the Northwest Territories the South Nahanni River thunders over a precipice almost twice the height of Niagara. This little-known river descends 915m (3,000ft) over a distance of 595km (370 miles) in a series of tumbling rapids and deep gorges.

The Hunlen Falls and the Helmcken Falls are both in British Columbia. At the Helmcken Falls, the Murtle River cascades over a cliff of ancient rock to a spray-filled basin 137m (450ft) below. The Hunlen Falls are seven times the height of Niagara, and drop in a curtain of spray 366m (1,200ft) to the rocks below.

ABOVE: *The Skylon Tower's observation deck offers a bird's-eye view of the Horseshoe Falls.* RIGHT: *Floodlighting transforms the falls by night.*

Over the Falls

Some people have taken the sheer power and size of the Niagara Falls as an irresistible personal challenge. Several adventurers have gone over the falls, in a variety of different vessels including barrels, boats and sealed capsules.

One of the most famous death-defying escapades took place on 30 June 1859, when Jean François Gravelet, better known as Charles Blondin, crossed the falls on a tightrope. The rope was 335m (1,100ft) long, and suspended 49m (160ft) above the falls. Evidently Blondin found the whole experience a little too tame: a year later he made the crossing again, but this time with his agent on his back.

See also:
Angel Falls 194
Iguaçu Falls 202-3
Victoria Falls 140-1

67 **The CN Tower,** Canada

- The Tower measures 553.3m (1,815ft 5in) to the top of its antenna and took 40 months to build.
- Visitor figures to the Tower currently average around two million a year.
- Initial proposals for three towers interlinked by bridges were rejected as impractical.

the **facts**

The **CN Tower**

Canada's National Tower, the world's tallest building, receives and transmits signals at a point well above the mass of Toronto's high-rise buildings. It is also a world-famous landmark, entertainment complex and tourist attraction.

Before work began on the Tower in February 1973, members of the planning team embarked on a fact-finding world tour to inspect other towers. Theirs was to be the biggest, and it was also to be the very best possible in terms of visitor facilities. Far from keeping the public at bay, it would welcome large numbers of them and offer the opportunity to look out over not just Toronto but distances up to 100 miles. The designers produced a scheme for a fine, needlelike tower equipped with a so-called Main Pod—a circular capsule housing indoor and outdoor observation galleries, the Horizons restaurant, and a revolving restaurant, called 360 The Restaurant, at a height of 351m (1,151ft). The world's highest observation gallery, known as the SkyPod, provides even more remarkable views at 447m (1,465ft). At this height it is sometimes possible to feel the building move at the top due to the Tower's wind resistance, but don't worry—this is as it should be. All very tall structures are designed to cope with turbulence at altitude—they would be dangerous if they did not yield slightly.

Although many of the construction problems faced by the designers, engineers and builders were similar to those tackled in other high-rise buildings, because of its height, this project was a venture into uncharted territory, and it was essential that the expertise of everyone involved could be relied upon completely. No individual architect or engineer is credited with the overall design. The CN Tower as it stands today evolved over a number of years as a result of teamwork.

The story of the Tower's construction is well illustrated through a series of displays and kiosks on the Mezzanine. It is a tale of scarcely believable statistics involving 40,523.8 cu m (53,000 cubic yards) of concrete, 128.7km (80 miles) of post-tensioned steel and 4,535 tonnes (5,000 tons) of reinforcing steel. The total weight of the building is calculated at 117,910 tonnes (130,000 tons) and the whole thing was built by 1,537 workers. For the foundations alone it was necessary to move over 63,000 tonnes (69,440 tons) of earth and shale, digging up to 15m (50ft) deep.

The Tallest Towers

The Eiffel Tower held the record for the world's tallest building from 1889 until 1931, when the Empire State Building succeeded to the title. Forty years later, in 1971, the Ostankino Tower in Moscow rose to 537m (1,761ft), only to be surpassed in 1975 by the CN Tower—a record it still holds. While a century ago a tower of 305m (1,000ft) was considered an astonishing achievement, today a building of 610m (2,000ft) appears to be well within the bounds of possibility. One day, perhaps, a new structure will relegate the CN Tower to second place.

Psychology and Elevators

Six elevators travel up the Tower at a speed of 6m (20ft) a second; they transport approximately 1,200 people up and down in a single hour. The journey to the Main Pod takes 58 seconds, a rate of ascent similar to that experienced at takeoff in a jet plane.

The designers of the Tower realized that the combination of speed, height and restricted space could unnerve some visitors, so psychologists were called in to offer advice. As a result the design of the elevator cars gives the sense of being in a safe, secure cocoon, and their speed, calculated for maximum comfort, can be reduced during windy conditions. Each elevator has one glass wall which gives spectacular views.

ABOVE: *A retractable roof on the Skydome Stadium, home of the Toronto Blue Jays, allows spectators a great view of the Tower.*
LEFT: *Looking down over Toronto from the SkyPod.*
ABOVE RIGHT: *Dominating the skyline of Toronto, the CN Tower looms above the skyscrapers.*

See also:
The Eiffel Tower 26-9
The Empire State Building 162-3
The Leaning Tower of Pisa 44-5

68 The Statue of Liberty, USA

The Statue of Liberty

The best known statue in North America—perhaps in the world—was dedicated by President Grover Cleveland on 28 October 1886 to the roar of a 21-gun salute, the blasts of ships' foghorns and a din of fireworks. Ever since that day, the towering figure holding Liberty's torch has been the first sight of America for passengers entering New York Harbour, and for many thousands of immigrants it has represented a promise of freedom from oppression and poverty.

The statue had its origins in French politics. In 1865, when Emperor Napoleon III was on the throne, an academic named Edouard de Laboulaye and his circle hatched the idea of a 'Statue of Liberty', to express approval of the great republic across the Atlantic and underline their own hopes for an end to the monarchy and the establishment of a new French Republic. A sculptor from Alsace, Frédéric-Auguste Bartholdi (1834-1904), was encouraged by Laboulaye to consider the project. He was helped in his task by engineer Gustave Eiffel, creator of the Eiffel Tower, and Eiffel's head of research, Maurice Koechlin.

Bartholdi had planned to build a lighthouse for the Suez Canal in the form of a colossal female figure holding a torch aloft to symbolize the light of progress coming to Asia. He adapted this idea to the new project with enthusiasm, inspired in his modelling of Liberty by Delacroix's famous painting *Liberty Guiding the People*, and basing her stern features on his own mother's face.

The huge size of the statue and its exposure to wind and weather posed severe technical problems for Bartholdi and the engineering team. Eiffel built an ingenious iron framework supported by a central pylon, and onto this flexible interior skeleton was attached the statue's visible outer layer of copper, only 2.4mm (0.09in) thick. Starting with a model 1.2m (4ft) tall, Bartholdi then made three

the facts

- Marking the entrance to New York Harbor, the Statue of Liberty is seen as the symbol of freedom.
- Liberty's star-shaped pedestal was designed by American architect Richard Morris Hunt.
- The statue is 46m (151ft) high.

Vital Statistics

The Statue of Liberty itself is 46m (151ft) high and stands on Richard Morris Hunt's pedestal which is 47m (154ft) high. The tip of the torch is 93m (305ft) above the ground. The statue weighs a huge 229 tonnes (225 tons) and is 10.6m (35ft) around the waist.

The mouth is 91cm (3ft) wide and the right arm (which is the one holding the torch), is 12.8m (42ft) long. The index finger alone is 2.4m (8ft) long, which is far taller than the average man. The tablet in the statue's left hand is 7.2m (23ft) long, 4.1m (13ft) wide and 61cm (2ft) thick.

RIGHT AND BELOW: *There are plenty of images of the statue in NYC.*

the **history**

1884
Frédéric-Auguste Bartholdi completes his sculpture of Liberty.

1886
Pedestal construction completed in the US.

1901
Statue placed in care of the War Department.

1924
Fort Wood's star-shaped walls and the statue within it decared a National Monument.

1956
Bedloe's Island renamed Liberty Island.

1984
Designated a World Heritage Site.

ABOVE: *The statue was first constructed in Paris, then dismantled for reassembly in New York.*

ABOVE: *The statue dominates the skyline of New York.*
LEFT: *The monument attracts more than four million visitors a year.*

THE GOLDEN DOOR

The Statue of Liberty inspired Emma Lazarus to write her poem *The New Colossus* (1903), describing the 'huddled masses' and 'wretched refuse' of the Old World coming to be welcomed by Liberty's lamp, lifted 'beside the golden door'.

From 1892 onwards the huddled masses actually arrived at nearby Ellis Island, where boatloads of immigrants were processed through a succession of bureaucratic and health checks, in an intense atmosphere of nervous apprehension mingled with hope and excitement. An average of 2,000 new arrivals a day passed through the great hall in the busiest period in the early 1900s. In its peak year of 1907 Ellis Island handled more than a million people.

Not everyone had a chance of becoming an American citizen, however. In 1790 a law was passed stating that only white people could be naturalized, and this law was not overturned until 1952. The Ellis Island immigration station closed in 1954, and the complex has been restored as a national monument.

LEFT: *There are 168 steps in the spiral staircase inside the statue, with rest areas at every third turn of the spiral.*

more, each bigger than the last, until the full magnificent size was reached. The final statue was constructed in Paris, where it was formally presented to the American ambassador on 4 July 1884 as a gift from the French to the American people. It was then taken to pieces and shipped in crates to New York, where it was reassembled on the massive pedestal built for it at American expense on Bedloe's Island (now Liberty Island).

The figure has the broken shackles of tyranny at her feet. In her left hand she holds a tablet which represents the Declaration of Independence. She wears a crown of seven rays, with the rays standing for freedom spreading across the seven continents. A spiral staircase inside the statue leads to the crown (a climb equivalent to walking up a 12-floor building), but this has been closed to the public since September 2001.

See also:
The Lincoln Memorial 158-9
Mount Rushmore 160-1

the facts

- Lincoln's statue is 5.8m (19ft) high and the same wide.
- The memorial colonnade is 57m (188ft) long by 36m (118ft) wide.
- There are 38 columns. Each is 13.4m (44ft) high with a diameter of 2.26m (7ft 5in) at the base.
- The inner chamber is 28m (60ft) high.

The Lincoln Memorial

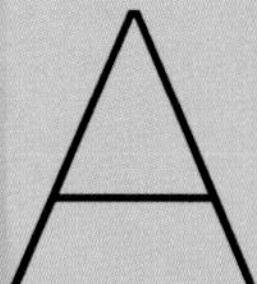

Abraham Lincoln's monument in Washington DC is a dignified, restrained and moving tribute to the man and to the virtues of tolerance, honesty and constancy that he represented. Within two years of the American president's death in 1865 there were proposals for a memorial in Washington, but not until 1915 was the foundation stone laid. The memorial was dedicated on 30 May 1922.

The Last Act

On the evening of 14 April 1865, five days after the surrender of the Confederate Army under General Robert E Lee at Appomattox Court House, President Lincoln and his wife attended Ford's Theater in Washington to see a comedy called *Our American Cousin*. At 10.15pm a deranged actor called John Wilkes Booth shot and wounded the President. Lincoln was carried to the house across the street, where he remained unconscious in one of the bedrooms. Mrs Lincoln, who was in a hysterical state, waited as members of the Cabinet gathered at the house. At 7.22am Edwin M Stanton, Secretary of War, emerged from the bedroom to announce the President's death with the words: 'Now he belongs to the ages'. Lincoln was 56. Ford's Theater has been restored, with a museum of Lincoln relics and objects. The house where Lincoln died is also open to the public.

Daniel Chester French

French (1850–1931) was one of the most popular and successful sculptors of his day. Born in Exeter, New Hampshire, he started on his career path as a boy, carving comical figures out of turnips. He studied in Boston and New York and at the age of 24 received his first commission—a statue of *The Minute Man,* which stands on the Green in Concord, Massachusetts, commemorating the Battle of Lexington and Concord (1775) during the American Revolution.

After spending a year in Italy French returned to Washington, where he opened a studio and made his reputation as America's foremost monumental sculptor, making him a natural choice for this important memorial.

LEFT: *The Lincoln statue looks out through the colonnade.*

LEFT: *Daniel French, America's most admired sculptor of the day, carved out the massive statue from 28 separate blocks of Georgia marble.*

Its designer was architect Henry Bacon, a specialist in monuments who was also responsible for a memorial to Lincoln in the city of Lincoln, Nebraska.

A Fitting Memorial

Washington's Lincoln Memorial is in the form of a classical Greek temple, echoing the design of the Parthenon in Athens. The rectangular building is flanked by 38 doric columns of white Colorado marble, two of which are set back slightly and mark the entrance. The remaining 36 stand for the 36 states of the Union at the time the memorial was dedicated.

Inside, a colossal statue by Daniel Chester French shows the President seated in a massive chair, in a mood of contemplation that visitors can interpret as they will. The whole statue seems to be carved from one immense block of marble, but is in fact made of pieces so smoothly fitted together that the joints are invisible.

Beyond the President's head is an inscription: 'In this temple, as in the hearts of the people for whom he saved the Union, the memory of Abraham Lincoln is enshrined forever'. Also cut into the walls are the words of two of his great speeches, the Gettysburg Address of 1863 and the Second Inaugural Address of 1865. There are murals by Jules Guérin on the themes of the reconciliation of North and South after the American Civil War, and the freeing of the slaves.

The monument is floodlit at night to spectacular effect and a wreath is placed every year on 12 February, Lincoln's birthday. There are guided tours of the caves underneath the building, with their stalagmites and stalactites. The Lincoln Memorial is close to the Potomac River, aligned with the Capitol and the Washington Monument, toward which stretches the beautiful Reflecting Pool. To the west, crossing the Potomac, is the Arlington Memorial Bridge, itself a symbol of the reconciliation of North and South on which President Lincoln set his heart.

LEFT: *The monument, in the style of a Greek temple, has 38 doric columns.*

See also:
Mount Rushmore 160-1
The Statue of Liberty 154-7

The monument cost almost $1m to create.

The presidents' faces are carved 18m (60ft) high on the rockface.

Sculptor Gutzon Borglum was determined to include Roosevelt in the group because of the sculptural challenge posed by his glasses.

the **facts**

Mount Rushmore

Carved in the granite of Mount Rushmore in South Dakota, four huge faces of American presidents gaze out upon the world: George Washington, Thomas Jefferson, Theodore Roosevelt and Abraham Lincoln.

The idea of the monument was originally conceived by local historian and publicist Doane Robinson as a spectacular project to draw tourists to the beautiful Black Hills. In 1924 he interested sculptor Gutzon Borglum in this mammoth project, and it was decided to create a 'shrine to democracy'.

Borglum was 60 when work began at Mount Rushmore in 1927 and it preoccupied him for the rest of his life. He designed the monument and directed the sizeable workforce of local masons and miners, who blasted the mountain face with dynamite and shaped the great heads with hammer and chisel, while dangling precariously on swaying platforms. Borglum intended the presidents to be shown down to waist level. As the project was never finished, it has been remarked that it was just as well that he started with the heads.

At Mount Rushmore, Borglum had fierce arguments with the National Park Service, and his work was constantly interrupted by shortage of funds and bad weather. All the same, Washington's head was formally unveiled in 1930, Jefferson's in 1936, Lincoln's in 1937 and Roosevelt's in 1939. After Borglum died in 1941, his son, Lincoln, worked on it for a while until the money ran out.

Gutzon Borglum's Vision

Borglum had ideas as grandiose as his name, which in full was John Gutzon de la Mothe Borglum. He was born in 1867 near Bear Creek, Idaho, of Danish Mormon immigrants. At his Roman Catholic boarding school in Xavier, Kansas, Borglum impressed his Jesuit teachers with his drawing skills and later he studied art in Paris, where he met the great sculptor Auguste Rodin. After returning to the US he was invited, in 1915, to carve a giant head of General Robert E. Lee at Stone Mountain, near Atlanta, Georgia. Borglum transformed this project into a parade 0.5km (0.25 mile) long of Confederate infantry and cavalry to be carved out of the mountain, with heroic figures of Stonewall Jackson and Jefferson Davis as well as Lee himself, all on horseback. However, Borglum and the committee could not come to terms, and the project never came to fruition.

BELOW: *Film director Alfred Hitchcock made the most of the presidential faces in a famous scene in his 1959 movie,* North by Northwest, *in which actors Cary Grant and Eva-Marie Saint flee across the giant features.*

Sacred Ground

The Black Hills were sacred territory to the Sioux, and the United States government confirmed this in a treaty of 1868 for 'as long as rivers run and grass grows and trees bear leaves'. This proved not to be as long as expected, because in 1874 gold was discovered in the hills at French Creek.

Prospectors swarmed in and the Native Americans went to war. They won a famous victory at the Battle of Little Bighorn (1876), where General George Armstrong Custer and his force of cavalry were wiped out to the last man. However, the Native Americans eventually lost the war and white settlers took over.

BELOW: *A visitor centre has been built into the rock below the massive heads, but the best views are from the regular helicopter trips.*

Indian Shrine

Not far from Mount Rushmore and just a few miles north of the town of Custer, another enormous figure is being carved in the living rock of a mountain. Designed by the late Korczak Ziolkowski, it is to depict the great Native American leader Crazy Horse (1849-77), bare-chested and on horseback, in a carving 172m (563ft) high and 195m (641ft) long. The sculptor was commissioned in 1939 by Sioux chiefs, who wanted to show that 'the red men had great heroes too'.

Since Ziolkowski's death in 1982 at the age of 74, work has continued, as the great sculptor left detailed instructions for the completion of the project.

See also:
The Lincoln Memorial 158-9
The Statue of Liberty 154-7

The world's tallest building between 1931 and 1971, and the tallest building in New York City.

On a clear day, you can see as far as 130km (80 miles) away.

The TV antenna on the top of the building, installed in 1985, is 22 floors high.

the **facts**

The **Empire State Building**

This towering edifice is a potent symbol of the excitement, glamour and sheer exuberant excessiveness of New York City. For more than 40 years it lodged itself firmly in everyone's mind as the world's tallest building, and although it has been overtaken by younger rivals, it is still for many people the skyscraper of skyscrapers. To make way for the building the most select hotel in town, the Waldorf-Astoria, was demolished.

The building's statistics are appropriately awesome. Its 102 floors rise to a height of 381m (1,250ft) and the television tower on top makes the total height 449m (1,472ft). It was originally planned to moor airships to the top of it, but the idea was abandoned. The building occupies a site of some 0.8ha (2 acres) on Fifth Avenue. Although it weighs a mammoth 331,000 tonnes (325,704 tons), the foundations are only two floors deep, but it is held upright by steel beams weighing 54,400 tonnes (43,530 tons). The staircase from the ground level to the top (the 102nd floor) has 1,860 steps; once a year there's a race up the 1,576 steps to the 86th-floor observatory (the winning time is just under ten minutes).

Viewing a Modern Icon

With so many other tall office blocks all around it, it is difficult to get a good view of the great building at ground level. It was designed in a simple and elegant Art Deco style. The stone façade has strips of stainless steel running up it, and the higher levels are neatly set back. Inside, the

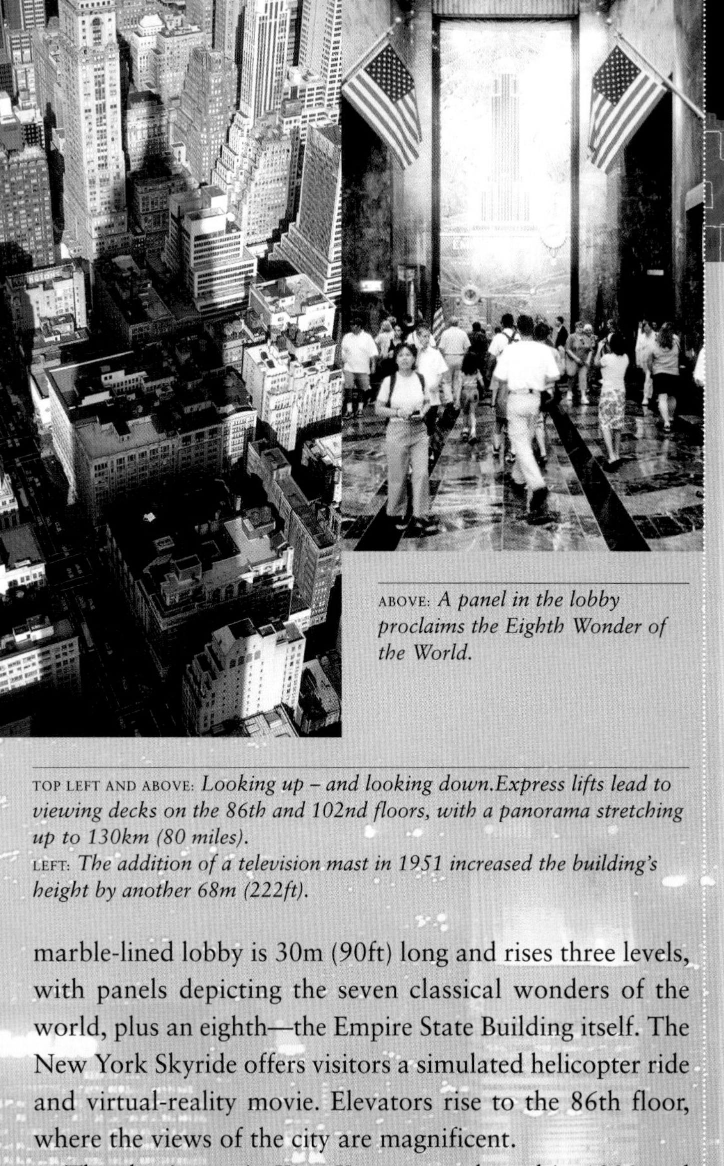

ABOVE: *A panel in the lobby proclaims the Eighth Wonder of the World.*

TOP LEFT AND ABOVE: *Looking up – and looking down.Express lifts lead to viewing decks on the 86th and 102nd floors, with a panorama stretching up to 130km (80 miles).*

LEFT: *The addition of a television mast in 1951 increased the building's height by another 68m (222ft).*

marble-lined lobby is 30m (90ft) long and rises three levels, with panels depicting the seven classical wonders of the world, plus an eighth—the Empire State Building itself. The New York Skyride offers visitors a simulated helicopter ride and virtual-reality movie. Elevators rise to the 86th floor, where the views of the city are magnificent.

The classic movie *King Kong* was released in 1933 and planted the building's image firmly in audiences' minds by showing the monster gorilla clinging to it while beating off attacking planes, but it was also the year of the building's first suicide. Catastrophe followed in 1945 when a plane crashed into the 79th floor, causing 14 deaths and $1 million worth of damage.

Reach for the Skies

Named in compliment to the state of New York (nicknamed the Empire State) and designed by Shreve, Harmon and Lamb, the building cost $41 million—well below estimate—and was erected at a speed that has never been surpassed. It rose at the rate of over four floors a week, and in one hectic period, over 14 floors were added in 10 days.

The building was opened in May 1931, but with the United States in the grip of the Depression the space proved hard to rent. For a while it was sardonically known as the Empty State Building. In fact it took ten years for the office space—which can accommodate 15,000 people—to be fully occupied.

See also:
The CN Tower 152-3
The Petronas Towers 225
Taipei 101 Tower 225

Buildings are much more than just floor, walls and roof. They may represent political power or personal wealth or provide refuge or a space for contemplation. Some are simply functional, while others are objects of beauty. Yet architecture has the potential to provoke controversy, as it forms such a vital part of our everyday environment.

the facts

- In 2003 Taiwan's 101 skyscraper became the latest record-holder as the world's tallest building, standing at 508m (1,676 feet).
- The 1997 Guggenheim Museum in Bilbao is coated in 30,000 glittering titanium sheets.
- The Winter Palace in St Petersburg is made of five million bricks and has over 700 rooms.

Great Architecture

GRAND PLANS

When the Palace of Versailles near Paris was built, it was the envy of heads of state the world over. Built for Louis XIV in the 17th century, it combines immensity, regularity and sheer splendour to convey his status and harmonious reign. Over a thousand years earlier Emperor Vespasian had used the construction of the Colosseum in a similar way. However, as well as flaunting his power, the Colosseum provided entertainment for Rome's grateful citizens.

It was personal indulgence that inspired Bavarian King Ludwig II's castle at Neuschwanstein near Munich, which is a riot of mock-medievalism, and it was newspaper magnate William Randolph Hearst's private wealth which enabled him to spend vast amounts on examples or copies of the world's great art and architecture for his 1919 Californian mansion Hearst's Castle.

ORIGINALS

Some of the greatest modern buildings are truly original, such as Richard Rogers' Pompidou Centre in Paris which wears its innards—pipes, vents and ducts—on the outside. Other unique buildings are Jørn Utzon's Sydney Opera House, which floats on Sydney Harbour like a surreal swan or a flotilla of yachts, and Antoni Gaudí's Sagrada Família church in Barcelona, with its exuberant, organic coronet of towers, which is still taking shape over a century after work began.

PEACE AND QUIET

Many buildings celebrate faith, and as such, are designed to provide a tranquil place for prayer and peaceful contemplation. They can also be incredibly beautiful because of their scale, their design or the art on the walls. In Istanbul in Turkey the Blue Mosque's symmetrical exterior conceals interior decoration of overwhelming intricacy, namely thousands of tiles. Chartres Cathedral in France uses rich blues to sublime effect in its stained-glass windows, adding to an overall impression of height and space.

Secular architecture can also encourage serenity. Think of the streams and tranquil courtyards of the Alhambra in Granada in southern Spain. Perhaps the best-loved (and most recognizable), place of peace is the Taj Mahal, a tomb and memorial of exquisite grace, whose appeal, though indefinable is universal.

CLOCKWISE FROM TOP LEFT:
Photographing the Guggenheim Museum in Bilbao, Spain; the Acropolis in Athens, Greece; Hindu deities on the Sri Mariamman Temple in Singapore; Roman remains at Ephesus, Turkey; the old city of Ayutthaya in Thailand; the Golden Pavilion of the Kinkakuji Temple in Kyoto, Japan; the futuristic Burj Al Arab Hotel, part of the Jumeirah Beach Resort complex, in Dubai; the Reichstag Dome, designed by Sir Norman Foster, in Berlin, Germany.

See also:
Sagrada Familia 60-1
Sydney Opera House 214-17
Versailles 24-5

the facts

- Zion Canyon in Utah is only 24km (15 miles) long, but in places reaches a depth of 762m (2,500ft).
- At its northern end, in a section known as the Narrows, only 6m (20ft) separates the cliffs.
- It is possible to hike along the Narrows in the dry season, although there is a danger from flash floods.

Zion National Park

Thousands of years ago, a small stream meandered its way across the soft young rocks of a plateau on its way southwards. As the land rose, the stream began to cut itself a path, scouring the underlying rock with particles of grit and sand eroded from further upstream. The result of this was Zion Canyon, a winding gorge slicing through the Navajo sandstone to the older, underlying Kaibab limestone.

The Mormons discovered and named Zion Canyon in the 1860s, though it was not surveyed until 1872. In 1919, 383sq km (148 square miles) of the wilderness surrounding the canyon was designated as a national park. In 1956 this was enlarged to include an area of 596sq km (230 square miles). Zion National Park is a fascinating array of rock formations, mainly carved out of the predominant Navajo sandstone. The overwhelming image of the park is of towering cliffs, forbidding domes and deep chasms, ranging from deep glowing red to a delicate rose-pink.

Stunning Natural Features

Zion has many extraordinary natural features. Checkerboard Mesa is a great slab of sandstone looming over the road, its surface intricately carved into squares by the effects of wind and water. In Verkin Canyon, a natural

America's National Beauty

About 310,000sq km (120,300 square miles) of the US in about 320 different sites come under the care of the National Park Service, which covers historical sites as well as sites of natural wonder. These include battlefields (such as Saratoga and Gettysburg), early trading posts and archaeological sites where evidence of Indian settlement has been discovered.

The first national park, founded in 1872—and which remains one of the most popular in America—was Yellowstone. Since then many other sites have been considered important parts of America's heritage, and their protection has been assured by their designation as national parks or national monuments.

BELOW: *A spectacular view of Zion Canyon from Canyon Overlook shows the erosion of the red sandstone, scoured out by the North Fork Virgin River.*

BRYCE CANYON

Bryce Canyon National Park lies only a short distance from Zion. Water has raged across the sedimentary rocks, eroding them into a complex system of ravines and gullies, a process that is continuing today as flash floods cause walls to split and columns to collapse. Metallic minerals mixed in with the sediments have produced rocks of rich reds and oranges, and even pale mauve in places.

The Pink Cliffs escarpment is perhaps the best-known area, containing a fantastic jumble of pinnacles, ravines and oddly shaped pillars. The first European pioneer to explore the area, Ebenezer Bryce, remarked this is 'one heck of a place to lose a cow'.

LEFT: *The Great Arch is one of several extraordinary natural features in the rock.*

arch spans between two cliff faces, while Great White Throne stands flat-topped and massive among towering red cliffs. The highest point in the park is the West Temple, towering 1,158m (3,800ft) above the canyon base. The Towers of the Virgin are a group of jagged sandstone peaks ranging along the west wall of the canyon, and the natural amphitheatre of the Temple of Sinawava provides splendid views of the surrounding cliffs and domes.

Another well known feature is the Weeping Rock, where water from springs higher up the rock trickles across its surface, dropping like tears from its overhangs. A similar phenomenon occurs at Hanging Gardens, but instead of dripping away, the water is absorbed by the plants that cling precariously to its slopes.

The pale sides of Zion Canyon's west rim show clear lines where the Navajo sandstone has been formed in neat, regular layers. Fast-running water has scoured out caves, which provide shelter for a variety of birds, small mammals and insects. In some of the larger caves, archaeologists have discovered items from ancient Pueblo Indian settlements.

See also:
Redwood National Park 178
Sequoia National Park 178
Yosemite National Park 166-7

73 The Hoover Dam, USA

the facts

- There is as much steel in the Hoover Dam as in the Empire State Building.
- When formally dedicating the dam in 1936, President Roosevelt called it the Boulder Dam, which it remained until 1947, when Congress restored the original name.
- The dam drains an area covering 7.7 percent of the US.

The Hoover Dam

From its headwaters in the Rocky Mountains the mighty Colorado River flows southwest across the states of Colorado and Utah and through the Grand Canyon, to form the border between Arizona and Nevada and then between Arizona and California, before crossing into Mexico and finally reaching the sea in the Gulf of California. In 1905 this unpredictable river abruptly changed course, creating the 777sq km (300 square miles) of the Salton Sea and threatening to inundate the entire Imperial Valley in California. To bring the river under control and improve irrigation, and at the same time generate electricity, it was

Boulder City

When word of the dam project first got out legions of unemployed men made their way to the site and camped out in the desert in the hope of being given work. Those who were engaged endured horrific conditions, and lived in improvised shelters, some along with their wives and children.

Eventually the long-promised new homes were built for the dam's workforce, giving simple accommodation to 4,000 people, and Boulder City, a pleasant little community, grew up. Part of the motivation for building it was to segregate the workers from the nearby fleshpots of Las Vegas.

decided to build a vast dam on the river along the Arizona-Nevada border. Congress provided the money in 1928, and construction work began in 1931. As Herbert Hoover was president at the time and had taken a vigorous interest in the project, the dam was given his name.

The dam, at that time the biggest ever built, is a huge mass of 2.5 million cu m (3.25 million cubic yards) of concrete. Over eight million tonnes (seven million tons) of rock had to be excavated to build it. It is 201m (660ft) thick at the base and stands 221m (726ft) high—about the height of a 70-floor skyscraper. It measures 379m (1,244ft) along the top and is 14m (45ft) thick at that point.

Immediately to the north, the dam created Lake Mead, one of the largest manmade reservoirs in the world. Today it is run by the National Park Service and used for sailing, boating and other water sports.

Valley of Fire

North of Lake Mead lies the spectacular 14,165ha (35,000-acre) Valley of Fire National Park, so named because the sandstone rocks here are a fiery shade of red, before toning down to shades of tangerine and lavender. Wind and weather have carved these sandstone rocks into domes, beehives and other weird shapes, including a particularly dramatic one that looks like the head and trunk of an elephant. On some of the rocks are mysterious carvings and paintings made centuries ago by the Anasazi people, ancestors of today's Pueblo Indians and best known for their remarkable cliff dwellings. Whether the marks are a language or a form of map is not known. Ten thousand or more of these people lived in a 'lost city' on the banks of the Muddy River near by, in an area now partly covered by Lake Mead.

See also:
Aswan High Dam 121
Itaipú Dam 224
The Three Gorges Dam 90-1

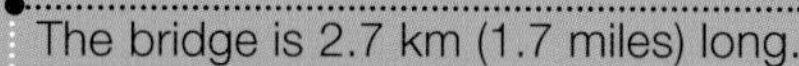

the facts

- The bridge is 2.7 km (1.7 miles) long.
- For over 20 years it had the longest suspension span in the world—1,280m (4,200ft).
- The towers rise 227m (746ft) above the level of high tide.
- Each cable is 93 cm (36.5in) in diameter and composed of 27,572 separate strands of wire.

The Golden Gate Bridge

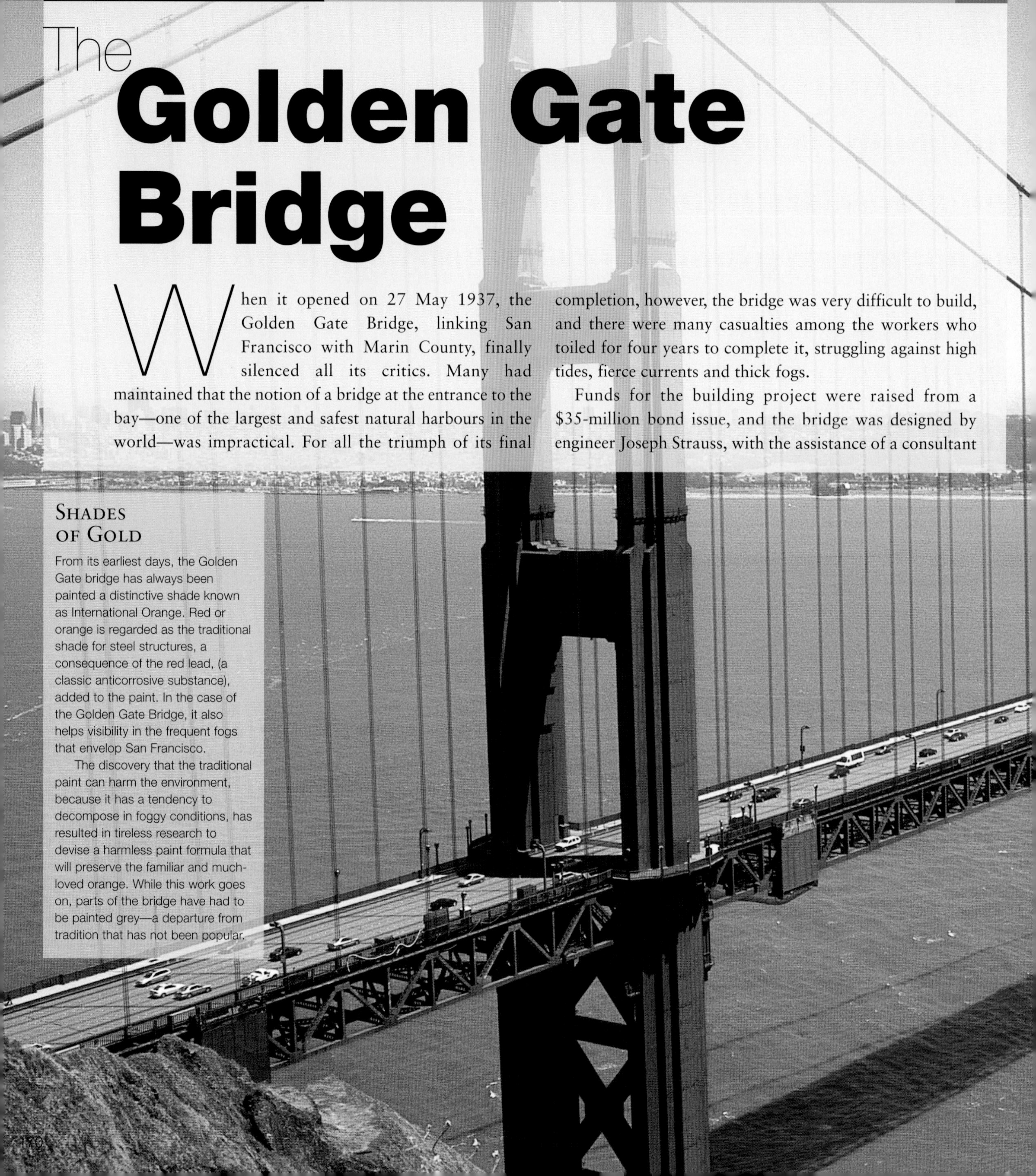

When it opened on 27 May 1937, the Golden Gate Bridge, linking San Francisco with Marin County, finally silenced all its critics. Many had maintained that the notion of a bridge at the entrance to the bay—one of the largest and safest natural harbours in the world—was impractical. For all the triumph of its final completion, however, the bridge was very difficult to build, and there were many casualties among the workers who toiled for four years to complete it, struggling against high tides, fierce currents and thick fogs.

Funds for the building project were raised from a $35-million bond issue, and the bridge was designed by engineer Joseph Strauss, with the assistance of a consultant

Shades of Gold

From its earliest days, the Golden Gate bridge has always been painted a distinctive shade known as International Orange. Red or orange is regarded as the traditional shade for steel structures, a consequence of the red lead, (a classic anticorrosive substance), added to the paint. In the case of the Golden Gate Bridge, it also helps visibility in the frequent fogs that envelop San Francisco.

The discovery that the traditional paint can harm the environment, because it has a tendency to decompose in foggy conditions, has resulted in tireless research to devise a harmless paint formula that will preserve the familiar and much-loved orange. While this work goes on, parts of the bridge have had to be painted grey—a departure from tradition that has not been popular.

architect, Irving Morrow, who introduced some Art Deco detailing. The foundations for the south tower proved the most hazardous part of the job. Workers had to balance on barges, tossed by huge tidal swells, as they constructed a vast concrete fender into which the bridge caissons could be sunk.

Once the two towers were in place, equally courageous workmen had to clamber along catwalks slung between them in order to position the suspension cables. For the first time on a major building project a safety net was installed and as a result 19 men survived after falling off the catwalks. Tragically, on 17 February 1937 a platform fell onto the net and broke it, killing ten men.

The strength of the bridge is awesome, with each tower carrying a vertical load of 95 million kg (210 million lb) from each cable, and each shore anchorage block required to withstand a pull of 28.5 million kg (63 million lb). The main parts of the tower legs were riveted in place at their manufactories in Pennsylvania to check that they fitted, before being dismantled and transported to the site.

The Golden Gate Bridge has become a key symbol of San Francisco. Despite the noise and pollution generated by the 125,000 cars that cross it every day, the pedestrian path along the bridge is a popular one, and it provides a setting much used by film directors. During a party held to celebrate the 50th anniversary of the bridge in 1987, the whole structure was closed to traffic so that all the party-goers could walk across. As it happened, there were simply too many of them, and the idea had to be abandoned on the grounds of practicality and safety.

Golden Gate Park

A 405-ha (1,000 acre) park lies south of the Golden Gate Bridge and stretches eastward almost halfway across San Francisco. Work on the park began in 1870. The park's original designer, William Hammond Hall, was succeeded by Scotsman John McLaren, who devoted 56 years to its care and nurture. McLaren, who is estimated to have planted two million trees, successfully transformed an unpromising area of shifting sand dunes into mature and thriving gardens.

He is reported to have made a number of rules for the administration of the park. No workman was to wear gloves or to smoke during working hours, signs forbidding people to walk on the grass were outlawed, and garden statuary was treated with suspicion and likely to be hidden behind thick shrubs or bushes.

ABOVE: The high tidal swell in the Golden Gate channel added to construction difficulties.
LEFT: Around 125,000 vehicles cross the toll bridge every day.

See also:
The Kapellbrücke 38-9
Sydney Harbour Bridge 217

the facts

- The base of the Devil's Tower is 305m (1,000ft) in diameter.
- From its base the tower is 264m (865ft) tall.
- It rises 396m (1,300ft) above the Belle Fourche River.
- On clear days the tower can be seen from 160km (100 miles) away.

The Devil's Tower

The Devil's Tower is truly a giant, rising majestically out of the trees at its base on the rolling plains of Wyoming near the pine forests of the Black Hills. An Indian legend relates how seven maidens fled to the flat summit of the tower to escape

Chimney Rock

About 25 million years ago a deposit of sandy clay was laid down in western Nebraska. It was later covered with sandstone. Subsequent erosion has removed many of these deposits from the area, and only small, slightly more durable segments remain. One such remnant is Chimney Rock, a dome topped with a sandstone pinnacle 99m (325ft) high. It was a landmark for pioneers heading west on the Oregon Trail, who were able to see it from a distance of 48km (30 miles). Although other geological formations on the route were also named, Chimney Rock is often regarded as the symbol for America's westward migration in the 19th century.

a huge bear. The bear, desperate to catch the maidens, scored deep marks in the tower with his claws as he attempted to scramble to the top. When he finally succeeded in reaching the summit, the maidens jumped onto a low rock that saved them from the bear by soaring away into the sky. Another myth suggests that the tower gained its name because an evil demon pounded his drums on the summit, making thunder and terrifying anyone within earshot. More recently, the Devil's Tower featured as the backdrop for the landing site for aliens in the film *Close Encounters of the Third Kind*.

Formation of the Rock

The Devil's Tower was formed about 50 million years ago when Wyoming was under the sea, and layers of sedimentary rock such as sandstone, limestone, shale and gypsum were being deposited. At the same time, pressures from deep within the earth's crust forced a mass of magma to intrude into the sedimentary rock. The magma began to cool and crystallize, and as it did so it contracted and cracked, forming polygonal columns much like those at the Giant's Causeway in Northern Ireland. A similar process is often seen in dried-up streams and ponds, where water has evaporated from the crust, forming small polygonal saucers of mud with slightly upturned edges.

The igneous rock formed by the magma intrusion was much harder than the surrounding sedimentary rock, and over millions of years, as the sea bed rose from the water to become solid land, the forces of erosion began to eat away at the sedimentary rocks, leaving this great block of igneous rock standing proud. Water later seeped into the spaces between the columns, expanding and contracting with changes in temperature, and forcing some of the columns to fall away from the main body of rock. Broken columns litter the base of the tower, forming talus slopes. As this process of weathering continues, Devil's Tower will eventually collapse completely—but it's likely to be around for a good few million years yet.

BACKGROUND: *The Devil's Tower was formed tens of millions of years ago.*

Monument Valley

Rising dramatically out of the flat desert floor in northeast Arizona are strangely shaped blocks of sandstone, standing up to 305m (1,000ft) high. These towering monoliths were sacred to the Navajo Indians, and watching them glow red in the setting sun in the empty expanses of desert, it is easy to see how they have inspired a sense of awe for thousands of years. The monuments were formed in a similar way to the Devil's Tower, except that the rock here is sandstone. The entire area was once covered by sedimentary rocks, which were worn down over millions of years, leaving behind only the more resistant parts as free-standing towers and blocks.

See also:
Uluru (Ayer's Rock) 218-19
The Giant's Causeway 16-17

the facts

- In 1864 Yosemite Valley became the first state park in the United States.
- In 1890 the area around the valley was designated a national park.
- At 739m (2,425ft), Yosemite Falls is the third longest waterfall in the world.

Yosemite National Park

Few places in the world can have as many spectacular features in one small area as Yosemite Valley, a 12-km (7.5 mile) long natural masterpiece of staggering beauty and diversity nestling in the heart of the Sierra Nevada mountain range of California. It is home to the Merced River, Yosemite Falls and many splendid domes and peaks, with some of the largest rock walls in the world including El Capitan, a granite buttress that rises almost straight up, 1,099m (3,605ft) from the valley.

The Yosemite Valley is only a small part of the Yosemite National Park, which covers an area of 3,080sq km (1,189 square miles). Near the southern entrance to the park, Mariposa Grove contains huge sequoia trees that are thousands of years old. To the east is the popular high country of Tuolumne Meadows, where huge rock domes tower over lush, green meadows, and lakes have a pristine clarity. Past Tuolumne Meadows is the 3,031-m (9,945ft) Tioga Pass, the high point in the park, which leads down a steep road through the Inyo National Forest to the eastern side of the Sierra Nevada.

To the north of all of this is the rarely visited High Sierra region, including the Grand Canyon of the Tuolumne River and the Hetch Hetchy Reservoir, which was created in 1913 by flooding a valley almost as beautiful as Yosemite Valley. Campaigners are still calling for the reservoir to be drained and for water supplies to be provided elsewhere, so that the valley can be restored to its former glory.

LEFT: *The John Muir walking trail leads to the base of the distinctive peak known as Liberty Cap.*

The Discovery of Yosemite

Yosemite lay unknown to Westerners until 1851, when the volunteers of the Mariposa Battalion entered the valley in pursuit of a number of Ahwahneechee Native Americans, whom they had been assigned to take to a reservation. The park's name came from the corruption of the local Native American word for grizzly bear, *uzumati*.

Within a few years sightseeing parties were coming to admire the views down into the valley, and they are the same views that visitors see today upon emerging from the Wawona Tunnel. To the left the majesty of El Capitan and to the right, the elegant 189m (620ft) Bridalveil Falls which pour down from the back of the Cathedral Rocks. There's also the seemingly unassailable Sentinel Rock and, straight ahead, the glacier-carved face of Half Dome.

The man who really made Yosemite part of the American consciousness was the Scottish environmentalist, John Muir. He spent a great part of his life in this part of the country and was a key figure in the establishment of a United States forest conservation policy.

BELOW LEFT: *The Vernal Falls on the Merced River tumble 97m (317ft), and are just one of several popular wedding locations in the park.*

Rock Climbing in Yosemite

Yosemite Valley offers all types of climbing: cracks, chimneys, faces, overhangs, artificial aid, high angle, low angle—whatever a climber could desire, including Sentinel Rock, Royal Arches and El Capitan, one of the largest granite faces in the world.

Yosemite became the focus for rock-climbing in the US in the 1950s and 1960s, when Royal Robbins, Yvon Chouinard and Warren Harding first made ascents on climbs that had previously been thought impossible. Robbins, Jerry Galwas and Mike Sherrick were the first climbers to conquer the sheer, 610-m (2,000ft) northwest face of Half Dome in 1957, and Harding, Wayne Merry and George Whitwore made the first ascent of the Nose Route of El Capitan the next year. Famous climbers in the 1970s and 80s included Bev Johnson, one of the greatest female climbers.

See also:
Redwood National Park 178
Sequoia National Park 178
Zion National Park 166-7

the facts

- The main canyon is 365km (227 miles) long and about 29km (18 miles) across at its widest point.
- The North Rim Headquarters and Grand Canyon Village, on the south rim, are less than 19km (12 miles) apart across the canyon, but it takes a diversion of 322km (200 miles) to get from one to the other.

The Grand Canyon

No description can ever truly prepare the visitor for the sheer size and magnificence of this massive gorge, stretching as far as the eye can see in a vast, spectacular complex of canyons, waterfalls, caverns, towers, ledges and ravines. The Grand Canyon never seems to look the same twice, and the sun and the shadows of passing clouds constantly change the shades of the rocks through a delicate spectrum from black and purple-brown to pale pink and blue-grey.

Peering down at the bottom of the canyon from one of the many vantage points, it is difficult to imagine that the tiny brown stream of water up to 1.6km (1 mile) below was responsible for this huge gorge. However, if you can, view the river from the canyon floor itself, where you'll see the Colorado River as a swift and powerful force—the Lava Falls Rapids are said to be the fastest navigable rapids in the world—and where it is easier to envisage how it was able to carve itself a path through the rocks.

Less than ten million years ago the Colorado River meandered over a huge plain. Then movements in the earth's surface caused the land to rise, and the river began

BELOW LEFT: *A trip by mule offers a precipitous route through the canyon.*
BELOW RIGHT: *Rafting is a cooler way to explore the canyon.*

The Grand Canyon Discovered

Native Americans knew about the Grand Canyon for thousands of years before it was discovered by Europeans. The caves and caverns in the park are rich in archaeological remains, and include rock paintings, pots and wooden figures. In 1540 a small group of Spanish adventurers arrived looking for gold, but finding none they moved on.

An expedition was mounted in 1857 to travel down the canyon by boat, but had to proceed on foot when the boats were wrecked almost before the trip had started. The most famous expedition was led by Major John Wesley Powell in 1869. Powell, a Civil War veteran and college professor, took nine frontiersmen with him to map the huge canyon, but his account of the journey remained unpublished for more than 20 years.

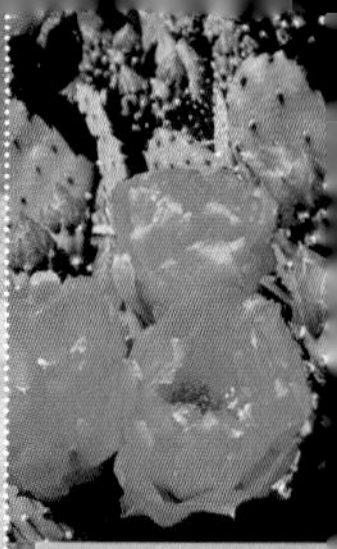

to cut a channel through the rocks. The soft two-million-year-old limestones were the first rocks to be eroded, then the older shales and sandstones lying in layers underneath. The oldest rocks are the two-billion-year-old granites and schists that form the bottom of the canyon today.

Exploring the Canyon

The Grand Canyon is not just one gorge. Many other canyons run into it, each one different from the others, and together they make up the Grand Canyon National Park. The Vulcan's Stone, a black cinder cone formed by volcanic activity about 10,000 years ago, stands high above the river, while the Esplanade is a heavily eroded terrace of red sandstone that glows scarlet in the evening sun. In many places, pinnacles of layered sandstone teeter at the edges of precipices, affording the most incredible views.

Although millions of tourists visit the most famous parts of the Grand Canyon, there are many places where you can find complete solitude. Fern Glen Canyon is famous for its micro-climate, and surprisingly, lush flowers and plants flourish there in the middle of the desert. North Canyon Wash has silent green pools of water that lie at the base of creamy-white canyon walls.

BELOW RIGHT: *Overlooking the Grand Canyon from the West Rim drive.*

Roosevelt and the Grand Canyon

One of the early visitors to the Grand Canyon was President Theodore Roosevelt, who first came in 1903, and made it a national monument in 1908.

Roosevelt was influenced by the writings of the conservation campaigner John Muir, and pursued policies aimed at protecting vast areas of American wilderness and maintaining the balance of their delicate ecology. Even at the turn of the 20th century, Roosevelt was aware of the delicate ecology of the area. He commented that the wisest course was for Americans to 'leave it as it is. You cannot improve on it. The ages have been at work on it, and man can only mar it'.

See also:
The East African Rift Valley 128-9
Zion National Park 166-7

the facts

- The Californian forests originally covered about 6,131sq km (2,367 square miles).
- *Sequoia sempervirens* is the tallest living tree; *Sequoiadendron giganteum* is the largest living organism.
- Redwoods can live for up to 3,000 years and giant sequoias can live for up to 4,000 years.

Redwoods and **Giant Sequoias**

Redwoods are now restricted to a narrow coastal strip stretching from the Klamath Mountains in southern Oregon to Monterey Bay in northern California, and giant sequoias grow on the slopes of the Sierra Nevada mountains. The best redwood trees are in Redwood National Park on the north California coast, and the largest sequoias are in Sequoia National Park in central California. Fossil records show that these giant trees were present in the Jurassic period, between 208 and 144 million years ago, when they were distributed over large areas of the northern hemisphere.

The giant sequoia grows to around 95m (312ft), and the trunk can have a diameter of 5m to 11m (15ft to 35ft). The largest of these trees, General Sherman, weighs about 2,995,796kg (4,400,000lb). In addition to these majestic trees, the forests of the Redwood and Sequoia National Parks are also important for a wide range of animals including moose, elk, black bear, beaver and white-tailed and mule deer.

Exploiting the Forest Giants

The redwood and giant sequoia produce very high-quality timber, prized as a multi-purpose wood suitable for a range of uses including house-building, furniture-making and rail sleepers. They are straight-growing, with very few knots and a fine grain, making them light but strong, and a combination of natural oils and resins makes them almost rot-proof and resistant to attack from termites.

In the latter half of the 19th century these trees were heavily exploited, and at risk of extinction. Exploitation continues today, although the US National Parks Service continues in its efforts to annex remaining tracts of forest to the existing protected areas.

79 **Meteor Crater,** USA

the facts

- Meteor Crater is a saucer-shaped hole 1,220m (4,000ft) in diameter and 180m (600ft) deep.
- A recent estimate is that the meteor was about 41m (135ft) across and weighed 300,000 tons.
- The meteor hit the ground with incredible force and parts of it have been found 10km (6 miles) away.

Meteor Crater

ABOVE: *The giant saucer-shaped depression left by the meteor measures 1,200m (4,000ft) across, with the edge rising 46m (150ft) above the Arizona plain.*

Thousands of years ago a bright trail flared in the sky over northern Arizona. The fireball crashed into the earth at about 19km (12 miles) per second, hurling millions of tons of rock into the air and creating Meteor Crater. The destructive energy of the explosion was a thousand times that of the atomic bomb dropped on Hiroshima. Fortunately, such enormous missiles from outer space do not often crash into the earth—but meteoroids penetrate the atmosphere each day. Most of these are small particles of dust, vaporized before they reach the surface by the heat generated by friction in the outer atmosphere.

Most of the few metereoids that are found contain iron, which is better able to withstand the great heat generated as it plummets downwards. A meteorite found at Cape York in western Greenland had been used for many years by the local Inuit people as a source of iron for their tools.

Big Bang

Some scientists believe that a meteorite may have been responsible for the mass extinction of dinosaurs that occurred 65 million years ago. According to this theory a huge piece of space debris tore through the earth's atmosphere to cut a crater 40km (25 miles) deep and 200km (125 miles) across under the ocean. Volcanic material and hot gases joined the millions of tons of dust and rock that were hurled into the air.

The dust rose high into the atmosphere and blocked life-giving solar energy, causing a disruption in plant growth and a shortage of food, and subsequently led to the deaths of many animals and plants, including the dinosaurs. A large crater discovered off the coast of Mexico may finally provide the proof for this theory.

See also: **Ngorongoro Crater** 128

the facts

- The Everglades take in freshwater marshlands which once covered around 10, 360sq km (4,000 square miles).
- The area is one of the largest remaining freshwater marshlands in the world.
- Native Americans call this area *pa-hay-okee*, which means 'grassy waters'.

The Everglades

This unique sub-tropical wilderness is fed by water from Lake Okeechobee, the largest lake in North America after the Great Lakes. The water from the lake seeps into the underlying limestone, and from there feeds this vast wetland area through a series of aquifers. The Everglades is dominated by dense, and in places impenetrable stands of sawgrass that grow up to 4m (13ft) high, covering vast areas. The region is criss-crossed by channels and small lakes of open water, where other plants such as water lilies and bladderworts thrive. The bladderworts are specially adapted for living in these nutrient-poor waters: they have small air bladders that trap insects and larvae that the plant then absorbs to obtain vital nutrients.

Small islands, or hammocks, where the underlying limestone rises above the water table, support a variety of hardwoods together with many species of orchids, ferns and animals. At the coast, the freshwater marsh, or glade, gives way to a fringing strip of red mangroves, to form the only forested marine wetland in North America.

The large range of habitats is reflected in the highly diverse flora and fauna of the area. There are over 1,000 seed-bearing plants, including 25 varieties of orchid and 120 species of trees, which range from tropical palm and mangrove through temperate forest species such as oak and ash to desert plants such as yucca and cactus.

Many creatures depend on more than one element in this mosaic of habitats—for example, colonial birds use the cypress and mangrove forests as nest sites, while feeding in the sawgrass marshes. The Everglades is an exceptionally important area for birds, with over 320 different species recorded. These include such rarities as the wood stork, the reddish egret and the southern race of the bald eagle. The Everglades kite feeds exclusively on snails, using its specially adapted, long, curved and sharply pointed bill to extract the flesh of the snail from the shell. Many species of fish-eating birds also frequent the freshwater swamps, and the coastal mangrove fringe is home to anhingas, roseate spoonbills, pelicans, wood ibis, herons and egrets.

Over 150 fish species are found in the coastal waters, providing good feeding for the many birds, reptiles and mammals. The American alligator is the main predator in the swamp, but there are others such as the American crocodile, the rare Florida panther and various otters.

TOP RIGHT: *An air-boat takes visitors into the interior of the Big Cypress National Preserve, a vast area of wet and dry prairie to the north of the Everglades.*

The Florida Manatee

Among the animals taking advantage of the abundant fish in the Everglades' coastal waters are 12 species of turtle, including giant loggerhead turtles and green turtles. The Florida manatee is a gentle, plant-eating mammal and is a member of the group of animals known as the *Sirenia*, which were once believed by sailors to be mermaids.

Manatees feed on the seagrass beds in the shallow waters fringing the mangrove forests. These harmless creatures face a threat from marina developments, which decrease their feeding area, and bring with them pollution and the increased danger of death or injury from boats.

Encroachment on a Wilderness

Despite a variety of human pressures on this area it is still relatively unspoiled, but protecting an area as complex as the Everglades is a difficult task. The Everglades National Park faces constant threats from drainage works and flood defences that cut off the life waters to the swamps. With less water and reduced flooding the area of swamp has already decreased, and so, in turn, have the numbers of wildlife. In the 1930s an estimated 1.5 million birds nested here; now their numbers have decreased to fewer than 50,000, and the alligator population has declined by over 90 percent in the same period.

TOP: *Alligators are a familiar sight in these wetlands.*
LEFT: *Grey herons are among the birds which feed in the reedbeds.*

See also:
The Camargue 22-3
The Okavango Delta 142-3
The Waddenzee 21

81 Hawaiian Islands, Pacific Ocean/USA

the facts

- The Hawaiian Islands stretch for about 2,415km (1,500 miles) across the north Pacific Ocean.
- Mauna Kea is the tallest mountain in the world when measured from its base on the ocean floor, 5,998m (19,680ft) below sea level.
- In 1992, Cyclone Iniki destroyed 10,000 Hawaiian homes.

Hawaiian Islands

BELOW: *A sulphurous steam-cloud hangs in the crater of a cinder cone in the Hawaii Volcanoes National Park.*
BOTTOM: *The 137-m long (450ft) Thurston Lava Tube, on Big Island, was created when molten lava continued to flow through a cooled crust of rock.*

Hawaii's Emerald Island

Kauai is the lushest and most beautiful of the Hawaiian Islands, with dense green vegetation, golden beaches and turquoise seas. At its heart is an extinct volcano called Mount Waialeale.

However, this is also one of the wettest places on earth with an average of 1,170cm (460in) of rain every year. The high precipitation means that Kauai is fantastically green, and more than 70 percent of the island is devoted to plantations, national parks and open space.

The island's main industry was traditionally the growing of sugar cane. The first sugar cane mill opened in 1835 and workers were recruited from China, Japan and the Philippines, as well as from the local population. Many settled in Kauai, which accounts for the island's richly multicultural background.

The Hawaiian Islands extend from Kure and Midway Island in the west to the island of Hawaii itself in the east, and seem unrelated to any of the other volcanoes that lie around the margins of the Pacific—the Ring of Fire. Most of these are associated with deep sea trenches, where the oceanic crust is being dragged under the continental margin. The Hawaiian Islands sit above a hot-spot in the earth's mantle, a point source of heat. Geologists believe there are about 30 such hot-spots that are relatively static and produce lines of volcanoes as the oceanic crust passes over them. That is exactly what happened with the Hawaiian Islands. The crust of the western part of the Pacific is moving steadily westward, and seems to have shifted about 2,414km (1,500 miles) during the life of this hot-spot. All the islands in the Hawaiian chain are volcanic; the oldest are at the western end and the youngest—and hence the most active—are on the island of Hawaii itself, at the eastern end of the chain.

The island of Hawaii is shaped like a triangle balancing on one of its points, and is about 130km (80 miles) by 153km (95 miles). Its highest point is the summit of Mauna Kea, at 4,205m (13,796ft) above sea level. Its height and its clear, unpolluted atmosphere have made it an ideal place to site several of the most powerful astronomical telescopes in the world.

Islands of Fire

Most of the current volcanic activity in Hawaii is at Kilauea, a subsidiary vent on the flanks of Mauna Loa, the second highest mountain, about 32km (20 miles) east of the summit. This volcano was in virtually continuous eruption during the 19th century and has been active since 1983. The volcanic crater is 152m to 183m (150ft to 160ft) deep and covers an area of 10.4sq km (4 square miles).

Kilauea is believed to be the home of Pele, the Hawaiian goddess of volcanoes, and anyone detecting the low-pitched humming or roaring noise that precedes some Hawaiian eruptions is said to be 'hearing Pele'. Another detectable sign of imminent eruption is a change in the local magnetic and electrical fields: magma heated above about 600°C (1,100°F) loses its natural magnetism, implying that a large body of molten rock has developed within the volcano.

BELOW: *Scuba-diving in a crystal-clear freshwater pool formed above a lava field in the Volcanoes National Park.*

THE BANZAI PIPELINE

Waves are caused by a combination of winds, currents, and the gravitational pull of the earth. As they roll towards the land, other factors determine their size and shape, such as the shape of the sea bed over which they travel. A gently sloping sandy beach has waves very different from those where the beach rises sharply.

The sea bed on the northwest coast of the Hawaiian island of Oahu gives rise to huge Pacific waves that roll towards the shore, growing taller as they reach shallower waters, eventually toppling over themselves. The toppling effect occurs at a slight angle, forming a blue-green tunnel known as the Banzai Pipeline. As a result Oahu is a popular place for surfers, who use great skill to skim along the inside of the tunnels, surrounded by the translucent walls.

See also:
Deception Island 236-7
Volcanic Iceland 14-15

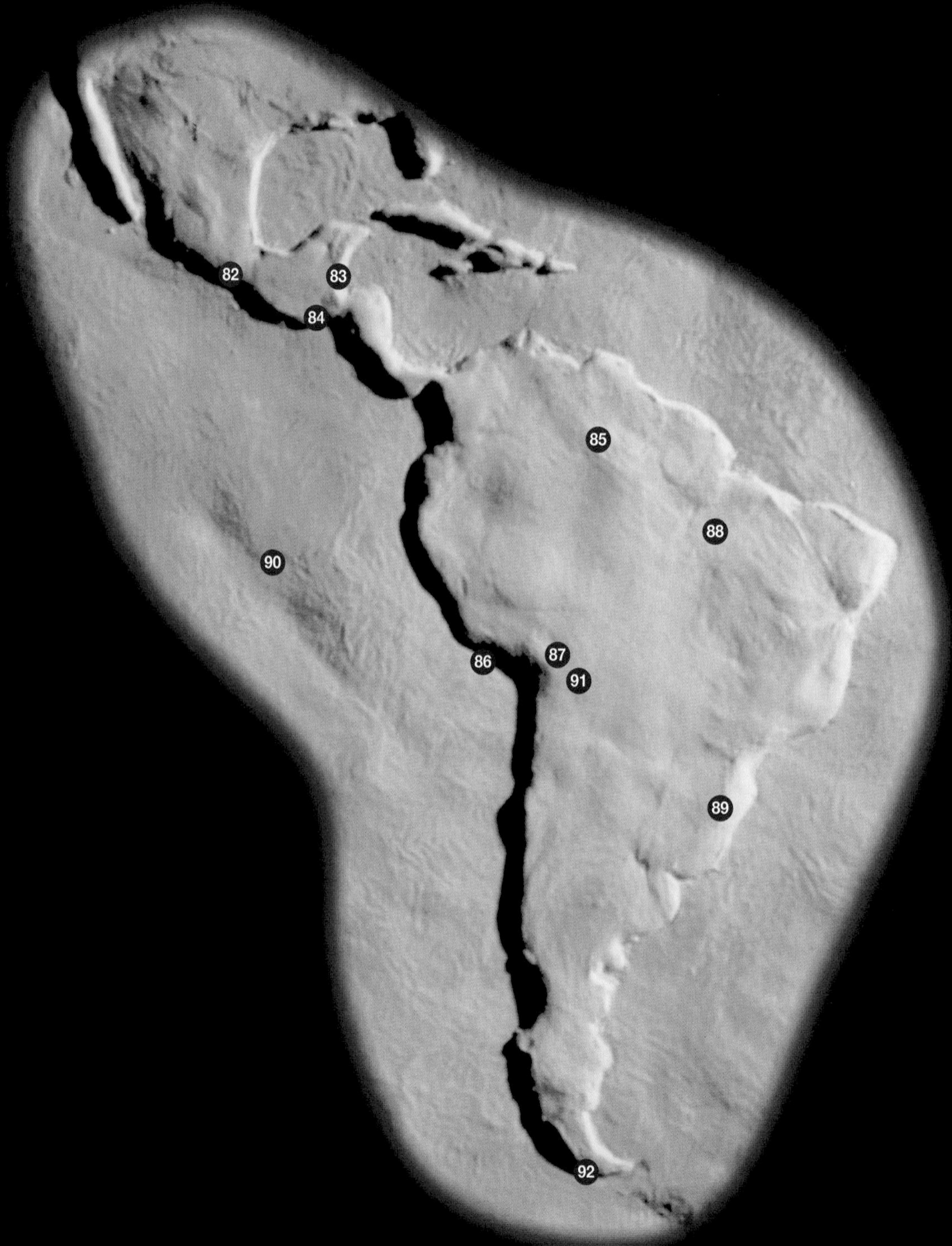

82 **Teotihuacán**

83 **Chichén Itzá**

84 **Tikal**

85 **Angel Falls**

86 **The Nazca Lines**

87 **Machu Picchu**

88 **The Amazon Basin**

89 **Iguaçu Falls**

90 **Galapagos Islands**

91 **The Inca Trails**

92 **Tierra del Fuego**

Central & South America

Central and Southern American history remains enigmatic, though its early inhabitants left an impressive legacy of art, treasures and monuments. From the fourth century AD to the tenth the Mayan civilization reached its apogee in Guatemala, eastern Mexico and the Yucatán, with Tikal as perhaps its largest city. Further west, the city of Teotihuacán was bigger than imperial Rome. The Aztecs built up their empire and by 1450 they controlled almost all modern Mexico from their capital at Teochtitlan. They were infamous for starting wars, capturing prisoners for sacrifice and enslaving the peasantry. Resentment of Aztec oppression helped the Spanish in their conquest of Mexico in 1521, after which they ruled Mesoamerica for 300 years.

Spanish and Portuguese rule was also imposed on South America, a 7,403-km (4,600 mile) long landmass embracing a remarkable range of climate and landscape, from the jungles of the Amazon to Tierra del Fuego, near the icebergs of the Antarctic. In the Andes, snowcapped peaks rear up close to the equator, running parallel to the western coast like a great wall. In Peru and Bolivia there are two parallel ranges, and between them is the Altiplano, a high plateau of plains, hills and valleys, where some of the first city–states developed. The Nazca people created astonishing works of art in the barren plain near the southern coast of Peru, forming huge patterns and animals clearly visible only from the sky.

From their capital at Cuzco the Incas built up the largest empire in the Americas, linked by an efficient road system. In 1531 Francisco Pizarro landed on the Peruvian coast in search of the gold city of El Dorado and conquered the empire in a few months. But the Inca Empire has not given up all its secrets, as became apparent when the settlement of Machu Picchu, a site whose purpose is still unknown, was uncovered in the Andes.

- Teotihuacán is an Aztec name meaning 'place of the gods'.
- It covers an area of over 21sq km (8 square miles).
- The city's population once numbered 50,000–100,000.
- According to local legend, the sun and the moon were born in Teotihuacán.

facts

Teotihuacán

This remarkable site dates back to the first century BC. By AD500 Teotihuacán had grown larger than the imperial city of Rome and was the biggest city in Mesoamerica. It was a sophisticated city, with wide streets, monumental religious buildings, artisans' quarters and private houses, but despite tireless archaeological investigation little factual evidence has been uncovered revealing the daily life and customs of its people. It has been possible to determine by studying the engravings and statues on religious temples that this highly developed civilization worshipped a rain god and revered the jaguar.

Teotihuacán was meticulously planned according to a grid system, so strict that a river was diverted into a channel to prevent it from interrupting a network of parallel streets. The main axis, which runs north–south, is a vast avenue 40m (130ft) wide and 2.3km (1.5 miles) long, known as the Street of the Dead. Lined with temples and

Pyramid Power

Extravagant claims have been made regarding the mystical power of pyramids. It is said, for example, that organic material can be preserved, razor blades sharpened and a person's mind stimulated when they are positioned close to the ancient monument's apex.

Some believe that ancient cultures had an understanding of cosmic energies that we lack today, and that there is a significance in the way monuments were aligned in relation to the sun, the moon, and the stars. Certainly the orientation of the grid plan at Teotihuacán is very precise, and it does seem likely that the people of Teotihuacán were aware of the movements of the celestial bodies and attatched considerable importance to them.

RIGHT: *Detail of a painted mural, now preserved in the site's museum.*

shrines, it is dominated by two pyramids: the Pyramid of the Moon—actually several interlocking pyramids with an overall height of 46m (150ft)—at the north end, and the Pyramid of the Sun standing further south. Two monumental public places of assembly stand at the heart of the city—the Citadel and the Great Compound.

The Great Compound, with two large platforms on which a number of buildings once stood, seems to have had an administrative function, while the Citadel clearly played a religious role. Approached by a grand stairway, the Citadel platform, 365-m (400 yard) square, supports another pyramid, the Temple of Quetzalcoatl (the Feathered Serpent, a major god), which originally rose to a height of about 21m (70ft) in tiers of richly carved sculpture. Stone serpents, their heads projecting menacingly from the tiers, appear alarming even today—they must have made an even greater impression during their prime, when their shining obsidian eyes were still in place and the whole structure was covered in stucco and paintwork. Local supplies of obsidian were an important trading commodity in a chiefly agricultural economy.

High-quality murals suggest that the people had artistic talent, but evidence of human sacrifice during the years of decline points to a more barbaric side of their culture. No one knows precisely how Teotihuacán came to an end, but by the eighth century the city had been sacked and burned.

BACKGROUND AND LEFT: *Awesome carvings of the plumed serpent Quetzalcoatl guard the front of the temple of the same name.*
BELOW LEFT: *The Pyramid of the Sun is the second of two great temples in the city, and is laid out on the Avenue of the Dead.*

Esperanza Culture

Esperanza culture is the term used to describe an amalgam of Teotihuacán and Maya culture that can be seen at Kaminaljuyu, near the heart of modern Guatemala City. Once an important Maya site, it was apparently conquered by the people of Teotihuacán at the beginning of the fifth century AD. The area lacked suitable stone for building so the victors built a planned city—an imitation of Teotihuacán—from the local clay.

Rather than wipe out Maya culture, the new inhabitants absorbed and developed aspects of it and furnished their tombs with Maya-style pottery.

Elsewhere in the Maya region, Teotihuacán influenced art and architecture, and there are examples of Maya and Teotihuacán deities on their ceramic ware.

See also:
Chichén Itzá 188-9
The Great Pyramid 116-19
Tikal 192-3

83 Chichén Itzá, Mexico

the facts

- The site at Chicén Itzá was inhabited by the Maya and later by the Toltecs.
- The days and months of the year are represented on the pyramid temple, El Castillo, by the number of steps and terraces. 52 panels symbolize the Maya 52-year cycle.
- El Castillo has nine tiers and 91 steps up each side.

Chichén Itzá

Chichén Itzá was an important Maya site until the tenth century AD. At some later point, as Maya civilization went into decline, Toltec warriors appear to have seized control and turned Chichén Itzá into a bigger and better version of their own capital, Tula. The extensive remains at the site today are neither purely Maya nor purely Toltec, but rather an intriguing fusion of the ideas and motifs of both cultures.

Chichén Itzá is thought to have been built as a new capital for the ruler-god Topiltzin Quetzalcoatl, known here by the Maya name Kukulcan. A pyramid temple dedicated to him, called El Castillo (The Castle), dominates the complex. The careful alignment of the building, whose

Toltecs

The Toltecs were a nomadic people who are believed to be behind the destruction in the eighth century AD of the civilisation based at Teotihuacán (see pages 186–7). Their own capital was established at Tula, but this in turn was destroyed by enemies, and for a long time their future was in doubt.

Despite this they went on to rule over Mexico from the mid-10th to the mid-12th century AD.

Their legendary skills and achievements survived them. Toltec art, dismissed by some as crude, is full of representations of warriors and illustrates the power and extent of their empire, but the line between myth and fact is unclear.

BELOW LEFT: *Chac-mool figures like this acted as altars.*
BELOW RIGHT: *The pyramid temple, El Castillo.*

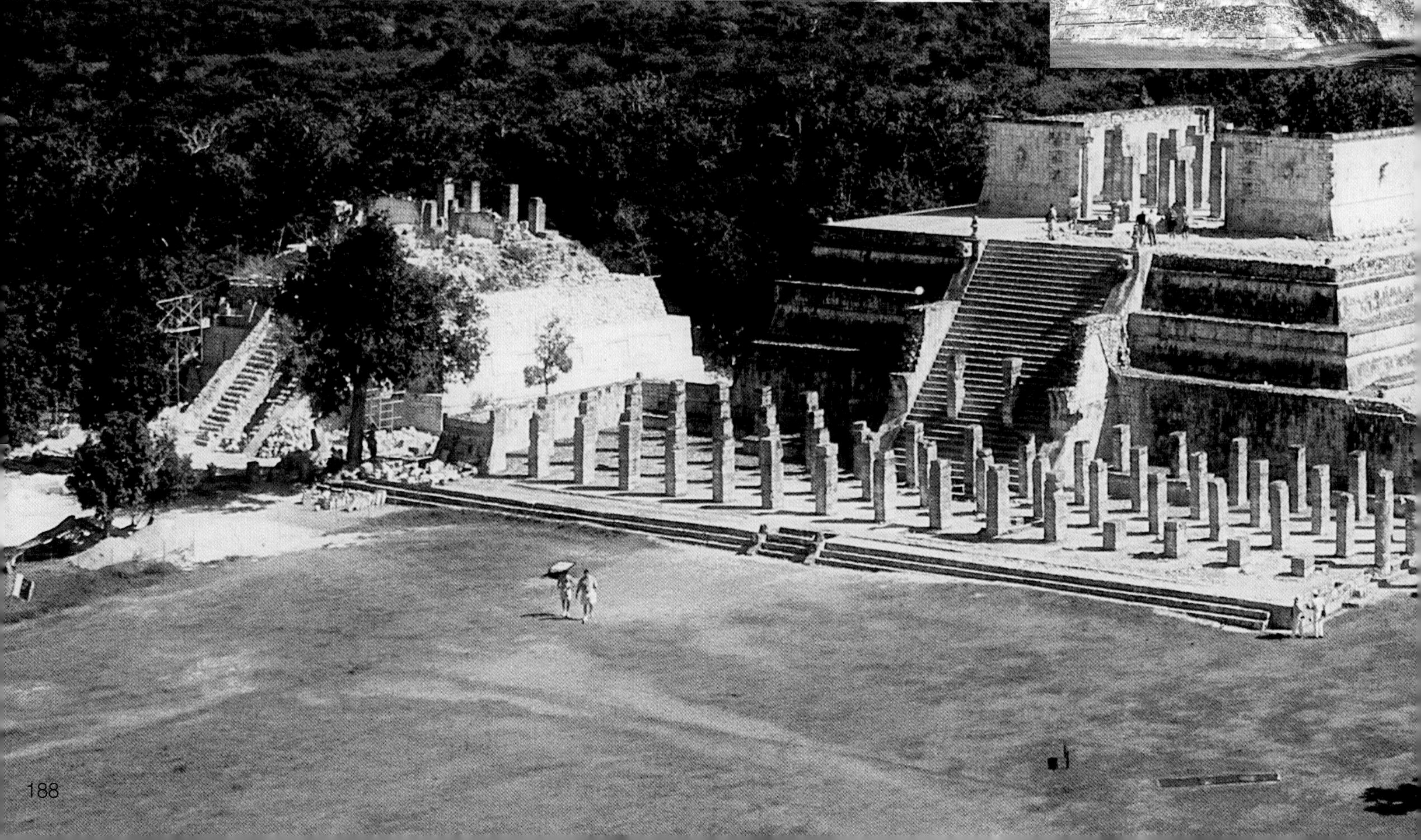

stairways face exactly north, south, east and west, creates an extraordinary effect at the spring and autumn equinoxes, when shadows fall on the serpent god's carved head and tail, at the bottom and the top of the main staircase, supposedly bringing it to life.

Detecting Amid the Ruins

Chichén Itzá has perhaps the finest ball court in Mesoamerica. It is vast, with two parallel walls 83m (272ft) long and 8.2m (27ft) high, set 27m (90ft) apart. Temples stand at each end of the court, but the exact religious significance of the game is not known. Bas-relief panels on the side walls showing decapitated players suggest that these were contests fought to the death. A later account of the game indicates that the winner was the player who got the ball through one of the stone rings high up on each side wall. The victor was rewarded with the spectators' clothes.

The Temple of the Warriors is approached through a colonnade, and countless such pillars, carved to represent Toltec warriors, once supported a roof. The temple is decorated with carvings and frescoes, and the familiar jaguar and eagle motifs of Toltec art are both in evidence. Chichén Itzá also has a Temple of the Jaguars, with a fine specimen of the species carved out in stone guarding the approach.

The overgrown area known as Old Chichén contains some equally interesting buildings, which include an observatory—a tower supported on a double platform—and a pyramid in which a number of tombs were found. The settlement is thought to have been abandoned in about 1224 after an attack by the rulers of a rival power.

BELOW: *There are 91 steep stone steps to the top of El Castillo.*

BELOW: *The carved stone heads of big cats adorn the Temple of the Jaguar.*

Human Sacrifice and the Sacred Cenote

Chichén Itzá's sacred *cenote*, or well of sacrifice, is approached along a 274-m (900ft) causeway. A natural well, 23m (75ft) deep, it supplied fresh water and was treated as a place of pilgrimage.

In times of drought, victims were thrown alive into the well in an attempt to provoke the rain god into action, and offerings of precious metals, jade and sacred images have been retrieved from its depths. Many children drowned during the ritual, but those who survived the ordeal were treated with respect, as it was believed that they had communicated with the gods.

See also: Tikal 192-3

Great civilizations rise and, however mighty their rulers and cities, they eventually fall. Our landscapes are littered with the remains of civilizations that, at their height, must have seemed all but indestructible to those who lived within them. All we know of some of these ancient societies are the monuments they left behind.

the facts

- The four primary civilizations of the Old World (in Mesopotamia, Egypt, the Indus Valley and northern China), all developed at a similar latitude.
- The Roman Empire extended north to Britain, south to North Africa and east as far as modern-day Syria.

Great Civilizations

AGE OF STONE

Popular myth has long dismissed the people of the Stone Age—a term covering many thousands of years, between 7000 and 2200BC—as little more than savages. But they lived in complex and sophisticated societies which used precision tools, international trade and symbolic structures.

Remnants of the Stone Age can still be seen in many parts of Europe. There are exquisite cave paintings in the Dordogne in France, and the labour that went into the accurate placing of the monoliths at Stonehenge in England speaks for itself. In Ireland, the megalithic passage grave at Newgrange is known for the distinctive geometric patterns in the stone.

CLOCKWISE FROM RIGHT: *Teotihuacán, Mexico; ancient Minoan fresco c1700BC, Knossos, Crete; mystical Stonehenge, England.*

ANCIENT EGYPT

While Stonehenge was receiving its third or fourth renovation, the pharaohs of Egypt's Old Kingdom (2686–2181BC) were building their pyramids at Giza. The Egyptian Empire that grew from the Nile's fertile banks lasted nearly 3,000 years and recorded its history in writings that baffled the modern age until Jean Barthélemy cracked the hieroglyphic code in 1785.

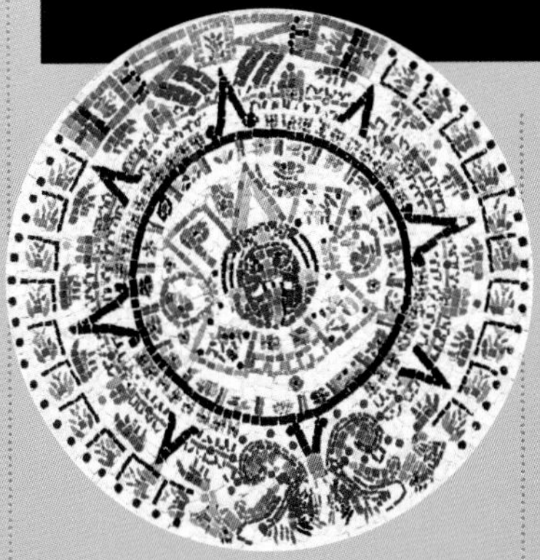

CHINA

Ancient Chinese dynasties flourished over 11,000 years, producing gunpowder, paper, the compass and the philosophies of Confucius.

In the third century BC the cruel but successful Qin Shihuangdi overcame rival warring kingdoms to create a unified empire, securing its boundaries with the Great Wall. The name of the unified empire, China, derives from the name Qin.

OLD AND NEW WORLDS

The first Spanish adventurers to reach Central and South America were astonished to find the impressive cities of the Maya, Aztec and Inca civilizations. However, within the space of only a few years these peoples were to disappear, helpless against the new diseases and superior weaponry of the European empiricists.

Today fabulous gold museum pieces and the ruins of settlements such as Tula and Chichén Itzá in Mexico, Tikal in Guatemala and Machu Picchu in Peru survive as clues to the histories of once formidable and wealthy empires.

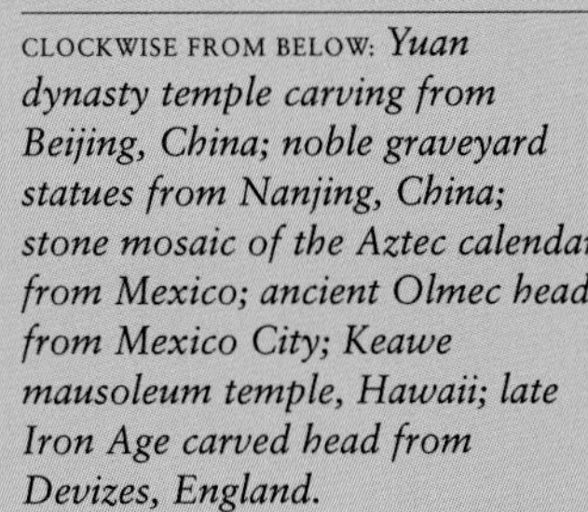

CLOCKWISE FROM BELOW: *Yuan dynasty temple carving from Beijing, China; noble graveyard statues from Nanjing, China; stone mosaic of the Aztec calendar from Mexico; ancient Olmec head from Mexico City; Keawe mausoleum temple, Hawaii; late Iron Age carved head from Devizes, England.*

See also:
Chichén Itzá 188-9
Machu Picchu 196-9
Pont du Gard 30

the facts

- A total of 16 temples remain in Tikal today.
- The ceremonial area covered 1 square mile (2.5sq km).
- Tikal's largest pyramid, known simply as Pyramid IV, is 70m (228ft) high.
- At its peak the settlement's population is thought to have numbered between 10,000 and 45,000.

Tikal

Tikal lies on the Yucatán Peninsula in a region first entered by Europeans in 1517, and gradually conquered by Spain over the next 30 years. Set in the northern lowland area of Maya territory, Tikal was perhaps the largest settlement of Classic Maya civilization. At its heart was a huge square, bordered by pyramid temples on the west and east sides and an acropolis on the north. Beyond this complex there were some 3,000 buildings within an area of 16sq km (6 square miles). The acropolis shows signs of having been occupied continuously for 11 centuries, and the temples to be seen there now stand on the buried remains of countless other earlier buildings, including some elaborate painted tombs.

The word city is perhaps not the best description of Tikal; rather, it was an important ceremonial centre on whose outskirts large numbers of people chose to live. Although the majority of people did not live in any great affluence, the Maya devoted tremendous energy to the construction of their tombs and temples. In paying tribute to their gods, their elite and their dead, they created monuments that are still awe-inspiring today.

Buildings of Tikal

The buildings occupying the large, central ceremonial area were linked by causeways to more squares and their

The Mayans

The Maya people, ancestors of the present-day Maya Indians, belonged to a civilization that inhabited a wide area of highland and lowland Mesoamerica. Their culture, dominated by religious ceremony, was presided over by ruler-priests.

The highly elaborate Maya calendar, the Long Count, involved a cycle of 52 years, and attempts to reconcile this with the European system have produced conflicting results. Radiocarbon dating supports the view that the Classic Maya period, when the civilization reached its peak, was between the fourth and the tenth century AD.

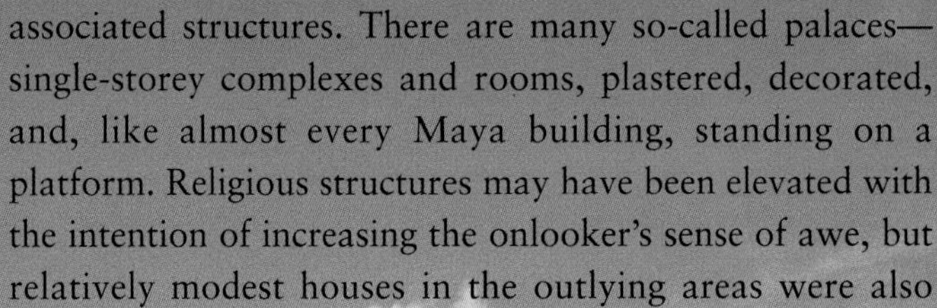

associated structures. There are many so-called palaces—single-storey complexes and rooms, plastered, decorated, and, like almost every Maya building, standing on a platform. Religious structures may have been elevated with the intention of increasing the onlooker's sense of awe, but relatively modest houses in the outlying areas were also built on mud platforms, presumably as a safeguard against floods during the rainy season.

Glimpses of Maya rulers and their religious ceremonies can be seen in stone sculpture as well as in fine carvings on sapodilla wood. This woodwork was used for decorative beams in some of the palaces and for ornate lintels over the doorways of the pyramid temples. Stone stelae in front of the palaces and temples were often symbolic, depicting a ruler or warrior trampling an enemy underfoot.

Tikal has six steep pyramids, with chambers at the top approached by steps and crowned with elaborate 'roof combs'. The pyramids were tombs for the wealthy and important, who were buried with sumptuous grave goods and food for their journey to the next world.

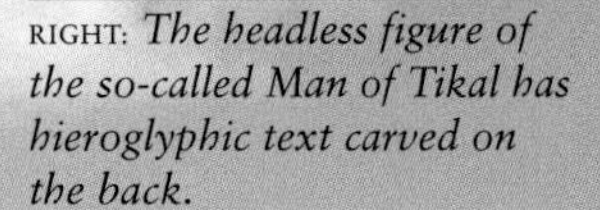

RIGHT: *The headless figure of the so-called Man of Tikal has hieroglyphic text carved on the back.*

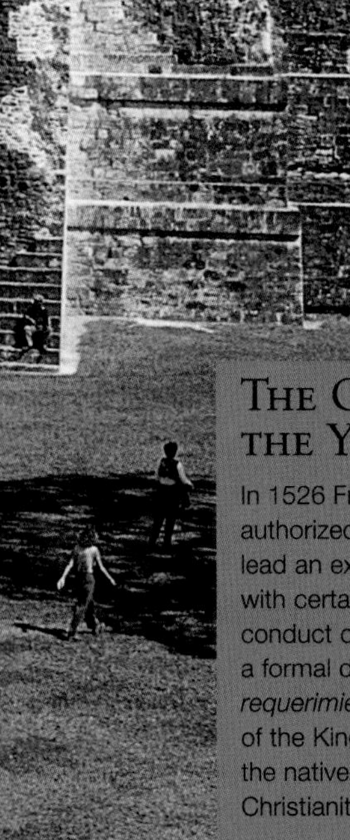

The Conquest of the Yucatán

In 1526 Francisco de Montejo was authorized by the King of Castile to lead an expedition to the Yucatán, with certain conditions for the conduct of this expedition laid out in a formal document known as a *requerimiento*. It stated that the aim of the King of Castile was to convert the natives of the New World to Christianity by means of understanding and good treatment. These intentions were to be explained clearly to the natives through an interpreter. If they failed to comply, the Spaniards would declare war against the land and subject the people to the authority of Crown and Church.

There followed years of guerrilla warfare, and resistance to the *conquistadores* and their ways continued long after they had imposed their rule on the Yucatán.

See also:
Chichén Itzá 188-9
Teotihuacán 186-7

the facts

- Salto Angel in the Venezuelan jungle is the highest waterfall in the world with a total fall of 979m (3,212ft).
- The first drop is 807m (2,648ft) to an obstruction; a second stage plunges 172m (564ft) into a jungle pool.
- The falls are named after an American pilot, Jimmy Angel.

Angel Falls

In the remote southeastern corner of Venezuela, close to the borders with Guyana and Brazil, torrential tropical rains feed the Rio Churún, a tributary of the Caroní River, that winds slowly over Auyán Tepuy, a high plateau above the jungle, until it reaches the cliff on the northern edge. The river then gathers pace down a short incline and rushes into space. From a distance the thin white line at the cliff edge gradually broadens into a blur of spray, until the water drops out of sight into the jungle.

For a long time the entire area was virtually inaccessible to all and was only reached by the most determined jungle explorers, but today it is possible to reach the falls in a motorized dugout canoe or in a light aircraft. Adventurous modern day explorers also come here to leap off the plateau in a hang-glider or sail off the cliff under a paraglider.

Finding the Falls

The existence of the falls has always been known to local American Indians, who call them Churún-Meru. Their name for the plateau, Auyán Tepuy, means Devil's Mountain.

The first documented sighting of the falls was in 1910, when Ernesto Sánchez la Cruz reported his discovery, but it was an American pilot, Jimmy Angel, who brought them to attention of the wider world. Angel was seeking gold in 1933 when he noted the falls in his logbook. Shortly after the falls were given his name: Salto Angel in Spanish, Angel Falls in English. Jimmy Angel failed to find gold, but he did achieve lasting fame.

BELOW: *The fractured red sandstone peak of Auyán Tepuy reaches a height of 2,515m (8,250ft).*

In 1926 Alfred Kroeber and Mejia Xesspe were the first people to notice the lines.

Stone cairns mark the points where the lines converge, possibly indicating a ceremonial purpose.

German scholar Maria Reiche spent 30 years in the pampas studying the lines.

the **facts**

The **Nazca Lines**

Geometric shapes, birds and animals are etched in the Pampa Ingenio desert in the Nazca Valley in Peru. From the ground they appear to be a network of pathways, but from above they appear as a gigantic menagerie—a 50m (164ft) spider, a giant condor, a hummingbird, a lizard and a monkey 100m (328ft) long.

This maze of designs, spread over 500sq km (193 square miles), was created by removing the surface crust of stones to expose the yellowish-white layer beneath. Archaeologists estimate that the Nazca Lines date back to the first century AD, but their purpose remains a mystery. One theory is that the patterns represent constellations, another (and fanciful) theory is a suggestion by Erich von Däniken in his book *Chariots of the Gods*, that the lines mark entry ports for visitors from outer space.

The Pyramids of Cahuachi

The Pyramids of Cahuachi are part of an extensive archaeological site in the Nazca Valley. Among workaday constructions of adobe and *quincha* (mud-covered cane) rise several public or ceremonial buildings, the most prominent being the Great Temple, a stepped pyramid 20m (66ft) high, faced and capped with walls made of elongated adobes. Around the base are adobe-walled rooms and plazas, the largest measuring 45m by 75m (148ft by 246ft). Burial pits on the site were found to contain offerings of food and pottery.

In the early stages of Nazca culture, which lasted from AD100 to 800, the priestly function seems to have been important. Portrayals of animals on Nazca pottery and textiles imply that certain creatures, such as felines, were regarded as sacred.

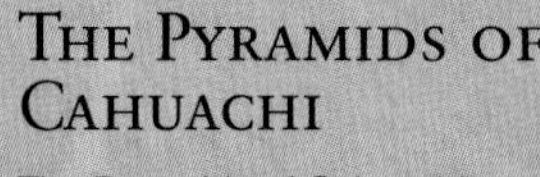

LEFT: *Strong designs are a feature of this Nazca pot.*

See also: Easter Island 212-13

87 **Machu Picchu,** Peru

Machu Picchu

A long-lost ceremonial site sits high in the Peruvian Andes, 475m (1,500ft) above the Urubamba River. This mysterious place, perched on the saddle between two mountains, is known today as Machu Picchu—The Old Peak—but its name gives no clues to its origins, having been borrowed from a nearby mountain and attached to the remarkable settlement. The real name of Machu Picchu, its origin and purpose, are matters for speculation.

When Machu Picchu was rediscovered in the early 20th century it was first thought to be Vilcabamba, where the Incas survived for 36 years after Spanish conquerors had driven their emperor from his capital at Cuzco, but the identification of the site as the Incas' last refuge is now thought to be wrong. Machu Picchu appears to have been more an important ceremonial or religious complex than a city. The date of its construction is uncertain, but it probably originates from the rapid period of expansion of the Inca Empire at the end of the 15th century.

ABOVE: *The Hitching Post of the Sun is linked to an ancient winter solstice ritual.*

Little is known about the purpose of the site, but it is possible to determine that Machu Picchu was a place of gardens and terraces, grandiose ceremonial buildings and palaces. The different levels and terraced gardens were connected by hundreds of steps and there is evidence of aqueducts, fountains and bath buildings and the cultivation of maize, potatoes and other vegetables. Skeletons discovered on the site suggest that the female-male ratio was 10:1, leading to the theory that Machu Picchu was a place of sun-worship and a sanctuary for women known as Virgins of the Sun.

Further evidence of the importance of the sun at Machu Picchu is provided by the Intihuatana (Hitching Post of the Sun). This curiously shaped stone structure seems to have been a complex astronomical device. Nothing else like it

the facts

- Machu Picchu covers an area of 2ha (5 acres).
- There are 18sq km (5 square miles) of terraced stonework on the site, linked by 3,000 steps.
- Machu Picchu has about 200 buildings, including residences, temples and storehouses.
- According to one estimate, as few as 1,500 people may have lived here.

1460-70
Machu Picchu is built, probably for Incan ruler Pachacuti Inca Yupanqui.

1527
Incan population reduced by half, mainly due to smallpox brought by Spanish invaders.

1911
Hiram Bingham, an archaeologist from Yale University, rediscovers the site.

1983
Declared a World Heritage Site by UNESCO.

2001
Geologists warn that Machu Picchu is in danger of destruction by a landslide.

BELOW: *Connecticut senator Hiram Bingham discovered Machu Picchu while searching for the last Inca refuge of Vilcabamba.*
BELOW LEFT: *The national flower of Peru, the kantuta.*

survives, but it is thought to have been used to calculate significant dates, such as the solstices. Its name seems to refer to a ceremony in which the sun was said to be tethered to the post at the winter solstice.

Solar observation also seems to have taken place at the Tower of the Sun—a building with a horseshoe-shaped plan and a special window oriented to catch the sun's rays at the winter solstice—and the Temple of the Three Windows. The alignment and arrangement of these windows, with an upright rectangular stone at the centre of the building, has clearly been carefully thought out. An Inca sun festival, known as Inti Raymi, is known to have taken place here during the summer and winter solstices.

MIRACULOUS MASONRY

One of the most remarkable aspects of Machu Picchu is its amazing stonework, and the skill with which the huge white granite blocks were laid without the use of mortar. Many of the shaped stones are locked together, their edges carefully contoured so that one stone fits into another with perfect precision. The result is a wall with joints of almost imperceptible width, and the buildings constructed in this way have proved remarkably resilient, with many still standing.

Machu Picchu lay abandoned for several hundred years before its rediscovery, but although the jungle had encroached during that time and much clearance work was necessary, structural damage to the site was surprisingly limited. Some archaeologists refuse to accept that the Incas, who apparently had no iron tools, no beasts of burden and no knowledge of the wheel, could have produced masonry of such quality, and suggest that this is the work of some pre-Inca community.

Whatever the method used to build it, Machu Picchu provides a tantilizing glimpse into the way of life of an enigmatic people.

LEFT: *Despite the ravages of time and jungle, the skilled stonework of Machu Picchu has survived.*

See also:
The Inca Trails 206-7

the **facts**

- The Amazon River flows for 6,565km (4,080 miles)—the second longest river in the world after the Nile.
- Its area of tropical rainforest covers nearly 6 million sq km (2.3 million square miles).
- A 10-sq km (3.9 square mile) area of rainforest can contain 1,500 species of flowers and 400 bird species.

The **Amazon Basin**

The Amazon Basin contains the world's largest tropical rainforest and extends into nine different countries. The lifeblood of this vast expanse of rainforest is the mighty River Amazon and its tributaries, which together contain about 25 percent of all the water carried by the world's rivers.

This vast expanse of tropical rainforest contains over a million species of plant and animal life and is the repository of the genetic inheritance of the world. Even within a relatively small area the diversity is staggering, with many species still to be recorded and identified.

The Amazon and its tributaries support over 2,000 species of fish, and many unusual mammals and reptiles, including the Amazonian manatee, the pink river dolphin, the giant otter and the spectacled caiman. The diversity of fish is extraordinary, ranging from the small but infamous red-bellied piranha—a feared and voracious carnivore that occurs in large shoals—to other, closely related species which eat seeds and fruits that fall into the water from the fringing trees. The arowana, which can grow up to 1m (3ft) in length, leaps out of the water to pick off beetles from low-hanging branches of trees. The giant otter, a gentle, curious creature, is now one of the rarest animals on earth, as a result of over-hunting and the destruction and pollution of its habitat. They live in extended family groups, containing as many as 30 individuals, and an adult male can measure up to 1.8m (6ft) in length.

Habitat under Threat

The exploitation of the rainforest continues at an alarming rate, with over 4sq km (1.5 square miles) of irreplaceable forest disappearing every hour. Plans to construct highways, railways and hydroelectric schemes have been

Not Enough Trees

Exploitation of the forests has resulted in the loss of many species of tree, and others are now on the brink of extinction.

The Brazilian rosewood has long been in demand for its beautiful timber, used in making furniture. It is now used only as a very thin veneer over other woods, but the trees have been cleared so much that there are not even enough left to supply this market. As a result the Rio Palenque mahogany is listed as one of the ten most endangered plants in the world. Only 12 mature trees remain, but there is hope for the future as many young seedlings are now beginning to sprout.

RIGHT: *Native American Indians have lived in the Amazon Basin for hundreds of years.*

fiercely opposed by conservationists. The destruction of this complex ecosystem has global implications, threatening the survival of the wildlife, the way of life of the Native American Indians who have lived in the forest for centuries, and the opportunities for future generations to enjoy and unlock the mysteries that these forests hold.

One gleam of hope is offered by the Colombian government. Recognizing that the Indians are the best custodians of the forest, in 1989 they created Chiribiquete National Park, an area of 10,000sq km (3,900 square miles) where all external exploitation is banned and the land management is left to the Indians.

Gardens in the Forest

Local American Indian tribes live in harmony with the Amazonian rainforest, exploiting it in a sustainable way by mimicking nature. The traditional Indian custom involves clearing small areas known as *chagra*, or 'gardens in the forest', where the inhabitants cultivate yuccas, peppers, mangoes and other crops. After a short period of fertility the tribe moves on to clear another chagra, leaving the old one to revert to rainforest.

A natural clearing which may have been caused by fire will revert to mature natural forest in as little as 40 years; a chagra may take as long as 200 years. Nevertheless, this is still far preferable to the complete, irreversible destruction caused by clear felling.

BELOW: *An aerial view of the river, winding its way slowly through the forest.*

See also:
The Zaire River 136-7

89 **Iguaçu Falls,** Brazil/Argentina

- The River Iguaçu rises in the Serro do Mar, close to the Brazilian coast south of São Paulo.
- It flows inland (westward) for about 1,320km (820 miles).
- As Niagara Falls straddle two countries (the USA and Canada), Iguaçu Falls form part of the boundary between two countries in South America, Brazil and Argentina.

the **facts**

Iguaçu Falls

The River Iguaçu follows a winding course across the Paraná Plateau until, swollen by tributaries, it drops down via 70 waterfalls that punctuate its path. Where the river eventually reaches the edge of the plateau it plunges over the Iguaçu Falls, shortly before joining the Paraná River. The water here is about 4km (2.5 miles) wide, and the whole width of the river tumbles down a magnificent crescent-shaped cliff. There are as many as 275 separate cascades, some plunging directly 82m (270ft) into the cauldron below, others crashing over a series of smaller cataracts before reaching the river. These smaller cataracts are broken by ledges of resistant rock that disperse the tumbling water into clouds of mist and spray; sunlight then completes the display, creating brilliant ever-changing rainbows.

Between the cascades the rock outcrops are covered in trees and dense foliage—palms, bamboo and lacy tree ferns forming outposts to the surrounding jungle. Beneath the trees, wild tropical flowers—begonias, bromeliads and orchids—splash vivid colours through the undergrowth,

Salto dos Sete Quedas

On the Alto Paraná River, about 160km (100 miles) upstream of the confluence with the Iguaçu, is the Salto dos Sete Quedas or Guairá.

This waterfall, which has an average height of only 34m (110ft), may seem an unlikely contender for the world's greatest fall, but when measured on its average annual flow of water it outstrips all others.

The lip of the Salto dos Sete Quedas is 5km (3 miles) wide and the estimated flow of water is 13,300cu m (470,000cu ft) per second. At this rate of flow, the falls could fill the dome of St Paul's Cathedral in London in less than a second.

BELOW: *Brilliantly-coloured macaws live in the tree canopy around the falls.*

and parrots, macaws and other gaudily feathered birds fly through the canopy.

Viewing the Falls

National parks in both Brazil and Argentina flank the falls, and access to the area is normally through one of these. Perhaps the best view is achieved from a helicopter, when the whole breathtaking panorama is spread out below. But the most thrilling way to experience the falls is from the catwalk that extends over the river, passing the falls at close range and crossing to the far side. At these close quarters you can feel the immense power of the water as it plunges into the abyss below.

The falls are at their most spectacular during the rainy season, from November to March, but there is usually a good show at any time of year. Despite the impression of permanence given by the constant rush of water, the falls have been known to stop. In May and June 1978, during a period of particularly dry weather, the river gradually ceased to flow, and for 28 days not a drop of water passed over the lip. This was the first time that the falls had dried up since 1934, a serious blow to visitors at the time but an excellent demonstration of the delicate balance of nature.

BELOW: *The viewing facilities on both sides of the falls are superb.*

The World's Largest Dam

The Paraná River, the fifth largest in the world, flows with great force, and a huge dam has been built to harness its powers and produce hydroelectric power. Itaipu, on the border between Paraguay and Brazil, was the site selected.

Once the construction work had been completed, sluice gates closed for 40 days to allow the reservoir to fill, creating a new lake 161km (100 miles) long, and covering an area of 1,554sq km (600 square miles). After 14 years of work, during which million of tons of concrete were poured, the world's largest dam and hydroelectric scheme was completed in 1988. Its generators have a capacity of 12,600 megawatts—sufficient to power the whole of Paraguay and the industrial cities of Rio de Janeiro and São Paulo in Brazil.

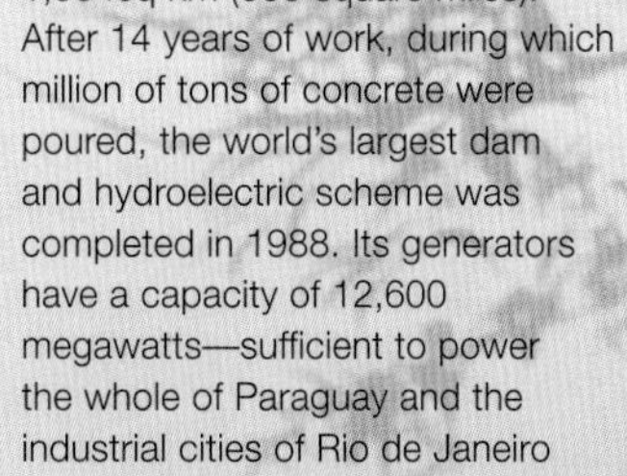

See also:
Angel Falls 194
Niagara Falls 150-1
Victoria Falls 140-1

- The Galapagos Islands in the Pacific Ocean, cover about 7,800sq km (3,012 square miles).
- There are 15 main islands, 42 islets and a further 26 rocks or reefs.
- The archipelago extends 300km (186 miles) from north to south.

the **facts**

Galapagos Islands

Visitors to the Galapagos Islands are always impressed by their beauty, variety and uniqueness. When Charles Darwin came to the islands in 1835 during his epic voyage of discovery on HMS *Beagle* he was particularly inspired by the peculiar nature of the flora and fauna. Darwin saw much here that would subsequently inspire his great thesis, *On the Origin of Species* (1859), in which he formulated his theory of evolution, based on observations made during the voyage.

The Galapagos are a group of oceanic islands formed from lava rising from the sea bed. Over 96 percent of the archipelago is now a national park, with a surrounding marine reserve of 79,900sq km (30,850 square miles).

Darwin's Finches

Galapagos finches are descended from common ancestral stock which arrived by chance from South America. They found a large number of vacant niches in various habitats throughout the islands, and have evolved into 13 species of distinguishable size, shape of bill, plumage, song, diet and habits.

This adaptive radiation is best illustrated by the differences in the beaks of the various species. Some have the typical seed-eating bill; others, that feed on cacti, have developed a long, pointed bill; and yet more have a small tit-like bill for feeding primarily on insects. The woodpecker finch has developed not only a specialized bill, but also a complex behaviour pattern which includes the ability to use a cactus spine to prize larvae out of cracks and crevices.

RIGHT: *A panga (dinghy) brings tourists ashore on Santiago Island.*

Exploring the Islands

The contrast in island habitat is notable. The lowland coastal fringes are arid and dry, and the vegetation here is dominated by cacti. The humidity increases with altitude, and the hillsides between 200m and 500m (650ft and 1,600ft) are covered by lush evergreen forest, while the higher regions have open areas dominated by sedges and ferns.

The flora and fauna of these islands, as with all oceanic archipelagos, depends on chance arrivals by sea or air, although recently humans have also played their part. Many of the animal species found on the islands are unique not only to the archipelago but to specific islands in the group. Two species of seals are found in the waters around the Galapagos Islands, both of which are only found in the area. The Galapagos fur seal is the only tropical representative of a sub-Antarctic genus and is active by night, while the other, the Galapagos sea lion, is active by day. Even more remarkably there are two species of bat which are also endemic to the islands, together with three races of native rat, including a recently discovered giant race, previously known only from fossil remains.

The bird populations of the Galapagos include migratory sea birds, such as the waved albatross, which visits the islands to breed, and no fewer than 28 native species of land birds. Over 750,000 pairs of breeding sea birds make the island their home, including the largest known colony of masked booby in the world, the indigenous Galapagos penguin and the Galapagos dark-rumped petrel.

ABOVE: *A Sally Lightfoot crab shows off its colours on Española Island.*

Island Reptiles

The Galapagos Islands are the only place on earth where you can find marine iguanas. These lizards feed exclusively on seaweed, and have adapted to their marine way of life by developing partially webbed feet. Seven different races of marine iguana, each showing marked variations, have evolved on the different islands. On six of the islands there is also a species of land iguana peculiar to the Galapagos.

The islands are also famous for another reptile, the giant tortoise. Mature individuals can weigh 135kg to 180 kg (300lb to 400lb). Fifteen distinctive races have evolved to adapt to niches for which there are no other competitors—despite this four races are now extinct and a fifth is now represented by a single male.

LEFT: *A marine iguana on the shore of Española Island.*

See also:
Madagascar 138-9
The Great Barrier Reef 220-3

the facts

- Half of the Takesi Trail's length of 40km (25 miles) is made of irregular pieces of stone fitted together.
- Altogether the Inca Empire had about 40,000km (25,000 miles) of roads, varying in width from 50cm (20in), where there were steps, to 6m (20ft), where the land was flat.

The Inca Trails

The Incas, like the Romans, were builders of roads. Like the Romans, too, they preferred to take the most direct route, but unlike them they had to surmount the obstacle of the Andes. This meant that engineers had to perfect techniques that could cope with the often precipitous mountain terrain: where the gradient was steep, they cut steps; where outcrops of rock impeded the shortest route, they bored tunnels. They even cast suspension bridges over gorges. In the uplands, retaining walls were built of stone to keep back the snow; in the desert, adobe walls protected the roads from drifting sand.

Strictly speaking, however, it is incorrect to attribute every mile of paved trail to the Incas, because they inherited roads built by earlier civilizations. Whoever was first responsible for the construction of the roads, many can still be walked today. The finest preserved stretch of Inca paving is in Bolivia, on the Takesi or Inca Trail. During the two days required to complete the hike, the scenery shifts between extremes from black, bare granite mountains brooding over the start of the route to the jungle vegetation of the humid Yungas Valley on the final stretch.

From Ventilla the trail rises steeply to the pass at 4,650m (15,255ft). Although the steps up the mountainside are shallow, this is an arduous and chilly section, but once completed you are rewarded with magnificent views of snow peaks and the Yungas below. The trail then descends

The Inca Road Network

Good communications were key to establishing and administering the Inca empire, and roads traversed their territories from the Amazon in the east to the coastal plain in the west, from what is now Colombia in the north to Argentina in the south.

All roads led to Cuzco, the capital. From there the Sun King sent his messengers *(chasquis)* to the farthest outposts. The *chasquis* ran in relays, covering nearly 320km (200 miles) a day, exchanging the baton in rest houses *(tambos)* at regular intervals along the trails. The baton was a knotted llama wool string called a *quipu* and different shades and thicknesses of wool, along with the number of knots tied, conveyed different messages.

BELOW: *A modern hiking party on the flank of Mount Jirishanka.*

BELOW LEFT: *On the trail through the Villcabamba mountain range.*
BELOW RIGHT: *Pausing for water at Tambomachay.*

to the village of Takesi, after which encouraging signs of plant life reappear, beginning with carpets of moss on the rock. The trail follows the Rio Takesi, then curves around Palli Palli hill to Kakapi and heads down to the Rio Quimasa Chata. From here it crosses the Takesi again, the lowest point at 2,100m (6,890ft), and finishes at Chojilla.

The longer but less strenuous hike from La Cumbre (The Summit), at 4,725m (15,500ft), to Coroico offers a similar scenic contrast over four days. It begins where a statue of Christ helpfully points to a path leading to the highest point at 4,850m (15,910ft), marked by a stone cairn. From there it is downhill all the way along a clear trail to the village of Achura. After passing the tree line the path narrows and becomes progressively more overgrown as the vegetation becomes more tropical. After the suspension bridge at Choro, the path follows the Rio Huaranilla to Chairo, finishing among the citrus and banana plantations of Coroico.

The Litter Trail

The most well-trodden Inca trail is that leading to Machu Picchu in Peru from a point outside Cuzco. In the summer months anyone walking is unlikely to find solitude in the mountains or among the ruins; and even without running into other people, a hiker will surely stumble upon the litter they left behind.

In 1980 the South American Explorers Club arranged the first of several cleanups in which 400kg (880lb) of unburnable debris was collected. The obvious solution of placing a few litter receptacles along the route is simply not an option. The trail, part of the Historical Sanctuary of Machu Picchu, is designated a UNESCO World Heritage Site, and development—anything from bins to public lavatories is forbidden.

See also:
Machu Picchu 196-9

the facts

- The total area of the Tierra del Fuego archipelago is 72,520sq km (28,000 square miles).
- Chile owns 70 percent of the land and the rest belongs to Argentina.
- In the 1830s 3,000 Yahgan Indians lived here. Many died due to disease and the loss of hunting grounds.

Tierra del Fuego

Tierra del Fuego forms part of the hook at the tip of the South American continent, a finger of land reaching towards the vast icy wastes of Antarctica just 965km (600 miles) away. In winter fierce storms lash the desolate coast at the southern tip of South America, driven by the freezing, snow-laden winds from the Antarctic seas. In the summer the land near the coast is balmy and mild, though sudden squalls are a

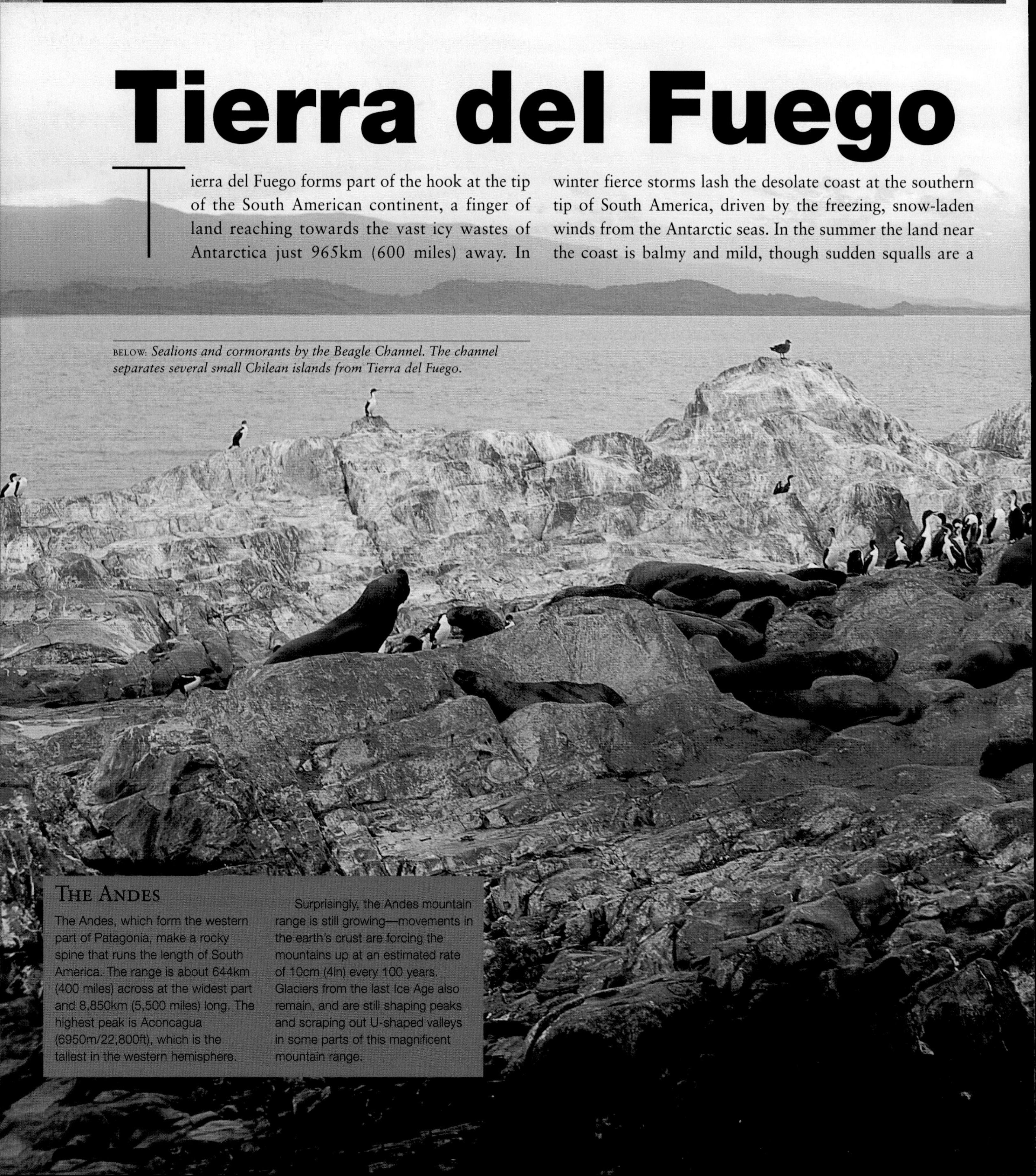

BELOW: *Sealions and cormorants by the Beagle Channel. The channel separates several small Chilean islands from Tierra del Fuego.*

The Andes

The Andes, which form the western part of Patagonia, make a rocky spine that runs the length of South America. The range is about 644km (400 miles) across at the widest part and 8,850km (5,500 miles) long. The highest peak is Aconcagua (6950m/22,800ft), which is the tallest in the western hemisphere.

Surprisingly, the Andes mountain range is still growing—movements in the earth's crust are forcing the mountains up at an estimated rate of 10cm (4in) every 100 years. Glaciers from the last Ice Age also remain, and are still shaping peaks and scraping out U-shaped valleys in some parts of this magnificent mountain range.

threatening reminder that Tierra del Fuego is not far from the wild shores of Antarctica.

Tierra del Fuego and the Antarctic Peninsula once formed a continuous stretch of land, but the continents began to move apart 25 million years ago. Corresponding rock structure and formations provide strong evidence that they were once joined, and fossils suggest that many animals and plants lived both in South America and in Antarctica.

Tierra del Fuego was discovered in 1520 by the Portuguese navigator Fernando Magellan (1480-1521), who named the land after the fires lit by the Indians along the coast as he sailed down what is now the Strait of Magellan. In 1578 Sir Francis Drake caught a glimpse of the small group of islands, later named by Dutch explorers as Cape Hoorn (Cape Horn). A full survey was not undertaken until the 19th century, when the British Admiralty sent two expeditions. The second of these voyages was undertaken by Captain Robert Fitzroy in a small barque named HMS *Beagle*. Fitzroy wanted to take a naturalist with him when he charted these little-known coasts, and he chose 22-year-old Charles Darwin.

Voyage of the Beagle

On 27 December 1831, the *Beagle* set sail from Plymouth in England on a journey that was to last almost five years. Tierra del Fuego was reached in December 1832. Darwin disembarked and remarked of the mountains and glaciers that it was 'scarcely possible to imagine anything more beautiful'. Fitzroy named the snow-dusted mountains that range down the Beagle Channel after Darwin.

As the tiny ship made its way down the channel, Darwin looked for native American Indians. He came across the Yahgan tribe and noted their harsh life. They survived by eating the plant life and taking fragile canoes into the cold and often mountainous seas.

INSET BELOW: *The high peaks of the Torres del Paine National Park in Patagonian Chile.*

Patagonia

Tierra del Fuego is sometimes counted as part of Patagonia, in the southern part of South America. This is a region of rugged beauty, shaped by spectacular mountains, two little-known ice fields and desolate plains. Geographically, the region is roughly divided into two: the Andes and the tablelands.

The tablelands rise from the coast to the foothills of the Andes in a series of steps, and the overlay of soft sedimentary rocks is deeply incised by a number of gorges that run from west to east. In some gorges saltwater lakes have formed, but few carry permanent rivers, and most of the canyons have dried up. The Chilean part of Patagonia on the other hand has magnificent fjords, carved out by the glaciers that once covered the region.

See also:
Galapagos Islands 204-5

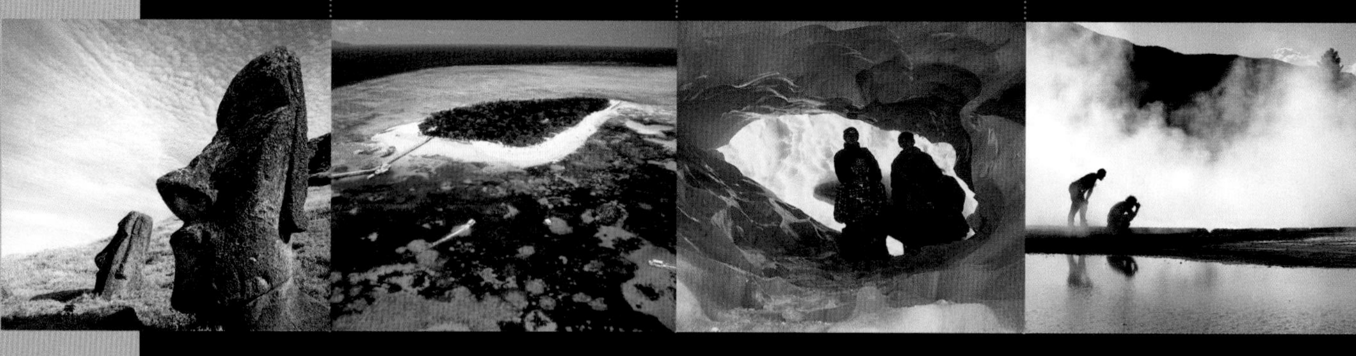

93 **Easter Island**

94 **Sydney Opera House**

95 **Uluṟu (Ayers Rock)**

96 **The Great Barrier Reef**

97 **Glaciers of the Southern Alps**

98 **Rotorua**

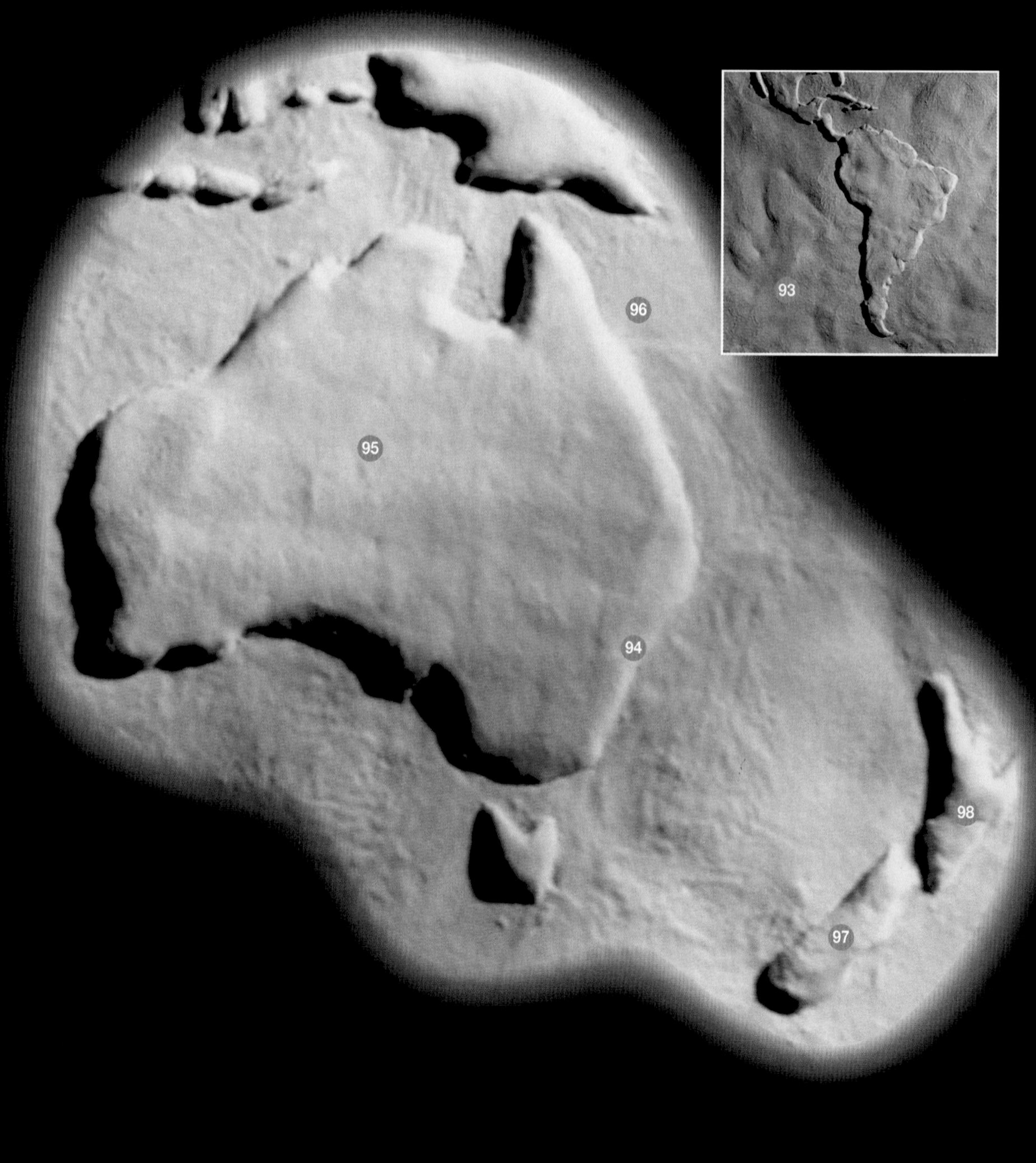

Australasia & Oceania

The Pacific Ocean is larger than the entire land area of the globe, covering an area of about 166 million sq km (64 million square miles). Scattered about it, mere specks of land in this vast sea, are more than 10,000 volcanic and coral islands. This was the last part of the earth to be permanently settled by human beings, the last to be colonized by Europeans, and the last to be freed from colonial dependence.

The Pacific Islanders rank among the greatest long-range seafarers of all time. They sailed their outrigger canoes confidently over enormous distances of empty ocean, navigating by the sun, the stars, sea currents and swells and the flight of birds. Over many centuries they populated all the habitable islands of Oceania. The first human beings in Australia arrived from the southeast of Asia perhaps as long as 40,000 years ago. They were the ancestors of the Australian Aborigines, who, when the first European colonists arrived, are thought to have numbered about 300,000. The earliest people to settle Oceania—maybe 20,000 years ago—were probably also of southeast Asian origin. Most of the main island groups in the western Pacific had been occupied by the first century AD.

Between the fifth and tenth centuries groups moved eastward across the Pacific in canoes tied together to form rafts. They brought bananas, breadfruit and pigs, and set up new homes in New Zealand and Hawaii. On Easter Island, over a period of centuries, enormous and enigmatic statues were created to gaze out over the ocean.

From the early 16th century European ships were charting these waters in search of gold and a navigable route to the Far East, and in 1788 a British colony was established at Sydney Cove in Australia. The dynamic city that grew from these small beginnings is now graced by one of the most beautiful buildings of modern times: the Sydney Opera House.

the facts

- Easter Island is volcanic and roughly triangular in shape, measuring 16km by 18km by 24km (10 miles by 11 miles by 15 miles).
- It lies 3,220km (2,000 miles) southwest of the Galapagos Islands and 4,200km (2,600 miles) west of Valparaíso in Chile, the country by which it was annexed in 1888.

Easter Island

Easter Island offers convincing evidence that truth can be stranger than fiction. It lies in the Pacific Ocean, thousands of miles from any other habitation. The first Europeans to approach it, on Easter Sunday 1722, were confronted with a ring of massive statues gazing out to sea; but the inhabitants appeared welcoming, and lit fires encouraging the visitors to come ashore. When they did so, Captain Roggeveen and his Dutch crew

The Statues

Many of Easter Island's statues stand 3.7m to 4.6m (12ft to 15ft) high. Some are up to 9.8m (32ft) tall and weigh 91.5 tonnes (101 tons). There has been much speculation about how the islanders managed to move these bulky figures into place. Local tradition fiercely insists that the statues walked. None of the statues is shown with legs and, intriguingly, the Easter Island language has a verb that means 'to inch along without the use of legs'.

Recent investigation has shown that the figures have a low point of gravity, and that a team of 15 people can heave one along with ropes at a surprising speed.

observed three different races among the islanders—some dark, some with a reddish skin, and some strikingly pale-skinned with red hair. Some of these people had curiously extended earlobes, into which large discs were fitted and they showed particular reverence for the giant statues. Very few women were seen, and a large part of the population kept out of sight, probably hiding in underground caves.

In 1770 a Spanish expedition from Peru made similar observations: the people were still friendly and the land well cultivated. But Captain Cook, reaching the island only four years later, encountered a very different scene. The land was neglected and barren, the people were listless and demoralized, and they now carried wooden clubs and spears. The huge statues had been overturned, and no one seemed to worship them any more. In the 19th century the island became a target for slave traders, and a massive Peruvian slave raid in 1862 proved appallingly destructive.

Ancestral Voyagers

Connections between the pre-Inca society at Tihuanaco, near Lake Titicaca in Bolivia, and Easter Island have been observed, and there also seem to be links with Peru, where the Spanish conquerors encountered tales of an island territory a long way to the west. Reeds found on Easter Island by some of the first explorers, and vegetables such as the sweet potato and the yucca, are native South American species.

Easter Island tradition speaks of the Long Ears, who came from the east, and the Short Ears, who came from the west later. This suggests original settlers from pre-Inca Latin America (where ear extension is known to have been practised) followed by Polynesians, who later overthrew the religiously minded Long Ears.

ABOVE: *The massive sculptures with their cap-stone 'hats' stare balefully out to sea, and may have been designed to intimidate invaders.*

ABOVE: *Each moai figure was carved from a single piece of rock, quarried on the island and inset with white stone eyes.*

An Unsolved Mystery

After coming close to destroying the Easter Islanders, the Western world finally began to study the people and their culture. Christian missionaries worked to convert the surviving population from their existing beliefs in a god called Make-Make, and in doing so discovered miniature idols that were kept in the people's homes, but apparently not worshipped with any great ceremony. When wooden tablets carved with hieroglyphic signs were discovered, it became clear that this had been a society that had known how to write. Some of the tablets were destroyed as instruments of paganism, but a few survived. Known as *rongorongo* tablets, they used signs representing humans, birds, fish and other items. Their precise meaning is still disputed by experts.

The most fascinating aspect of Easter Island, however, is the thousand or so huge statues, which the islanders call *moai*. What were they for? Do they represent gods or ancestors? Why do they stare out to sea? The statues are still keeping their secrets.

See also:
The Nazca Lines 195

94 Sydney Opera House, Australia

Sydney Opera House

In 1957 the competition to design an opera house for Sydney attracted 222 entries from 32 countries. The winner, a Danish architect named Jørn Utzon, had never seen the site and, like many other entrants, had to work from photographs. His design, inspired partly by the sails of yachts on Sydney's immense and beautiful harbour, and partly by Mayan and Aztec temples in Mexico, was to give Australia its most celebrated and recognizable manmade landmark.

Technically, Utzon's was the most difficult design to realize, though by far the most unusual and exciting. Both the appearance of the proposed building and its escalating cost provoked heated public debate. The opera house was supposed to open in 1963 and cost $7 million. It actually took ten years longer to construct and cost over $100 million. Most of the extra money was raised by lotteries.

Somehow the project kept moving forward amid incessant argument and violent storms of hostility and Utzon resigned in disgust in 1966. The beautiful concrete shells or 'sails'—elliptic paraboloids—proved impossible to construct as originally conceived and the design had to be modified. Thousands of hours of computer time went into solving the difficulties, and the final building is as much a triumph of Ove Arup's engineering as of Utzon's design.

BELOW: *An exuberant inflatable sculpture sets the party mood outside the Opera House.*

A Titanic White Swan

The end result is one of the most beautiful major buildings raised in any country since World War II—and indeed is one of the most beautiful of all time. It is seen at its best from the waters of the harbour, where it suggests a titanic white swan that might be about to take to the air. On the sails are more than a million Swedish antifungal ceramic tiles, which glint in the sun and never need cleaning, and after dark the building is floodlit.

the facts

- The Sydney Opera House complex covers an area of 1.8ha (4.5 acres).
- The highest roof vault, above the concert hall, is 67m (221ft) above sea level.
- The roof shells weigh 161,000 tonnes (158,424 tons) and are supported by 350km (217 miles) of cables.
- The concert hall organ is the world's biggest mechanical organ and has 10,500 pipes.

INSET BELOW: *Abseiling down the roof 'sails' as part of the Opera House's 25th birthday celebrations in 1998.*

the history

1954

Government sets up committee and appeal fund for new opera house.

1957

Jørn Utzon's design wins competition.

1959

Construction of the opera house begins.

1966

Jørn Utzon resigns.

28 Sep 1973

First performance in Opera Theatre.

20 Oct 1973

Sydney Opera House officially opened by Queen Elizabeth II.

The opera house stands by the harbour on Bennelong Point, named after an Australian Aboriginal friend of the colony's first governor. Inside, the effect has been dubbed Space Age Gothic, with steel ribs and concrete fans and 6,225sq m (67,000sq ft) of tinted glass. The biggest theatre curtains in the world are hung here, each covering close to 93sq m (1,000sq ft) and needing six men to lift it. Woven from wool in France in the Aubusson manner, they were designed by an Australian, John Coburn, to represent the sun and the moon. Within the building are five performing halls, an exhibition hall, a restaurant and a bistro. The opera hall seats 1,550 people, the concert hall 2,700, and the Sydney Symphony Orchestra, the Sydney Philharmonia Choir and Sydney Theatre all have their homes here.

LEFT *There are five different performance venues within the Opera House.*

THE COATHANGER

Sydney Harbour Bridge, near the opera house, was previously the city's best-known landmark. Functional in grey steel, its curving arch—locally nicknamed the Coathanger—has immense strength and a certain elegance. It was designed by an Australian railway engineer, John Job Crew Bradfield, who was born at Sandgate in Queensland. The road across the bridge, which also carries trains, was named Bradfield Highway in tribute to him.

Demand for a bridge over the bay, which had previously been crossed only by ferries, goes back almost to Sydney's earliest days; some called for a tunnel, rather than a bridge. Approval was eventually given to Bradfield's design in 1923 and it was completed in 1932. Work had progressed through the Depression years, hence the grey paint, the cheapest available. The bridge has a total length of 1,150m (3,770ft), the single main span being 503m (1,650ft) long. The crown of the arch is 134m (439ft) above the water of the busy bay. The walkway along the eastern side commands excellent views of both the harbour and the city.

LEFT: *Ceramic roof tiles on the Opera House reflect the sky.*

See also:
Feats of Engineering 224-5

95 **Uluṟu (Ayers Rock),** Australia

- Uluṟu is 2.4 km (1.5 miles) long, 1.6km (1 mile) wide and towers 348m (1,143ft) high above the desert plain.
- Uluṟu is the largest exposed monolith in the world.
- The custodians of Uluṟu and Kata Tjuṯa are Aṉangu, the Local Aboriginal people who live within Uluṟu-Kata Tjuṯa National Park.

the **facts**

Uluṟu (Ayers Rock)
& Kata Tjuṯa

Uluṟu (Ayers Rock) lies near the southwestern corner of Northern Territory in the dry, red heart of Australia. Dusty outback roads lead from Alice Springs to motels near Uluṟu, allowing spectators time to experience the spectacle of the rock in the changing light of morning and evening. As the sun sets the rock appears to glow from an inner fire as it changes from the dry brown of the day to an intense, fiery red, before becoming a black silhouette in the fading light. The dawn light reveals Uluṟu in even more beautiful pastel shades. When visiting this area, bear in mind the blistering heat of the Australian desert and remember to bring the most important item with you, water. In this region dehydration, sunstroke and heat exhaustion are potential hazards, as is the risk from prolonged exposure to excess ultra-violet (UV) rays.

BELOW: *Uluṟu stands in the Uluṟu-Kata Tjuṯa National Park, one of the few World Heritage properties listed for both its natural as well as its cultural values.*

Geological History

Uluṟu (Ayers Rock) is made from a coarse-grained sandstone, a sedimentary rock called arkose sandstone. Kata Tjuṯa is formed of conglomerate, a sedimentary rock which is a mix of boulders, pebbles and gravel held together by mud and sand. As a result it contains many minerals and different types of rock including granite and basalt.

The distinctive red colour of Uluṟu can be attributed to weathering of the rock. Time and environmental factors such as rainwater and oxygen affect the iron minerals in the rock (imagine how iron looks when it rusts). The weathering of the feldspar minerals inside the sandstone also contributes to the beautiful colour. It's also interesting to note that both Uluṟu and Kata Tjuṯa extend for several kilometres underground.

LEFT: *Kata Tjuta in the Uluru-Kata Tjuta National Park is also known as Mount Olga.*

Uluru was first seen by a European in 1872, when Australian explorer Ernest Giles crossed this part of the desert. However, long before Europeans came to Australia, and the British created settlements, Uluru had been a significant part of Anangu culture (Local Aboriginal culture), and there are many Anangu paintings around the base of the rock. Note that Anangu regard it as disrespectful to climb the rock, although it is not prohibited. The Uluru-Kata Tjuta National Park, in which Uluru stands, is governed by Tjukurpa, a word with no precise English translation, but which conveys law, tradition, ceremony, creation stories, religious philosophy and everything that has ever been, is and always will be.

The strata at Uluru are approximately vertical, while those at Kata Tjuta (Mount Olga), some 24km (16 miles) away to the west, are close to horizontal, a contrast that may explain the difference in patterns of erosion between the two outcrops. Two main types of erosion have affected both areas: rain and thermal erosion. Despite their desert locations, they do have a measurable rainfall of a few inches per year, but this tends to fall in one or two major storms every few years. During these storms, raging torrents of water flood down the sides of the rocks, washing away any loose particles in their path. Thermal erosion, on the other hand, is caused by the extreme temperature variation between very hot days and very cold nights, when the constant expansion and contraction of the rock eventually causes fragments to break away.

See also:
Devil's Tower 172-3

96 The Great Barrier Reef, Australia

The Great Barrier Reef

The Great Barrier Reef extends along the east coast of Australia from Lady Elliot Island to the tip of Cape York. This area of shallow coastal waters, where a staggering diversity of species thrives, is biologically, geologically and scenically one of the greatest natural wonders in the world. Its recognition as a World Heritage Site, a Biosphere Reserve and a marine park reflect the vital importance of this beautiful but vulnerable area.

Living animals or coral polyps make up the Great Barrier Reef, similar in design to the sea anemones found on the shore. These tiny, primitive animals live in vast colonies, each of which was derived from an individual polyp that has undergone innumerable divisions. The coral is actually made up of a soft body surrounded by a skeleton of limestone, which creates the fabric of the reef. A living reef is the product of thousands of years of life and death: the bulk of it is made up of the empty skeletons of past generations of polyps, which are covered by a thin veneer of living organisms.

Creature Comfort

Coral reefs are restricted to waters that maintain a temperature of between 22°C and 28°C (between 72°F and 82°F) throughout the year. This tropical habitat is capable of supporting very complex life systems—the most diverse ecosystem known on earth. The Great Barrier Reef contains over 400 species of hard and soft coral. Hard, reef-forming corals occur in many different shapes and sizes, and include mushroom corals, brain corals and staghorn corals, in shades ranging from vivid red to dazzling yellow to black. Over 4,000 species of molluscs have been identified—including chitons, snails, giant clams and octopus—as well as countless numbers of sponges, anemones, worms, crustaceans and echinoderms.

RIGHT AND BELOW: *Scuba diving on the Great Barrier Reef brings thousands of tourist dollars to the coastal resorts every year.*

the facts

- The Great Barrier Reef extends for a distance of over 2,011km (1,250 miles).
- It comprises around 2,900 reefs, ranging in size from 0.01sq km (0.004 square miles) to 100sq km (38.6 square miles).
- The total area covered is 348,698sq km (134,633 square miles)—greater than the land area of Great Britain.
- The coral's limestone skeletons create walls up to 100m (328ft) high.

TUSA

the **history**

17 million years ago
Reef-building corals begin inhabiting Australia's eastern coastal waters.

1768
First report of reef, by explorer Louis-Antoine de Bougainville.

1770
Captain Cook's ship *Endeavour* grounded on reef.

1960s
Mass tourism has adverse effects on reef.

1975
Great Barrier Reef Marine Park established to manage and protect reef.

1981
Declared a World Heritage Site by UNESCO.

More than 1,500 species of fish live in and around the Great Barrier Reef, presenting a kaleidoscope of colours and patterns as shoals dart one way and then another. The reef is also important for its numerous species of whale, including minke, killer and humpback. These waters are an important breeding area for the humpback whales, and mothers and suckling calves are sighted regularly. This is also a home to six of the seven species of sea turtle in the world, all of which are endangered and depend on the remote islands of the reef for safe nesting sites.

Over 240 species of waders and sea birds nest on the low islands of sand and coral, with shearwaters, tropicbirds, frigatebirds, six species of tern including roseate terns, as well as noddies, white-bellied sea eagles and ospreys among their number.

ABOVE AND LEFT: *A variety of shallow-drafted craft from huge catamarans to small dinghies take visitors to the best dive and snorkel sites between the coral atolls.*

TRAPPED ON THE REEF

The great British explorer Captain James Cook (1728–79) accidentally stumbled across the Great Barrier Reef during his epic voyage in 1770, which involved charting the waters off the east coast of Australia.

LEFT: *Around 1,500 species of fish live on the reef.*

The reef was very nearly the downfall of the expedition, for Cook had in ignorance sailed northwards for over 998km (629 miles) inside the reef itself. It was only when he reached Cape Tribulation that he became aware of the labyrinth of reefs that lay to his seaward side and the consequent danger to him and his crew. Their ship *Endeavour*, a converted coalship weighing 373 tonnes (368 tons), eventually grounded not far from Cape Tribulation on 12 June 1770. Over the following weeks guns, ballast, ammunition, old food, water and wood were jettisoned and a plug was made of a sail spread with sheep dung to mend the hole made by the reef.

Boats were dispatched to find the best routes out and on 4 August the ship set off, though it was still leaking. Not until 13 August did the *Endeavour* eventually sail clear of the reef.

See also:
Galapagos Islands 204-5
Madagascar 138-9

The urge to conquer distances, heights and inhospitable terrain has inspired some remarkable engineering achievements. Behind every new construction lies the imagination and invention of its designer, and the blood, sweat and toil of hundreds and thousands of workers who made the idea a reality.

the facts

- The Itaipú Dam in South America generates 75 billion kw of electricity a year and stands 643ft (196m) high.
- The Channel Tunnel between France and England is the longest underwater tunnel in the world.
- The Incas cut and transported huge blocks of stone to the site at Machu Picchu, without using wheels.

Feats of Engineering

WATER SUPPLY

Ancient Rome's expert engineers built not only long, straight, well-drained roads to carry the imperial troops, but also sturdy aqueducts and reservoirs to supply the ever-growing population of Rome.

The growth of modern conurbations has led to a demand for water-supply on a far greater scale, resulting in awe-inspiring projects such as the vast Hoover Dam on the Colorado River along the Arizona-Nevada border in the US and the Three Gorges Dam in China.

Crossing water presents a different set of difficulties. Pontoon (floating) bridges were used as early as the fifth century BC by Persians crossing the Bosphorus.

Ironmaster Abraham Darby III (1750–91) sparked an engineering revolution with the first cast-iron bridge, across the River Severn in England. San Francisco's Golden Gate suspension bridge, which was completed in 1937, used thick cables composed of thousands of separate wire strands to secure its immense span.

CLOCKWISE FROM ABOVE: *The Eden Project in Cornwall, England; underneath the Sydney Harbour Bridge in Sydney, Australia; the London Eye in London, England; the Skytower and AA building in Auckland, New Zealand; the Lovell Radio Telescope at Jodrell Bank, England; Musée du Louvre in Paris, France; a Roman aqueduct near Nerja in Spain.*

REACH FOR THE STARS

Building high presents unique engineering problems. Gustave Eiffel's decorative lacy ironwork in the Eiffel Tower was designed to minimize wind force. Malaysia's twin 451.9-m (1,482ft) Petronas Towers, built in Kuala Lumpur in 1996, use an innovative high-strength concrete and a damper on each tower. In January 2004 even these two giants were outdone by Taiwan's 508-m (1,666.6ft) Taipei 101 tower.

But the greatest construction jobs were those carried out by the ancient Egyptians and the Incas in Peru, whose enormous structures were erected without the help of sophisticated machinery and computer-aided design.

LAND

Before the advent of the railways, canals—artificial waterways punctuated by locks to allow for fluctuations in the terrain, which could take hours to negotiate—were the speediest means of commercial transport. The Suez Canal, built in the 1860s to provide a direct 190-km (118 mile) route from the Mediterranean to the Red Sea, was excavated by 1.5 million Egyptian workers without the aid of any sophisticated equipment—just picks and shovels.

Inconvenient geography is a constant challenge to rail engineers. On the Canadian Pacific Railroad, for example, they had to navigate a 1:22 gradient through the heights of Kicking Horse Pass to complete the connection between Montréal and Vancouver.

See also:
The Eiffel Tower 26-9
The Great Wall of China 82-5
The Three Gorges Dam 90-1

97 Glaciers of the Southern Alps, NZ

the facts

- Only 24km (15 miles) separate the Fox and Franz Josef glaciers.
- Westland National Park, which contains both glaciers, covers an area of 87,817ha (217,000 acres).
- The Tasman Glacier is the largest in New Zealand. In places it is 610m (2,000ft) thick.

Glaciers of the Southern Alps

The Southern Alps form a high mountain barrier along the western side of the South Island of New Zealand. The highest point is Mount Cook at 3,764m (12,349 ft); it is only 32km (20 miles) from the summit westward across the coastal strip to the Pacific Ocean. To the east the land descends more gradually for 130km (80 miles) across the Canterbury Plains to the coast. The westerly winds that blow in from the Tasman Sea are laden with moisture, and as the damp air rises against the mountains it drops heavy snowfalls along the range that feed the glaciers. The three most famous are the Tasman, Fox and Franz Josef glaciers.

The glaciers on the western side of the mountains are short and steep, tumbling downward like frozen cataracts that reach into the dense, subtropical evergreen rainforests in an extraordinary juxtaposition. On the eastern side of the range the glaciers are quite different in character, with the higher reaches typically steep and rugged, patterned by networks of crevasses that make travel difficult. Lower down, these glaciers flow to low altitudes, and the Tasman Glacier reaches almost as far as the central plain.

The Fox and Franz Josef glaciers flow to the west, the latter reaching 11km (7 miles) in length, although both have receded in recent years. Both are within the Westland National Park, an area that includes alpine peaks, snow fields, glaciers, forests, rivers and lakes. Lake Mathieson provides a famous view of the three major peaks—Cook, Tasman and La Perouse—reflected in its calm waters.

Crowning Glory

The Tasman Glacier, which flows down from Mount Cook, is its crowning glory. The glacier forms a narrow tongue of ice 27km (17 miles) long that widens in places to as much as 3km (2 miles), and is very active, flowing as fast as 51cm to 64cm (20in to 25in) per day. Despite its high speed the glacier is gradually retreating: its snout is only 762m (2,500ft) above sea level, where temperatures are relatively high, and the rate of melting and evaporation is greater than its flow. New Zealand underwent its most recent process of glaciation in the last Ice Age, and was covered in ice until the earth began to warm again about 10,000 years ago. Today, New Zealand's glaciers continue to retreat, and the long-term effects of current global warming may be to melt them completely.

ABOVE: *The Fox Glacier is a sea of ice which pours from the mountains down into the forest.*

Naming the Glaciers

Tasman Glacier takes the name of Dutch explorer Abel Tasman, who was sent on an expedition in 1642 by the Dutch East India Company to settle the vexed question of whether a great southern continent existed. No other European set foot in New Zealand for over 100 years.

Captain Cook arrived in 1769–70 and noted the existence of the Franz Josef Glacier, but another hundred years or so passed before its exploration by geologist Julius von Haast in 1865. He named the glacier—then 3km (2 miles) closer to the coast than it is now—in tribute to Emperor Franz Josef of Austria.

Fox Glacier was originally known as the Victoria Glacier, but was retitled during a visit by New Zealand's Prime Minister, Sir William Fox, in 1872.

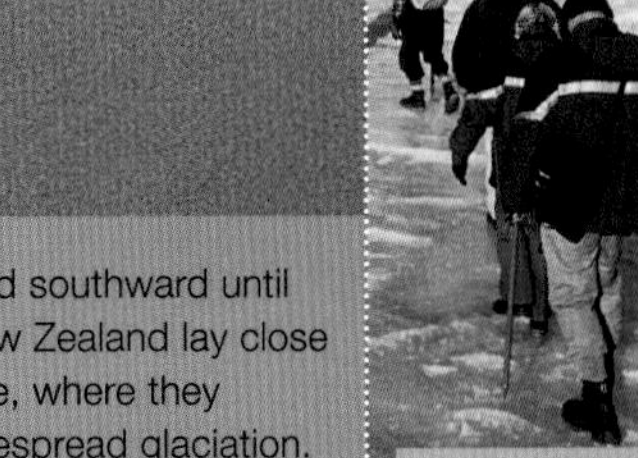

LEFT: *Helicopter tours make landing on the glaciers easy.*

BELOW: *Hiking on the Franz Josef Glacier.*

The Changing Climate of New Zealand

The climate of New Zealand, like that of many other regions, has gone through change over time. More than 500 million years ago New Zealand was a part of the ancient super-continent of Gondwana, and lay about 35 degrees north of the equator. During the next 250 million years Gondwana drifted southward until Australia and New Zealand lay close to the South Pole, where they experienced widespread glaciation.

The continuing rotation of Gondwana over the next 120 million years took New Zealand northward again into warmer temperate or sub-tropical regions, and the ice sheets disappeared. At about this time Gondwana began to break apart to form the different continents that we know today.

- Pohutu is the greatest geyser in New Zealand, usually spouting about every 20 minutes to a height of 30m (100ft).
- When the Waimangu Geyser appeared in 1900 it was the most powerful in the world, firing a mixture of mud, steam and water as high as 457m (1,500ft) into the air.

Rotorua

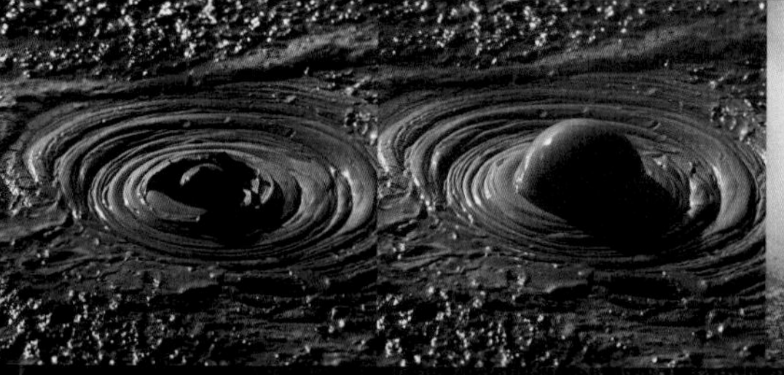

Geothermal activity at Rotorua, near the heart of New Zealand's North Island, has drawn tourists here for many years, and the Maori settlement and Maori Arts and Crafts Institute provide an added attraction, giving an insight into the tribal customs of the earliest New Zealand settlers. The Maoris have traditionally used the hot springs for cooking, washing and heating, but the springs are also reputed to have healing properties, particularly for arthritis and rheumatism, and the Queen Elizabeth Hospital still uses the sulphurous waters in its treatment regime.

Nowhere in Rotorua is far from thermal activity of some sort. The town's many spas include the former Bath House, founded in 1908, and now a museum. A popular boat trip takes visitors to Mokoia Island, in the middle of Lake Rotorua, where they can take a dip in Hinemoa's hot pool. On the edge of the town is the Whakarewarewa thermal area and Geyser Flat, where Pohutu, the splashing geyser, can be seen. Normally the smaller Prince of Wales Feathers geyser close by gives a display shortly before Pohutu erupts, like a prelude to the main act. Near by are bubbling, sulphurous mud pools, and the rock is hot underfoot.

Glorious Technicolour

About 10km (6 miles) southeast of Rotorua along Highway 5 are the famous blue and green lakes of Waimangu—hot water lakes in an extinct volcano crater. The water is heated at depth and dissolves different minerals in its upward passage, painting the water various vivid shades. The source of the water in each lake is probably different, and each has a separate route to the surface, leaching various minerals from the rocks to make the different colours. Iron oxides in the low cliffs surrounding the lakes produce a contrasting red, and in some places yellow is the result of

How Hot Springs Work

There are three basic criteria for hot springs: a good supply of ground water, a source of heat, and a suitable vent from the underground reservoir to the surface. New Zealand's wet climate ensures plentiful ground water, and the molten rock below ground provides a steady supply of heat. After a volcanic eruption residual lava frequently slips back into the magma chamber, leaving voids in the rocks above that can be filled with water, providing reservoirs for hot springs.

If there is no obstruction in the passage from the reservoir to the surface, a hot spring will form, gently bubbling as the hot water continually rises towards the surface.

LEFT AND BELOW: *Boiling mudpools and steaming sulphurous lakes at Wai-o-Tapu, Rotorua.*

sulphurous deposits. Throughout most of the 19th century the famous Pink and White Terraces in Waimangu covered an area of more than 5ha (12 acres) and attracted crowds of curious tourists. Tragically, an eruption of nearby Tarawera Mountain destroyed this famous landmark on 10 June 1886, along with several villages, burying everything under a huge shower of hot ash and debris, and killing 150 people. However, hot springs continued to bubble in the area, and in 1900 a new geyser, the Waimangu Geyser, appeared. In four years its power had decreased, and by 1908 the geyser had become extinct once more.

Geysers

Geysers work on a principle similar to that of hot springs, but they erupt scalding hot water fountains—some every few minutes, some separated by hours or even days—and they are not always regular.

The essential factor that changes a hot spring into a geyser is an obstruction in the passage leading to the surface. As the water in the reservoir heats it expands: if that expansion is confined by an obstruction the pressure increases, and so does the temperature of the water. The water becomes super-heated until the pressure can no longer be contained and the water rushes upwards. The reduction in pressure promotes instant boiling and an explosive release of steam in the reservoir that forces the water upwards ever faster.

See also:
Beppu 103
Pamukkale 70-1
Volcanic Iceland 14-15

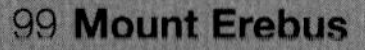

99 **Mount Erebus**

100 **Deception Island**

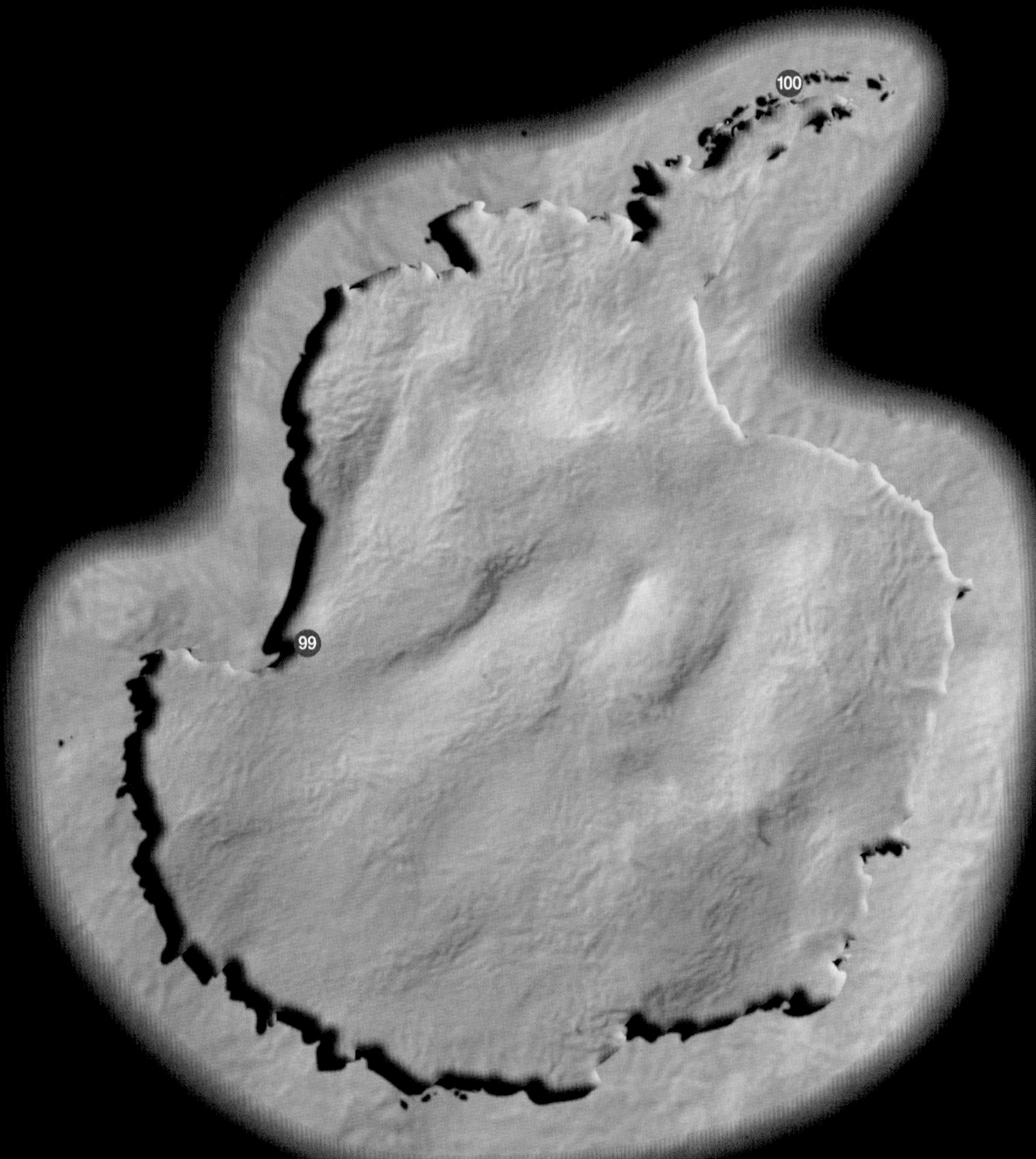

Antarctica

In 1820 the captain of a Russian ship, the *Vostok*, sighted a series of icy hillocks in the Southern Ocean. A couple of days later a British ship, the *Williams*, arrived and confirmed his sighting—the first record of the Antarctic mainland. There had been talk of a 'southern land' for hundreds of years, but not until 1840 was it established that this is a continent, rather than a group of islands.

In fact this cold continent is the fifth largest, exceeding Australia and Europe in size. Of its 14 million sq km (5,404,000 square miles), 13.72 million sq km (5,295,920 square miles)—about 98 percent—are made up of thick ice; the rest is barren rock. Its mountainous terrain ranges from the Bentley Subglacial Trench, at 2,555m (8,382ft) high, to the 4,987-m (16,361ft) Vinson Massif. About half the 17,968-km (11,165 mile) coastline is formed of glacier shelves, and over ten percent of the whole continent is made up of floating ice. This is the coldest, highest, driest and windiest of the continents—and in summer it receives more radiation from the sun than the equator. It is also a changing continent, at a rate that alarms some observers, who have noted the retreat of ice shelves due to global warming, and increased levels of ultraviolet light through the biggest hole known in the ozone layer.

Even this mainly uninhabitable region has not escaped human attention. Whalers have been active around the South Shetland Islands since the 18th century, and in the 1920s a sealing expedition set up a hut in Bouvetøya, one of the most inhospitable islands on earth as well as being the most remote. The late 20th century saw a flurry of scientific research stations being set up by several different countries. The Antarctic Treaty, which came into force in 1961, provides a code for all nations operating in the area, without giving any one nation territorial rights.

99 **Mount Erebus,** Antarctica

the facts

- The summit of Mount Erebus is 3,794m (12,448ft).
- Its crater is 805m (2,640ft) across and 274m (900ft) deep.
- At the bottom of the crater is a small lake of molten lava.
- The name 'Erebus' comes from the Ancient Greek word *erebos* which means darkness.

Mount Erebus

Mount Erebus on Ross Island forms a beacon for anyone venturing into this daunting area of Antarctica. The presence of an active volcano amid the ice and snow of a frozen continent seemed extremely enigmatic in the days when the science of geology was in its infancy, but today's geologists are no longer suprised by such phenomena. Volcanic rocks are quite common in Antarctica, although most of them are geologically very old and represent activity at times when the continent was not in its present polar position.

Volcanic rocks are important indicators of continental movements and can be a useful aid to plotting the ancient wanderings of the continents over the surface of the globe. The geologically young McMurdo Volcanic Province in the Ross Sea region and the related volcanoes of Marie Byrd Land are simply indicative of recent continental movement in Antarctica. Some Antarctic volcanoes—particularly the island volcanoes of the Southern Ocean—have been active during the last 200 years. Many eruptions have gone unwitnessed, to be recorded towards the end of activity or after the event, simply because the region is so sparsely populated. Only on Deception Island are there stations within the damage radius of the volcano.

Erebus—An Irresistible Draw

Ascent of this dramatic landmark rising above the sea ice has been a goal for explorers and mountaineers since its discovery. During Ernest Shackleton's 1907–9 expedition in the *Nimrod*, a party of six men made the first ascent of the mountain. They reached the summit on 10 March 1908. During the 1974–5 season a New Zealand geological party descended into the main crater and established a camp there, but a violent eruption prevented a further descent into the inner crater. On 17 September 1984 the volcano erupted again, throwing volcanic bombs outside the main crater. It is still the subject of intense geological research.

But it is not only geologists who are drawn to Mount Erebus. Modern explorers cannot resist the temptation to photograph the mountain in all its moods, and the early explorers—including Edward Wilson, doctor and naturalist on both of Captain Scott's expeditions—were compelled to commit its beauty to paper in watercolours. Botanists, too, have a special interest in Tramway Ridge, high on the mountain's flanks, where an area of fumaroles supports rich vegetation on the warm ground.

RIGHT: *Smoke rises from the crater of Mount Erebus on Ross Island.*
BELOW: *Mount Terror and Mount Erebus, both on Ross Island.*

The Discovery of Erebus

On 9 January 1841 James Clark Ross and Francis Crozier, in their ships HMS *Erebus* and HMS *Terror*, emerged with relief from the dangers of the pack ice into the open water of the Ross Sea. Three days later they saw a magnificent mountain range with peaks rising to 2,438m (8,000ft), which Ross christened the Admiralty Range.

The ships continued south, following the mountains. On 28 January 1841 the explorers were astonished to see, according to *Erebus* surgeon Robert McCormick, 'a stupendous volcanic mountain in a state of high activity'. The scientists on board were stunned to find an active volcano in this frozen land. The smoking volcano was duly named Mount Erebus, and a smaller extinct cone to the east Mount Terror, after the two ships.

Antarctic Volcanoes

Mount Melbourne, just across McMurdo Sound from Ross Island, has fumarole activity on its summit. The combination of steam and sub-zero temperatures has formed many delicate ice pillars, and despite the altitude there is a unique bacterial flora living around the fumaroles.

In 1893 the Norwegian CA Larsen, making a rare voyage south into the Weddell Sea along the east coast of the Antarctic Peninsula, reported seeing volcanic activity at Seal Nunataks. For many years this distant observation was regarded with scepticism by many geologists, who argued that it was probably a cloud that he had seen, but recent work has found evidence of fumarole activity in the area.

See also:
Mount Fuji 104-5
Mount Kilimanjaro 134-5

For those who live in temperate climates the weather is usually little more than a handy topic of conversation or, at worst, an inconvenience. Occasionally, however, Mother Nature reminds us all who's in charge, and volcanoes, earthquakes, floods or tornadoes strike even the most sheltered corners with devastating effect.

- Antarctica's lowest recorded temperature ever was -89.4°C (-129°F).
- Some parts of the Atacama Desert have had no rain for more than four centuries.
- The hottest place in the world is El Azizia in the Sahara. In 1922 the temperature hit 57.8°C (136°F).

The Elements

AIR

Hurricanes develop over tropical oceans, taking their energy from evaporating water and moving at speeds of over 120kph (75mph) before gradually losing their energy when they meet land. Tornadoes are violently spinning funnels of air that have been known to travel up to 483kph (300mph), leaving wide trails of destruction.

The US and Canada are especially vulnerable to tornadoes, which gather humid air from the Gulf of Mexico. The Great Plains area of the US, between the Rocky Mountains and the Appalachians, has so many tornadoes that it has become known as Tornado Alley.

CLOCKWISE FROM RIGHT: *Bryce Canyon National Park in Utah, USA; riding the waves off the Hawaiian island of Oahu; Wave Rock, Western Australia; an eruption of Mount St Helens in the USA; walking the ridge of Mingsho Shan, Inner Mongolia.*

WATER

Cherrapunji, 1,290m (4,232ft) above sea level and overlooking the plains of Bengal, has the world's heaviest rainfall with an annual average of 1,163cm (458in). Seasonal monsoons hit it with full force and ironically, since much of the torrential rains run into the valley below, residents often have to walk long distances for fresh water.

Antarctica is not only the coldest continent but also the windiest, the highest and, surprisingly, the driest. It has so little precipitation that it is statistically as dry as the Sahara. The Atacama Desert, on the coast of Chile, has the lowest known rainfall, with less than 0.01cm (0.004in) a year.

EARTH AND FIRE

The volcano, Mount St Helens in Washington State in the US, erupted with devastating force on 18 May 1980. A vast area was affected by the volcanic ash and 100 people were killed.

Earthquakes are closely associated with volcanoes and the volcanic islands on the Pacific Rim, known as 'The Ring of Fire', mean that countries such as Japan are particularly vulnerable. In 1906 the San Andreas Fault caused a quake which devastated San Francisco.

See also:
Antarctica 230-7
Sahara Desert 126-7
Volcanic Iceland 14-15

- Sir Hubert Wilkins made the first powered flight in the Antarctic on 16 November 1928 from Deception Island.
- Between 1912 and 1931 a post office operated on the island, and the first stamp was cancelled on 6 March 1913.

the **facts**

Deception Island

Sitting among the South Shetland Islands, Deception Island is shaped like a horseshoe, a roughly circular ridge open to the sea on its southern side. It is an ancient volcano whose central cone has collapsed to form a caldera, now occupied by a crater lake breached by the sea. Many minor vents have since been active around the rim of the caldera, reinforcing the island's shape. The South Shetland Islands are largely volcanic, formed in response to the consumption of oceanic crust along their northwestern margin.

Discovery of Deception Island and the Antarctic Mainland

The South Shetland Islands are so-called because they lie in the same latitude south as the Scottish Shetland Islands in the north. It is possible that Dirck Gherritz, a Dutchman, sighted the islands in 1599. They were rediscovered in February 1819 when William Smith's brig *Williams* was blown off course while rounding Cape Horn, en route from Buenos Aires to Valparaíso.

The Admiralty chartered the *Williams* and placed her under the command of Edward Bransfield, with Smith acting as the pilot. Charged with charting the South Shetland Islands, they sighted Deception Island on 29 January 1820. The following day, they sighted 'Trinity Land' (now known as Trinity Peninsula) and became, arguably, the first men to sight the Antarctic mainland.

Bransfield Strait is also volcanic in origin, but formed by sea-floor spreading behind the volcanic arc of the islands. Penguin and Bridgeman islands are young volcanoes but, unlike Deception Island, are no longer active.

A shore station, Aktieselskabet Hektor, was established at Whalers Bay on Deception Island in 1912. A Stipendiary Magistrate had been appointed by the Falkland Islands government for the 1911–12 and 1912–13 whaling season, and he was resident on Deception during the seasons until the station closed; whaling from the island ceased in 1931.

A Rapid Rescue

A British base was built at Deception Island in 1944, followed by Argentine and Chilean stations in 1948 and 1955. On 4 December 1967 a sudden eruption in the northwest corner of Port Foster showered ash and pumice over the Argentine station, and everyone was quickly evacuated onto the nearby Chilean vessel *Piloto Pardo*. Subsequent visits revealed that a new island had been formed by the eruption. Some personnel returned to Deception Island the following season to assess the damage, and the bases were partly reoccupied.

In 1969 and 1970 there were more eruptions and activity on Mount Pond, near the British and Chilean bases with heavy falls of ash over the buildings, and the entire Chilean station collapsed except for the brick-built entrance arch. A lahar, a river of mud, ash, blocks of ice and slurry, triggered by the heat of the eruption, flowed through the British base, knocking down one wall and creating a window with a view of the bay as it left. Earthquakes shook the ground and tilted some of the oil storage tanks. Once again the *Piloto Pardo* came to the rescue. Evacuees were grateful that the volcano had chosen to erupt during the summer season, while ships were about; had the eruptions occurred during the winter the story might have been quite different.

BELOW AND INSET: *A supply ship and a cruise ship anchor in the sheltered bay of Deception Island.*

Whaling and Deception

Whalers operated in the Southern Ocean in the 18th century, and it is conceivable that American sealers knew about the South Shetland Islands for some years before their official discovery, but kept their discoveries secret for obvious commercial reasons. In 1819 news of the discovery reached the sealers working in South Georgia, and they were quick to exploit the new, more profitable beaches farther south.

In the two hunting seasons of 1819–20 and 1820–1 the level of slaughter was so great that the fur seals were virtually extinguished, making further voyages unprofitable. However, Deception Island was now firmly on the map, and the scene was set for their future role in Antarctic exploration and exploitation. Today it's a popular stop for tourist ships.

See also:
Mount Erebus 232-3
Hawaiian Islands 182-3
Volcanic Iceland 14-15

Index

Acknowledgements

Abbreviations for terms appearing below: (t) top; (b) bottom; (c) centre; (l) left; (r) right.

The Automobile Association wishes to thank the following picture libraries, tourist boards and companies for their assistance with the preparation of this book.

Australian Tourist Commission 6b (iii), 6b (vii), 210tcl, 211tcr, 215 (Paul Steel), 216, 222/3, 223tl; **Bruce Coleman Collection** 103ct, 138/9, 143, 209b; **Corbis UK** 66/7 (Wolfgang Kaehler), 67tr (Wolfgang Kaehler), 67b (Wolfgang Kaehler), 198t (Bettmann), 232/3 (Galen Rowell), 233tr (Galen Rowell); **Dubai, Jumeirah International** 164br; **Frank Lane Picture Agency** 21b © Flip de Nooyer/Foto Natura; **Getty Images** 22/3 (Art Wolfe), 26l (Hulton), 26r (Hulton), 50 (Hulton), 94tl (Hulton), 118t (Hulton), 130/1 (Eastcott Momatiuk), 136/7 (Michael Nichols/National Geographic Image Collection), 137 (Michael Nichols/National Geographic Image Collection), 156tl (Hulton), 179tr (Harvey Lloyd), 179c (Harvey Lloyd), 180/1 (Randy Wells); **Grand Canyon National Park** 5cr, 147ctr, 176br, 177tr, 177cr; **IguassuFallsTour.com** 6t (v), 185tl, 203b; **National Parks Service** 161, 161tr, 173tr; **New Zealand Tourist Board** 132cl; **Photodisc** 4cl, 21tl, 21tr, 112tl, 132t, 133cr, 139tr, 142, 175tr, 181tl, 201cr, 202b, 203tr, 234r; **Pictures Colour Library** 13ct, 32, 33, 40t, 81bl, 83, 88/9, 101b, 104t, 105tr, 105br, 117, 134/5, 142b, 172/3, 192/3, 193c, 193tr, 199tl, 202/3, 213r, 213tr; **Tourism Queensland** 221; **Rex Features** 85tl, 90/1, 91tl, 104/5; **Romania National Tourist Office** 4b (vi), 11ctl, 36, 36tr, 36bl; **Western Australia Tourist Board** 235b; **World Pictures** 6b (i), 6b (ii), 12/3, 14/5, 15, 35tr, 35, 35c, 40b, 59b, 128/9, 140/1, 141, 148/9, 160/1, 194, 200/1, 200b, 201tr, 206, 208/9, 209tr, 210tl, 212, 213b/g, 213l, 230/1, 232, 236/7, 236b. 236tr.

The remaining photographs are held in the Association's own photo library (**AA World Travel Library**) and were taken by the following photographers:

Pat Aithie 75, 76, 78tl, 78/9, 78/9t, 98tr; **Kirk Lee Alder** 5cbr, 132/3b, 147tr, 182/3, 182t, 182b, 183tr, 183c, 183b, 191t, 235tr; **Frederick Arvidsson** 99tl; **Jon Arnold** 62b, 63t, 63bl, 64tr; **Adrian Baker** 4b (i), 10tl, 40/1, 210tr, 218/9, 219tl, 219tr, 219bl, 222bl; **Jeff Beazley** 4b (iii), 10ctr, 18/9; **Andy Belcher** 6b (iv), 6b (vi), 210ctr, 211tcl, 220, 223tr, 225tr, 226/7, 227tl, 228/9, 228tl, 228ct, 228tr; **Pete Bennett** 70/1, 73bl, 148t; **Malc Birkitt** 5ctr, 113ctr, 144/5; **Ian Burgum** 4tr, 5tl, 112tr, 113tl, 124/5, 124, 125bl, 125cr, 126/7, 126cb, 127tr, 127b; **Dirk Buwalda** 106, 106b, 133t; **Michelle Chaplow** 58l, 59t, 60/1; **Gordon Clements** 5b (vii), 68ctr, 84tl, 84/5, 86t, 86b, 87tr, 87br, 191br; **Chris Coe** 5tr, 16/7, 16ct, 16cb, 16t, 22tr, 113tr, 114/5, 115tl, 115tr, 115c, 119tl, 119tr, 120br, 121tr; **Douglas Corrance** 3, 5b (xi), 5b (xii), 7tr, 18ct, 69ctr, 69tr, 92, 92/3, 94/5, 95tl, 95tr, 96, 102, 154, 165bl; **Ben Davies** 107tr, 107bl, 107br, 132/3t; **Steve Day** 38/9, 39bl, 39tr, 60r, 61t, 61b, 122/3, 122cl, 122b, 123tr, 123bl, 123c, 123br, 126ct, 132bl, 214, 215cr, 217t, 225tl; **Fiona Dunlop** 139tl, 139c, 139b; **Jerry Edmanson** 4b (viii), 11tr, 58/9, 58r; **Richard Elliot** 5rl, 147tcl, 157tl, 163tcl; **Philip Enticknap** 27, 29tl, 190bl; **Jill Gocher** 94cl, 100b; **William Gray** 134br, 134b, 135cr, 135bl; **Van Greaves** 225br; **Terry Harris** 54/5, 55, 56, 57; **David Henley** 110bl, 110br, 111tr; **Nigel Hicks** 98br; **Jim Holmes** 43tr, 99br, 102br, 103, 103tr, 103bc; **John Howard** 145c; **Richard Ireland** 5b (i), 5b (ii), 146tl, 146tcl, 170/1, 174/5, 175tl, 175bc; **Max Jourdan** 4b (vii), 11ctr, 25tr, 25ct, 25cb, 25b, 27cl, 60l, 60c, 164c, 165br, 225bl, 225tc; **Paul Kenward** 6b (v), 6b (viii), 27cr, 70br, 71tr, 74, 128t, 128b, 129c, 129b, 155b, 156/7, 163tr, 210tr, 211tl, 211tr, 216/7, 217tr, 226, 227tc, 227tr, 229tl, 229tr; **Alex Kouprianoff** 5b (viii), 31cl, 31bl, 31br, 42, 48/9, 49tr, 49trb, 68tr, 88, 89bl, 91tr, 165tr; **Julian Loader** 75tr, 75br, 79cr, 79br, 80/1, 81tr, 81cr; **Guy Marks** 6t (ii), 6t (iii), 6t (vi), 6t (vii), 6t (viii), 131b, 131tr, 184tcl, 184tcr, 185tcl, 185tcr, 185tr, 195, 195b, 195tr, 196, 197, 198/9, 198b, 199tr, 204/5, 204b, 205tr, 205bl, 205bc, 206/7, 207tr, 207bl, 207br; **S&O Mathews** 191cr; **Simon McBride** 5b (iv), 34t, 34ct, 34cb, 34b, 42/3, 43tl, 47bl, 47br, 47t, 52b, 53t, 53bc, 125tr, 146ctr, 162/3, 163tcr, 164bl; **Eric Meacher** 4b (ii), 8/9, 10ctl, 20tl, 20c, 20; **Ingrid Morejohn** 5b (x), 69ctl, 82, 85tr, 86/7, 97, 97tr, 98bl, 191bl, 234l; **Kim Naylor** 13tl, 13tr; **David Noble** 24, 25tl; **Ken Paterson** 4b (v), 11tl, 52r, 62/3, 62t, 63cb, 64/5, 64bl, 64br, 65tr, 65cl, 65br, 89tr, 98tl, 171tr, 171bl, 171r, 178; **Jean-Francois Pin** 70bl, 152/3, 153cl, 153tr, 165cr; **Lanny Provo** 180, 181tr; **Erin Rooney** 155cbr; **Clive Sawyer** 4b (iv), 4b (x), 5tcl, 5b (iii), 5b (vi), 9tr, 10tr, 22tr, 22b, 23t, 37cl, 37, 37tr, 44, 45l, 46/7, 47bc, 50/1, 52t, 53r, 68ctl, 72/3, 73cl, 99bl, 113ctl, 129t, 145tr, 145b, 146ctr, 149t, 149c, 149b, 154/5, 155ctr, 156tr, 156c, 157tr, 158/9, 158l, 159b, 159tl, 159tr, 163tl, 163c; **Michael Siebert** 37tl, 37bl; **Barrie Smith** 30, 30b, 45br, 99tr; **Jonathan Smith** 18cl, 18cc, 19tr, 19br; **Tony Souter** 32bl, 32cr, 33c, 33tr, 45tr, 48, 73tl, 73tr, 76/7, 77t, 77cr, 79tr; **Karen Lee Stow** 97cl, 133bl, 222ct; **Rick Strange** 4c, 4cr, 4b (ix), 6t (i), 6t (iv), 22tl, 56/7, 68tl, 108/9, 108, 109tr, 109b, 110/1, 111tl, 112tcl, 112tcr, 114t, 114b, 115tc, 116, 118c, 118b, 118/9, 120c, 120/1, 120bl, 121tl, 121br, 184tl, 184tr, 186/7, 186, 187t, 187c, 187b, 188/9, 188c, 188cr, 189c, 189cr, 190r, 191cl, 191bc; **Nick Sumner** 5b (v), 147tl, 150, 150c, 150b, 151, 151tr, 151c, 151b, 152, 153cr; **Richard Surman** 54b; **Rupert Tenison** 224t; **James Tims** 27tr, 28/9, 29tr, 181bl, 224b; **Mamon Van Vark** 166/7, 166, 167tr, 167bl, 168/9, 168, 169, 173b, 176/7, 176bl, 235tl; **Steve Watkins** 5b (ix), 69tl, 100/1, 101tr, 194b; **Peter Wilson** 51cr, 165tl; **Jon Wyand** 190cl.